ANCIENT CHINESE THOUGHT, MODERN CHINESE POWER

The Princeton-China Series

DANIEL A. BELL, SERIES EDITOR

The Princeton-China Series aims to open a window on Chinese scholarship by translating works by the most original and influential Chinese scholars in the humanities, social sciences, and law. The goal is to improve understanding of China on its own terms and create new opportunities for cultural cross-pollination.

ANCIENT CHINESE THOUGHT, MODERN CHINESE POWER

Yan Xuetong

Edited by Daniel A. Bell and Sun Zhe
Translated by Edmund Ryden

PRINCETON UNIVERSITY PRESS
PRINCETON AND OXFORD

Copyright © 2011 by Princeton University Press

Published by Princeton University Press, 41 William Street, Princeton,
New Jersey 08540

In the United Kingdom: Princeton University Press, 6 Oxford Street,
Woodstock, Oxfordshire OX20 1TW

press.princeton.edu

Jacket photo: Night view of the China Pavilion during the trial operation of
the Shanghai World Expo, April 25, 2010. The China Pavilion has a distinctive
roof, made of traditional dougong or interlocking wooden brackets. It is a
modern adaptation of an architectural style that was widely used in the Spring
and Autumn Period (c. 770 BCE to c. 476 BCE). © Guo Changyao/XinHua/
Xinhua Press/Corbis.

Library of Congress Cataloging-in-Publication Data

Yan, Xuetong.
Ancient Chinese thought, modern Chinese power / Yan Xuetong ; edited
by Daniel A. Bell and Sun Zhe ; translated by Edmund Ryden
p. cm.
Chinese uniform title not available.
Includes bibliographical references and index.
ISBN 978-0-691-14826-7 (hardback: alk. paper)   1. China—Politics
and government—2002–   2. Political science—China—History—To
1500.   3. Confucianism—China—History.   I. Bell, Daniel (Daniel A.),
1964– II. Sun, Zhe, 1966–   III. Ryden, Edmund, tr, IV. Title.
JQ1510.Y46113 2011
327.101—dc22   2010031059

British Library Cataloging-in-Publication Data is available

This book has been composed in Perpetua

Printed on acid-free paper. ∞

Printed in the United States of America

2   3   4   5   6   7   8   9   10

∾

Contents

Acknowledgments

The idea for this book emerged from a conversation at Tsinghua University in 2007. Daniel Bell's old friend Sun Zhe (Sunny) had just moved to Tsinghua to direct the Center for U.S.-China Relations. They were having lunch at a restaurant called Yan near Tsinghua's main gate, and Sun mentioned that Yan Xuetong was working on a study of pre-Qin international political philosophy and thinking about implications for the rise of China. That sounded like a promising work for the translation series, and Sun helped to set up a meeting with Professor Yan at, yes, Yan restaurant (the characters in Chinese are different). The trio agreed to work closely on the book, with Bell and Sun as coeditors. Special thanks goes to Sun Zhe for helping to conceptualize the project and for ongoing invaluable advice about how it should be carried out. We are also grateful to Xu Jin, who helped to coordinate various parts of the book project.

Yan Xuetong, it turns out, has an office just down the hall from Daniel Bell's office. They have had many face-to-face meetings that made it easier to deal with issues and ambiguities. A panel on Yan's work at Tsinghua was presented in June 2009 as part of the first general conference of international relations scholars in mainland China, and Yan's three critics presented their papers. Yan's book and his critics' essays were revised, and the Princeton University Press sent the revised manuscript to three anonymous referees. We are grateful for the referees' reports, which helped to improve the book.

Perhaps the biggest challenge of a translation series is to find talented translators willing to work on the project. We were lucky to find Dr. Edmund Ryden, who translates brilliantly from classical and modern Chinese and who has himself written insightfully on the international political philosophy of the pre-Qin thinkers. Thanks to Axel Schneider and Matt Kawecki for helping us to get in touch with Dr. Ryden.

We owe special thanks to Ian Malcolm and Peter Dougherty of Princeton University Press for raising the possibility of this translation series and for their ongoing interest and support, and to Mr. P. H. Yu, chairman of the Tsinghua Fund for U.S.-China Research, who generously supports this project.

A Note on the Translation

This book has been expertly translated by Edmund Ryden. The authors and editors went over a couple of drafts with the translator and did their best to iron out ambiguities. We generally stuck with standard translations for key terms, except that the term 王 (*wang*)—the political ideal of pre-Qin thinkers that contrasts with 霸 (*ba*, hegemony)—was translated as "humane authority" rather than the more common "sage king." Obviously, Yan is not arguing for the reestablishment of a monarchical system led by one sage who would save the world with his moral goodness.

ANCIENT
CHINESE THOUGHT,
MODERN
CHINESE POWER

Introduction

Daniel A. Bell

If American neoconservatives are liberals mugged by reality, Chinese realists are idealists mugged by the surreal events of the Cultural Revolution. In the case of Yan Xuetong, he grew up in a family of morally upright intellectuals and, at the age of sixteen, was sent to a construction corps in China's far north, where he stayed for nine years. Here's how he describes his experience of hardship: "At that time, the Leftist ideology was in full swing. In May, water in Heilongjiang still turns to ice. When we pulled the sowing machine, we were not allowed to wear boots. We walked barefoot over the ice. Our legs were covered in cuts. We carried sacks of seed that could weigh up to eighty kilograms [about 176 pounds]. We carried them along the raised pathways around the paddy fields. These were not level; make a slight misstep and you fell into the water. You just thought of climbing out and going on. When you at last struggled to the end and lay down, your eyes could only see black and you just could not get up. . . . [W]e saw people being beaten to death, so you became somewhat immune to it." In 1969, the Voice of America predicted that war could break out on the Sino-Soviet border: "When we young people learned this, we were particularly happy. We hoped that a massive war would improve the country, or at least change our own lives. Today people fear war, but at the time we hoped for immediate action, even to wage a world war. That way we could have hope. In that frame of mind, there was no difference between life and death. There was no point in living."

Four decades later, Yan Xuetong has emerged as China's most influential foreign policy analyst and theorist of international relations (in 2008, *Foreign Policy* named him one of the world's hundred most influential public intellectuals). He openly recognizes that his experience of hardship in the countryside has shaped his outlook: "[It] gave people the confidence to overcome all obstacles. And this confidence is built precisely on the basis of an estimation of the difficulties faced, on the basis of always preparing for the worst case. Hence, many people who went down to the countryside are realists with regard to life. People who have not experienced hardship are more liable to adopt an optimistic attitude toward international politics."[1]

To the outside world, Yan may appear as China's "Prince of Darkness," the hawkish policy adviser who is the enemy of liberal internationalists. Mark Leonard, the author of the influential book *What Does China Think?*, labels Yan as China's "leading 'neo-comm,' an assertive nationalist who has called for a more forthright approach to Taiwan, Japan, and the United States." A "neo-comm" is China's equivalent of the American neocon: "The 'neo-comm' label will stick because there are so many parallels between Yan Xuetong and his analogues [the neocons] in the USA. Yan Xuetong is almost the mirror image of William Kristol. . . . Where Kristol is obsessed with a China threat and convinced that US supremacy is the only solution to a peaceful world order, Yan Xuetong is fixated with the USA and sure that China's military's modernization is the key to world stability."[2]

But Leonard's account—based on English-language sources—misrepresents Yan's views. Yan is neither a communist (or Marxist) who believes that economic might is the key to national power nor a neocon who believes that China should rely on military might rather than multilateral organizations to get its way. Yan's argument is that political leadership is the key to national power and that morality is an essential part of political leadership. Economic and military might matter as components of national power, but they are secondary to political leaders who act (at least partly) in accordance with moral norms. If China's leaders absorb and act on that insight, they can play a greater role in shaping a peaceful and harmonious world order. Yan is still a political realist, because he believes political leadership shapes international relations; it's the way the political world actually works, not just an ideal. Moreover, Yan believes that the global order is bound to be hierarchical, with some states being dominant and others less influential. But dominance is achieved mainly by morally informed political leadership rather than economic or military power.

Yan's theory was shaped by his groundbreaking academic research on ancient Chinese thinkers who wrote about governance and interstate relations during a period of incessant warfare between fragmented states, before China was unified by the first emperor of Qin in 221 BCE. In this way, too, Yan is different from the neocons: he is a scholar as well a political commentator. This book is a translation of Yan's work on the international political philosophy of ancient Chinese thinkers. The three essays by Yan are followed by critical commentaries by three Chinese scholars. In the last chapter, Yan replies to his critics and draws implications of pre-Qin philosophy for China's rise today. The book includes three appendixes: a short account of the historical context and the key thinkers of the pre-Qin period that may be helpful for nonexperts, a revealing interview with Yan Xuetong himself, and Yan Xuetong's discussion of why there is no Chinese school of international relations theory. Readers of this book may not agree with all of Yan's arguments, but the "neo-comm" label, we hope, will not stick.

THE INTERNATIONAL POLITICAL PHILOSOPHY OF PRE-QIN THINKERS

The Spring and Autumn Period (ca. 770–476 BCE) and the Warring States Period (ca. 475–221 BCE) were a time of ruthless competition for territorial advantage among small states. The various princely states still gave feudal homage to the Zhou king as their common lord but, as Yang Qianru notes in chapter 4, it "was rather like the relationship of the members of today's Commonwealth to Great Britain. They accept the Queen as the head of the Commonwealth but enjoy equal and independent status along with Great Britain." The historical reality is that "several large princely states already had two basic features of the modern 'state': sovereignty and territory. Not only did the states have independent and autonomous sovereignty, they also had very clear borders." Arguably, the Spring and Autumn and Warring States periods have more in common with the current global system than with imperial China, then held to be the empire (Middle Kingdom) at the center of the world. Hence, it should not be surprising that there emerged a rich discourse of statecraft that may still be relevant for the present-day context. As Yang puts it,

> on the grounds of protecting their own security, [the pre-Qin states] sought to develop and resolve the relationships among themselves and the central royal house and thus they accumulated a rich and prolific experience in politics and diplomacy. This complicated and complex political configuration created the space for scholarship to look at the international system, state relations, and interstate political philosophy. The pre-Qin masters wrote books and advanced theories trying to sell to the rulers their ideas on how to run a state and conduct diplomacy and military strategy while they played major roles in advocating strategies of becoming either a humane authority or a hegemon, making either vertical (North-South) or horizontal (East-West) alliances, or either creating alliances or going to war. Scholars who have researched the history of thought have looked only at one side and emphasized the value of the pre-Qin masters' thought as *theory* (philosophical, historical, or political), whereas most of these ideas were used to serve practical political and diplomatic purposes among the states. Their effectiveness both then and now is proven. Therefore, there is no doubt about the positive and practical role of researching the foreign relations, state politics, and military strategies of the pre-Qin classics or of applying the insights gleaned from studying these masters to international political thought.[3]

Chapter 1 is a comprehensive comparison of the theories of interstate politics of seven pre-Qin masters: Guanzi, Laozi, Confucius, Mencius, Mozi, Xunzi, and Hanfeizi. Yan deploys the tools of international relations theory to analyze their ways of thinking and what they say about interstate order, interstate leadership, and transfer of hegemonic power. Yan's analysis shows that there is a wide diversity of perspectives in pre-Qin international political philosophy. But there are also commonalities: "the pre-Qin thinkers hold that morality and the interstate order are directly related, especially at the level of the personal morality of the leader and its role in determining the stability of interstate order." Rulers concerned with successful governance in a world of shifting allegiances and power imbalances also need to employ talented advisors: "Confucius, Mencius, Xunzi, Mozi, and Guanzi all explain shifts in hegemonic power through the one mediating variable of the need to employ worthy people, that is, all of them think that employing worthy and capable persons is a necessary, even the crucial, condition for successful governance." And if the rulers want to strive for the morally highest form of political rule, the pre-Qin thinkers (with the exception of Hanfeizi) all agree that the basis of humane authority is the moral level of the state. Yan does not say so explicitly, but there is a strong presumption that areas of agreement among such diverse thinkers must approximate how international politics works in reality.

In her commentary (chapter 4), Yang Qianru objects to Yan's social scientific method on the grounds that it abstracts from concrete historical contexts and is driven by the aim of constructing an explanatory model that allows the researcher to draw normative conclusions of universal significance and to analyze China's rise. Yang does not object to the methods of international political theory per se, but she argues that "we need to correctly grasp the reality of historical texts and the thought of pre-Qin masters, and then deepen and expand the areas and perspectives of current research." But perhaps Yan and Yang are not so far apart; it's more a matter of two methodologies with different emphases that can enrich each other. Yan does aim to "grasp the *true picture* [my emphasis] of pre-Qin thought so as to make new discoveries in theory." In principle, he could distort the ideas of pre-Qin thinkers for the purpose of creating new theories or drawing implications for China's rise, but he doesn't do that: at some level, he is concerned with historical truth. So the more historically minded interpreters can help Yan's project by correcting and improving his account of pre-Qin thinkers; if they think his account is wrong, let them draw on detailed accounts of the historical context to explain the problem. As for the historically minded interpreters, they can learn from Yan's research so that investigations of the pre-Qin historical context will be guided by questions that are of greater theoretical and political relevance today.

In chapter 2, Yan focuses more specifically on Xunzi's interstate political philosophy. Xunzi (ca. 313–238 BCE) is the great synthesizer of international political philosophy of the Spring and Autumn and Warring States periods. Although he generally upholds Confucian moral principles, he begins with dark assumptions about human nature and is explicitly concerned with appropriate strategies for nonideal political contexts. In contrast to modern ideas of equality of sovereignty, Xunzi argues for hierarchies among states, with powerful states having extra responsibility to secure international order. Xunzi distinguishes among three kinds of international power, in decreasing order of goodness: humane authority, hegemony, and tyranny. Tyranny, which is based on military force and stratagems, inevitably creates enemies and should be avoided at all costs. In an anarchic world of self-interested states, the hegemonic state may have a degree of morality because it is reliable in its strategies: domestically it does not cheat the people, and externally it does not cheat its allies. But strategic reliability must also have a basis in hard power so that the hegemon gains the trust of its allies. For Xunzi, humane authority, meaning a state that wins the hearts of the people at home and abroad, is the ultimate aim. Humane authority is founded on the superior moral power of the ruler himself. Yan comments:

> We would have difficulty finding a political leader who meets Xunzi's standard, but if one compares F. D. Roosevelt as president of the United States during World War II and the recent George W. Bush, we can see what Xunzi means about the moral power of the leader playing a role in establishing international norms and changing the international system. Roosevelt's belief in world peace was the impetus for the foundation of the United Nations after World War II, whereas Bush's Christian fundamentalist beliefs led to the United States continually flouting international norms, which resulted in a decline of the international nonproliferation regime.

Yan agrees that humane authority should be the aim of the state, though he criticizes Xunzi for overlooking the fact that humane authority must also have a basis in hard power: "Lacking strong power or failing to play a full part in international affairs and having only moral authority is not sufficient to enable a state to attain world leadership."

In his commentary (chapter 5), Xu Jin argues that it is difficult for Xunzi to argue that hierarchical norms can be "implemented or maintained when there are evil persons (or evil states) that seek their own ends by flouting norms, especially when these people (or states) have considerable force." Xu suggests that it is easier to support Xunzi's political conclusions with Mencius's view that human beings have a natural inclination toward the good. Moreover, Mencius can contribute to the debate about how to implement humane authority: in addition to emphasizing the morality of the ruler, he puts forward detailed proposals such as light taxation and a land-distribution system meant to secure the basic requirements for life for the common people.

Yan's third chapter (cowritten with Huang Yuxing) provides a detailed picture of the hegemonic philosophy of *The Stratagems of the Warring States*. This book has not been regarded as a major philosophical treatise but it is a valuable historical resource for theorizing about the foundations of hegemonic power, the role of norms in a hegemony, and the basic strategies for attaining hegemony. Yan and Huang compare their findings with contemporary Western hegemonic theory and propose that ancient Chinese thinkers saw political power as the core of hegemony, with government by worthy and competent persons as its guarantee. Even a text that recounts the strategies of annexation and alliance of hard-nosed politicians stresses the importance of respect for interstate norms in attaining or maintaining hegemony: "Without the support of norms and relying only on power, the strategists of the Warring States Period could not have attained hegemony; hence, their emphasis on interstate norms is genuine and not primarily intended as a cloak for a profit motive." Yan and Huang draw on a recent case to illustrate the point that failing to respect interstate norms will have a negative influence on a state's hegemonic status: "The unilateralist foreign policy of President George W. Bush weakened the international political mobilizing capacity of the United States."

In his commentary (chapter 6), Wang Rihua expands on strategies for achieving hegemony by drawing on other texts from the pre-Qin period.

He points to the frequency of covenant meetings in the period that per-formed the political functions of affirming hegemony, controlling allies and preventing them from falling away from the alliance, and determin-ing international norms so that the will of the hegemonic state became the international consensus, thus institutionalizing the hegemony. More-over, political hegemonic theory of the period, like just-war theory today, preferred the military strategy of acting in response to aggression rather than launching wars of aggression. It also stressed that hegemonic states had the duty of providing security guarantees to small and medium-size states, and economic assistance in times of danger, such as famine. But Wang reminds us that "the ancient Chinese classics, including *The Strata-gems of the Warring States*, all acknowledge that the main distinction in power is between humane authority and hegemony." Pre-Qin thinkers held that the exercise of hegemonic power over other states within a frag-mented world, even if the power is informed by morality, is inferior to the exercise of humane authority in a world where there is a single ruler over everything under heaven.

RETHINKING CONTEMPORARY INTERNATIONAL RELATIONS THEORIES

Yan makes use of the analytical tools of modern international relations theory to sharpen understanding of the international political philosophy of pre-Qin thinkers. But the pre-Qin thinkers can also help to improve modern theories. International relations theory has been shaped primar-ily by the history and conceptual language of Western countries, and Yan aims to enrich it with the discourse of ancient Chinese thought. The pre-Qin era is a rich resource not just in the sense that the historical context approximates the contemporary world of sovereign states in an anarchic world, but also because they were writing for political actors, not their academic colleagues: "What pre-Qin thinkers have to say about interna-tional relations is all grounded in policy; their thought is oriented toward practical political policies." Yan is explicit, however, that the aim should not be to produce a distinctively Chinese school of international relations theory. Rather, scholars should aim to improve international relations theory with the insights of pre-Qin thinkers so that it can better understand and predict our interstate world. So what lessons can be drawn from pre-Qin international political philosophy?

Yan stresses that the pre-Qin thinkers discussed in the book, with the exception of Hanfeizi, were conceptual rather than material determinists: they believed that shifts in international power relations are explained more by ideas than by material wealth and military might. In today's international relations theory, in contrast, "the two well-developed theories are realism and liberalism, and both of these schools look at international relations from the point of view of material benefit and material force." Yan believes that such theories would become more realistic and have greater policy relevance and predictive power if they took more seriously the role of concepts and morality in shaping international affairs. Constructivism and international political psychology have recently emerged in response to concerns about the material determinism of international relations theory, but "these two theories are not yet mature . . . and they are stuck at the academic level."

Even Hanfeizi, notorious for his extreme cynicism, allows for the possibility that morality matters in certain contexts—when humans face nonhuman threats—and Yan argues that Han's view may become increasingly relevant in the contemporary world, with implications for theorizing about security in new ways:

> It shows that with, today's rise of nontraditional threats to security and the decline of traditional threats to security, morality may play a greater role in international security cooperation than in the cold war period of security attained between two opposing military blocs. Apart from terrorism, nontraditional security threats are basically nonhuman threats to security, such as the financial crisis, the energy crisis, environmental pollution, and climate change. Climate change especially is seen as an increasingly grave threat to international security. Reducing carbon dioxide emissions has become a moral issue. Research on security theory may have to take a moral angle to analyze conflict, cooperation, success or failure, and position shifts in the area of nontraditional security.

The pre-Qin understanding that the basis of international authority is the moral level of the leading state can also enrich modern theories: "The theory of hegemonic stability in contemporary international relations theory has overlooked the relationship between the nature of hegemonic power and the stability of the international order. . . . According to [the pre-Qin thinkers'] way of thinking, we can suppose that the level of morality of the hegemon is related to the degree of stability of the international system and the length of time of its endurance." Yan supports this hypothesis with examples from the imperial history of Western great powers: "Throughout history, Great Britain and France, respectively, adopted policies of indirect and direct administration of their colonies. Great Britain's colonial policy was gentler than France's, with the result that violent opposition movements were less frequent in British than in French colonies."

According to pre-Qin thought, the moral level of a state is determined primarily by the quality of the state's leaders. Yan spells out the implications for contemporary international relations theory: "The theory of imperial overstretch and the coalition politics theory both explain the fall of hegemonic power in terms of excessive consumption of the hegemon's material strength and overlook the fact that under different leaders the same state evinces a difference in the rise and fall of its power." Pre-Qin thinkers had specific views about what aspects of political leadership influence shifts in international power: "for the most part they think that it has to do with whether worthy people are employed." The competition for talent is a feature of the knowledge economy, suggesting that the pre-Qin thinkers may have hit upon a more universal rule that helps to explain the rise and fall of great powers: "If competitiveness among large states more than two thousand years ago and competitiveness among large states in the contemporary globalized world both involve competition for talent, this implies that competition for talent is not a phenomenon peculiar to the era of the knowledge economy but rather is the essence of competition among great powers." Yan is clearly persuaded by the pre-Qin view that the movement of talented persons among nations is the key indicator to assess national political power, and he adds that it is "an advance on the current lack of any standard to assess national political power in contemporary international relations theory."

Given variations in the moral levels of states and the quality of leaders and advisors, there will also be variations in the national power of states. Hence, pre-Qin thinking assumes that power in the international system has a hierarchical structure, in contrast to the principle in contemporary relations theory that demands respect for the equality of state sovereignty. Unexpectedly, perhaps, the accounts of pre-Qin thinkers may better model contemporary reality than theories of more modern origin: "If we look carefully at today's international system, . . . we will discover that the power relationships among members of the United Nations, the World Bank, and the International Monetary Fund are all structured hierarchically and are not equal. The United Nations distinguishes among permanent members of the Security Council, nonpermanent members of the Security Council, and ordinary member states. The World Bank and the International Monetary Fund have voting structures dependent on the contributions of the members." Yan does not deny that norms of equality direct state behavior in the international system, and he opposes practices like the traditional East Asian tribute system with China that make no room, however symbolic, for the principle of sovereign equality among nations. But he argues that the principle of hierarchy among states should play a key role in international relations theory, both because it fits the reality of our interstate world and because it helps theorists think about how best to deal with practical political problems, such as minimizing violent international conflict: "Pre-Qin thinkers generally believe that hierarchical norms can restrain state behavior and thus maintain order among states, whereas contemporary international relations theorists think that, to restrain states' behavior, norms of equality alone can uphold the order of the international system." Moreover, the case for equality on the ground that it helps to protect the interests of weaker states is not compelling because hierarchical norms can also perform that function: "Hierarchical norms carry with them the demand that the strong should undertake greater international responsibilities while the weak respect the implementation of discriminatory international rules. For instance, developed countries should each provide 0.7 percent of their GDP to assist developing countries, and nonnuclear states must not seek to possess nuclear weapons."

Pre-Qin international political philosophy also offers insights about how norms are disseminated in the international system. According to contemporary international relations theory, new norms are put forward by major powers, gain support from other states, and are internalized by most states after an extended period of implementation. But "contemporary theory still does not understand the process whereby international norms are internalized. According to the views of the nature of humane authority and hegemony expressed by pre-Qin philosophers, we know that humane authority has the role of taking the lead in implementing and upholding international norms, whereas hegemony lacks this. Based on this realization, we can study the path by which the nature of the leading state affects the internalization of international norms after they have been established." Yan's hypothesis is that humane authority is more likely than hegemonic power to succeed in influencing the norms of the international system.

In short, the key to international power is political power, and the key to political power is morally informed political leadership. Yan is a realist, but he believes that states which act in accordance with morality are more likely to achieve long-lasting success in the international realm. States that rely on tyranny to get their way will end up on the bottom of the pile; states that rely on hegemony can end up as great powers; but humane authority is the real key to becoming the world's leading power. As Yan puts it, "A humane authority under heaven relies on its ultrapowerful moral force to maintain its comprehensive state power in first place in the system." But Yan also rejects the idealistic view held by pre-Qin thinkers (with the exception of Hanfeizi) that morality alone can determine international leadership: "[A leading state's] hard power may not be the strongest at the time, but the level of its hard power cannot be too low. . . . It is unthinkable that a state could attain humane authority under heaven relying purely on morality and hard power of the lowest class. In the international politics of the twenty-first century, the importance of the area of territory ruled has already declined as a factor in gaining world leadership,

but a population of more than two hundred million does play an important role." Without the requisite population, the United Kingdom, France,
Germany, Japan, and Russia "have no possibility of becoming the leading
states of the system." For the moment, India and Indonesia may lack the
hard economic and military power. That leaves two states in contention
for global leadership: China and the United States. The United States is
clearly the leading power now. So what should China do if it wants to take
over "first place in the system"?

IMPLICATIONS FOR CHINA'S RISE

Given the importance of political power for international leadership, the
Chinese government should not assume that more economic power necessarily translates into the power to shape international norms. As Yan
puts it, "an increase in wealth can raise China's power status but it does not
necessarily enable China to become a country respected by others, because a political superpower that puts wealth as its highest national interest
may bring disaster rather than blessings to other countries." Since China
undertook its policy of reform and opening in 1978, however, "the Chinese government has made economic growth the core of its strategy." In
2005, it proposed a policy of a harmonious world and set the goal of building friendships with other countries, "but in August 2008, the report of the
Foreign Affairs Meeting of the Party Central Committee again said that
'the work of foreign affairs should uphold economic construction at its
core.'" Yan concludes his analysis of the status quo on a critical note: "The
Chinese government has not yet been able consciously to make building a
humane authority the goal of its strategy for ascent." Like contemporary
international relations theorists, the Chinese government seems to overes-
timate the political importance of economic power. In this case, the government may still be under the sway of Marxist economic determinism.

So what should be done instead? Yan proposes that China should learn
from Xunzi's recommendation of strategy for a rising power, which
"stresses human talent, that is, it focuses on competition for talent." Again,
there is a critique of the status quo: "At present, China's strategy of seeking

talent is still mainly used for developing enterprises and has not yet been applied to raising the nation as a whole. Talent is still understood as having to do with technicians rather than politicians or high-ranking officials. . . . The personnel requirements for the rise of a great power are not for technicians but for politicians and officials who have the ability to invent systems or regulations, because a pronounced ability to invent systems and regulations is the key to ensuring the rise of a great power." Talented people are available but they are not always chosen: "Xunzi thinks that there are many talented people with both morality and ability, and the key is whether the ruler will choose them."

Drawing on historical examples, Yan puts forward some strategies for finding talent that ensure the rise of a great power. First, "the degree of openness is high: choosing officials from the whole world who meet the requisite standards of morality and ability, so as to improve the capability of the government to formulate correct policies. For example, in ancient times, the Tang Dynasty in China and the Umayyad Empire in North Africa, Spain, and the Middle East, in the course of their rise, employed a great number of foreigners as officials. It is said that at its peak more than 70 percent of officials in the Umayyad Empire were foreigners. The United States has attained its present hegemonic status also by its policy of attracting talented and outstanding foreigners." Yan is a nationalist—he cares about the good of his country more than that of other countries—but he believes the best way to promote the good of his country is to employ more foreigners. Once China passes a certain baseline of hard power, the main competition with the United States will be competition for human talent rather than for economic or military superiority.

Second, Yan argues that officials should be held responsible for their mistakes. He opposes lifetime job security that increases the risk of officials becoming corrupt, lazy, and prone to repeating mistakes. In the more meritocratic societies, "unsuitable government officials could be speedily removed, reducing the probability of erroneous decisions. This applied to all politicians and officials if they lost their ability to make correct decisions for any reason, such as being corrupted by power, being out-of-date in knowledge, decaying in thought, suffering a decline in their ability to reflect, or experiencing deterioration in health. Establishing a system by which officials can be removed in a timely fashion provides opportunities for talented people and can reduce errors of policy and ultimately increase political power."

Yan also argues for the establishment of independent think tanks that would provide professional advice on policy. At the moment, "the research institutions attached to our government agencies are not think tanks in the strict sense. Their main task is to carry out policies, not to furnish ideas. To undertake the work of a think tank is to exercise social responsibility." Such think tanks existed in the past, but "since the founding of the new China in 1949, the state has not allowed high officials to have their own personal advisors or to rely on nongovernmental advisory organizations." If the think tank system of independent and public-spirited advisors is revived, Yan openly says that he would be willing to serve: "I would take part."

In short, China can increase its political power by adopting a more meritocratic system of selection of political officials and advisors. But this leads to the question of what exactly these talented and public-spirited politicians and advisors should aim for. In the West, political discourse is usually confined to two options: "good" democracy and "bad" authoritarianism. Pro-democracy commentators, whether hawkish or liberal, put forward proposals for a "community" or "concert" of democracies that would act together to promote democratic development in the world. The social scientific thesis that democracies do not go to war with one another has been the subject of much debate. In Yan's view, however, the two relevant options are hegemony and humane authority. The former is less good but it secures strategic reliability: countries that pursue hegemony in the pre-Qin sense are reliable international actors, even if they are not always striving for morally admirable goals. Humane authority is the best option—countries that lead with humane authority inspire the rest of the world with their morally superior ways—but it is more difficult to achieve.

So, should China strive for hegemony or humane authority? Yan allows for both possibilities. He regards the United States as a hegemonic power and argues that China should strive for a higher moral standing: "If China wants to become a state of humane authority, this would be different from the contemporary United States. The goal of our strategy must be not only to reduce the power gap with the United States but also to provide a better model for society than that given by the United States." Nonetheless, he also writes in favor of the pursuit of hegemony: "China can reflect on the alliance-building strategies of *The Stratagems of the Warring States* and adopt a strategy beneficial to expanding its international political support. The alliance-building strategies of *The Stratagems of the Warring States* and the Communist Party's United Front principle are very similar. This kind of principle was able to bring about victory in the War against Japanese Aggression [i.e., World War II], and it may also be successful in guiding China's rise." We can infer that China's aims would depend on the international context. In time of war, it should strive to build reliable alliances to maintain or increase its hegemonic status. In time of peace, it should strive to act like a humane authority.

But how can China act like a humane authority? In the pre-Qin era, the political ideal of humane authority was premised on the assumption that there would be one single ruling authority with sovereignty over the whole world. According to Yan, however, the ideal of world government is neither feasible nor desirable today. So how could China act like a humane authority in a hierarchical world divided into states that often have competing interests? In international relations, it should do as it says: "China should not adopt the United States' current way of acting, saying that all states are equal while in practice always seeking to have a dominant international status." The Chinese government also has resorted to some hypocrisy: "China's proposal for democratization of international relations has not been easily accepted by the international community because China could not abandon its special veto power in the United Nations Security Council." Instead, China should openly recognize that it is a dominant power in a hierarchical world, but this sense of dominance means that it has extra responsibilities, including the provision of economic assistance to poor countries and security guarantees to nonnuclear states. Rather than insisting on reciprocity with weaker states, China should try to gain their support by allowing for differential international norms to work in their favor. In the cooperation of the 10 + 1—the Association of Southeast Asian Nations (ASEAN) and China—for example,

"China is required to implement the norm of zero tariffs in agricultural trade before the ASEAN states do. This unequal norm enabled the economic cooperation of the 10 + 1 to develop more rapidly than that between Japan and ASEAN. Japan's demand for equal tariffs with ASEAN slowed the progress of its economic cooperation with the ASEAN states, which lags far behind that of China and ASEAN."

But it's not just a question of foreign policy: "For China to become a superpower modeled on humane authority, it must first become a model from which other states are willing to learn." In other words, China must act like a humane authority at home. Yan argues that the modern equivalent of humane authority is democracy: "I think that in their respect for norms, the modern concept of democracy and the ancient Chinese concept of humane authority are alike. . . . The electoral system has become the universal political norm today." Humane authority would also translate into a society that is more open to the rest of the world: "Stricter border controls lead to greater suspicion between nations and more pronounced confrontation. China should promote the principle of freedom to travel, to live, and to work anywhere in the world. People tend to move to the better place, and thus nations with better conditions will be attractive to talented people. Hence, China should expand its policy of opening to international society."

In appendix 2, Yan portrays himself as a hard-nosed scientific realist: "I am more concerned with how real life and real political behavior can verify explanatory theory. I do not like what cannot be verified, because there is no way of knowing if its conclusions are valid. For instance, in making predictions I like to set a timeframe: within five years, or within three years."[4] Yet his discussion of the "ultrapowerful moral force" of humane authority does seem to veer into normative thinking about a distant future. It's hard to disagree with his inspiring political vision for China: it would take on extra international responsibilities and help marginalized countries; its rulers would be chosen by some sort of electoral system; their political advisors would be chosen according to a meritocratic system that ensured promotion and demotion according to performance rather than political loyalty; and China's borders would be open for peoples of all nationalities to join the competition to attract talent. This vision does, however, seem quite far removed from the current reality. But maybe we can forgive a bit of methodological inconsistency. If America's most influential realists can dream of a world without nuclear weapons,[5] then Yan Xuetong can dream of a country that inspires the rest of the world with its humane values.

PART I
Ancient Chinese Thought,
Modern Chinese Power

A Comparative Study of Pre-Qin Interstate Political Philosophy

Yan Xuetong

There were several schools of thought on interstate politics among thinkers of pre-Qin (pre-221 BCE) China. Understanding the differences and commonalities among these schools may help us glean from their thought ideas to enrich contemporary theories of international relations. Given the great complexity of pre-Qin political philosophy—both in the number of schools and in their teachings—it is impossible to cover everything. Hence, this essay is limited to the works of seven thinkers: Guanzi, Laozi, Confucius, Mencius, Mozi, Xunzi, and Hanfeizi. It relies on the fruits of established research and examines these seven thinkers from four different angles: ways of thinking, views on interstate order, views on interstate leadership, and views on transfer of hegemonic power.[1] The nine concrete issues addressed are analytical method, philosophical concepts, cause of war, path to peace, role of morality, the nature of all under heaven, the basis for the right to leadership among states, unbalanced development, and transfer of hegemonic power. Finally, this essay will apply what has been learned from this study of Chinese thought to enrich contemporary international relations theory and present some findings relevant to China's foreign policy.

CURRENT RESEARCH: ITS FINDINGS AND LIMITATIONS

Early on, scholars noted the richness of pre-Qin ideas on interstate politics and did some research in this field. For instance, in 1922 Liang Qichao published a *History of Pre-Qin Political Thought*.[2] Two chapters of that book, titled "Unification" and "Antimilitarism," presented the views of Laozi, Mencius, and Mozi regarding world government and war. Liang Qichao interpreted the pre-Qin philosophers' idea of "all under heaven" as referring to the whole body of humankind. He saw this as a kind of universalism and illustrated it with Mencius's saying, "How can all under heaven be settled? It can be settled by being united," and Mozi's "Only the Son of Heaven can unify the standards in all under heaven."[3] The book also quotes Laozi's "Weapons are inauspicious instruments," and Mencius's "In the Spring and Autumn Period there were no just wars," and Mozi's chapter "Against Aggression" to prove that all three were pacifists, while holding that the Legalists were militarists.[4] Although scholars had begun to work on bringing together the interstate political thought of pre-Qin philosophers, in these studies domestic politics and foreign affairs were not clearly distinguished and there was very little in the way of systematic work, and thus this work had little impact on contemporary international relations theory.

There are four ways in which research in pre-Qin political thought has advanced. The first is the fruit of study of ancient Chinese history. While the emphasis here is placed on the pre-Qin period as such and on specific events, there are some studies analyzing pre-Qin thought though very few are undertaken from the point of view of interstate politics. For instance, a history book by Yang Kuan devotes twelve pages to summarizing Daoist thought but of this only some hundred words are devoted to interstate politics.[5] History books generally quote pre-Qin works to illustrate the political views of the philosophers but do not discuss the philosophies behind these views. For instance, by quoting Laozi's sayings that "It is better for the large to keep low" and "the ocean becomes the king of all the rivers because it is low-lying," a scholar argued that Laozi opposes the annexation of large states by small ones. But this kind of analysis cannot explain the logic of Laozi's thinking that a large state's ceding power can head off the outbreak of war.[6] If we look at this from the perspective of international relations theory, we will discover that the logical cause of Laozi's thinking is that he believed war originated from human desires and for a large state to cede power to others indicated that it had no desire to swallow up other states. When a large state has no desire to annex other states and small states have no power to do so, then wars of annexation can be avoided.

The second kind of study is that devoted to the history of Chinese thought. Here the emphasis is placed on analysis of the various schools: Confucian, Daoist, Mohist, and Legalist. There are also studies devoted to specific thinkers.[7] Books of this type enable us to understand the evolution of pre-Qin thought and the specific thought of the various pre-Qin masters. For example, scholars have discovered that "before Mencius, there was no clear opposition between 'king' and 'hegemon'; there was only a political difference."[8] A summary like this permits us to conclude that there were different kinds of hegemonic power and helps in improving contemporary hegemonic theory. This kind of research is undertaken from the point of view of domestic politics, however, and does not look at the thought of pre-Qin thinkers from the angle of interstate politics. For instance, Guanzi's theories on ruling the world in *Conversations of the Hegemon* have been summarized as discussing "rulers, power, and the relation between rulers and ministers" and understanding that "hegemons and sage kings have a sense of the right time. Having perfected their own states while neighboring states are without the Way is a major asset for becoming a hegemon or sage king." This illustrates the idea that there is a right time to exert hegemony.[9] If one looks at this statement from the point of view of international relations, it does not merely say that exertion of hegemony requires the proper time; more important, it points out the law of relative strength of a rising power to other states. In other words, whether a large state should exert itself to attain hegemonic status is determined by the relative proportion of strength between that state and others, not by an increase of its own absolute strength.

The third kind of study is dedicated to the history of China's foreign relations. This approach views the thought of the pre-Qin masters from the perspective of diplomatic relations, and holds that it is already evidence of "interstate political theory."[10] This kind of research has changed the idea that the relations of the feudal states were not interstate relations and, hence, has opened a new perspective for understanding the thought of the pre-Qin masters from the point of view of interstate politics.

Scholars adopting this approach use ideas from contemporary international relations theory to expound pre-Qin diplomatic thought and thus have opened up a new way of understanding these thinkers. For example, they use "idealism" and "realism" to differentiate the pre-Qin thinkers, taking Laozi, Mozi, and Confucius as "idealists" and Guanzi and Yanzi as "realists."[11] We must be very careful in applying concepts of contemporary international relations theory to the thought of the pre-Qin masters, however, because although there are instances in which these concepts and those of pre-Qin thought overlap, there are also differences. Hence, this kind of ticking off from a list may give rise to misunderstandings. Thus, in contemporary international relations theory, idealism refers to the idea of being founded on the notion of world government and hence avoiding war. This theory is compatible with that of Confucius—whereby the Zhou Son of Heaven is held in respect and the rites of Zhou are used to restrain war between the feudal lords—but it is not compatible with Mozi's rejection of all war nor with Laozi's opposition to the use of Zhou rites to uphold peace. Mozi's thought is closer to modern pacifism, whereas Laozi's is closer to anarchism.

The fourth kind of research is in international relations. This kind of research took off only in the twenty-first century. It employs ideas from contemporary international relations theory and undertakes comparative research into the political thought of the states of the pre-Qin masters. The initial results have focused on similarities between the pre-Qin masters and contemporary international relations theory. Some scholars maintain that as regards content there are many similarities between Western diplomatic thought and that of the pre-Qin masters. The West has moved from Grotius's international legal idealism to realism; China went from Guanzi's hegemonic order and Confucius's moral order to the realism of Hanfeizi. Wen Zhong's unlimited diplomacy and Machiavelli's theories are the same.[12] This work has provided us with a comparison of China and the West and has led us to recognize the richness of political thought among the feudal states of the pre-Qin masters.[13] Nonetheless, some features of this work of comparison can be challenged. For instance, to describe the conference of the various peoples in the Zhou era as like the United Nations, or to treat the feudal states as independent nation-states easily leads us to overlook the differences between the two.[14] At present the academic world accepts that the biggest difference between the nation-state and any other previous form of state is that the latter did not depend on international recognition. Previously, international recognition was not a prerequisite for acceptance as a state.

The results of international relations research have begun to head in a very revealing direction in recent years. Scholars are using pre-Qin thought and contemporary international relations theory to lead them to look for a way to shed new light on contemporary international relations theory. For instance, scholars have noticed that Hanfeizi adopts the view that the political system is an independent variable of the increase in a state's power, enabling us to realize that there is a need to deepen our understanding of the relationship of between the system and both hard and soft power.[15] Some scholars have studied the idea of intervention in *Zuo's Commentary* and found that successful intervention depends on the degree of intervention and the consistency of purpose, not on the amount of power exerted.[16] A Korean scholar has studied the *Record of Rites* and discovered that the idea of being a sage within and reigning without can help contemporary political leaders to undertake personal moral improvement and thereby enhance the international environment.[17] Some scholars have noted that the *Guanzi* emphasizes a combination of the development of power in economics, military affairs, and politics, which can be of value to researchers interested in the strategy of rising powers.[18] Having read the extracts in *Zhongguo Xian Qin Guojiajian Zhengzhi Sixiang Xuandu* (Readings in pre-Qin Chinese diplomatic thought), some scholars have remarked that the differences between the thought of the pre-Qin masters and contemporary international relations theory are more important than the similarities, because similarities simply reinforce each other whereas differences allow for the recognition of changes.[19] Although the revelatory nature of this kind of research is powerful, little has been accomplished so far in comparing the interstate political thought of the pre-Qin masters.

In fact, none of these four kinds of comparative research of the interstate political thought of the pre-Qin masters has produced much. The main purpose of undertaking a comparison is to be able to grasp the true

TABLE 1.1
Analytical Levels and Epistemological Ideas

	Analytical Level		
Epistemological Ideas	*System*	*State*	*Individual*
Conceptual determinism	Laozi, Mozi		Confucius, Mencius
Dualism		Guanzi	Xunzi
Materialist determinism		Hanfeizi	

picture of pre-Qin thought so as to make new discoveries in theory, not to assess the past. That is what this essay attempts to do.

ANALYSIS OF THOUGHT

The language and vocabulary of the pre-Qin thinkers were very different from those used today, yet their way of thinking about problems and their logic were very similar. In their works there is no clear methodology, their patterns of thought are heterogeneous, and their analytical logic is contradictory in places. Hence, to clarify and understand the logic of their thought, this essay relies on their basic concepts and categorizes them according to modern epistemological methods. The two axes are those of analytical level and epistemological ideas. In this way we can group the seven authors (Guanzi, Laozi, Confucius, Mencius, Xunzi, Mozi, and Hanfeizi) according to table 1.1.

Levels of System, State, and the Individual

Following the three levels of analysis of international relations, we can classify the analytical perspectives of Mozi and Laozi as on the level of the system, those of Guanzi and Hanfeizi as on the level of the state, and those of Confucius, Mencius, and Xunzi as on the level of the individual person.

Mozi and Laozi analyze interstate relations from the viewpoint of the whole interest of the whole world rather than from that of the advantage of each state. Mozi believes that using war to attain preeminence is beneficial only to a few states, not to most. War enables a very few states to become hegemons but at the cost of many, many small states that perish. Hence, he concludes that war is the greatest abuse. In refuting the idea that states should become strong and exert hegemony he says, "In the past the Son of Heaven enfeoffed the princes, more than ten thousand of them; today, because they have been annexed, the myriad and more states have been eliminated and only four states still stand. This is like the doctor who visits more than ten thousand patients but cures only four; such a one cannot be called a good doctor."[20] Laozi's model of the ideal world order is based on many small, weak states, not on strong, big states. He holds that if all states returned to the primitive era of recording events on knotted cords and the contacts between states were reduced, then the conflict between states would be reduced, and so he advocates small states with small populations. He says, "Let the people tie knots and use them, enjoy their food, embellish their dress, repose in their homes, rejoice in their customs. Neighboring states will look across at one another, calls of chickens and dogs will reply to one another. The people will reach old age and die but not communicate with others."[21]

Guanzi and Hanfeizi conduct their analyses largely at the level of the state. The starting point of their analyses is the state or the ruler, state and ruler being generally interchangeable. Guanzi and Hanfeizi both hold that relative power is the deciding factor in the rise and fall of states and in interstate relations. Guanzi says,

> Having perfected their own states while neighboring states are without the Way is a major asset for becoming a hegemon or sage king. . . . The early sage kings were able to reign as sage kings because the neighboring states made wrong decisions.
>
> There are conditions that mark out the hegemons and sage kings. They are superior in moral virtue, in wise stratagems, in war—knowing the terrain and moving accordingly—and thus they reign.[22]

Hanfeizi believes that human beings are selfish; hence, conflict cannot be eliminated and only if a state is strong can it uphold state interests. He maintains that the strength and size of a state are dependent on its legal governance: "There is no constant strength or constant weakness for a state. If the one who makes the law is strong, then the state will be strong. If the one who makes the law is weak, then the state will be weak."[23] He constantly reiterates that the authority of the state is the foundation, and even holds that diplomacy is of no help in making a state strong and large: "If today one does not exercise law or administrative techniques domestically while using one's wisdom externally, then one cannot arrive at strong governance."[24]

The method of analysis employed by Confucius and Mencius is on the level of the individual person, specifically, the ruler. Confucius believes that the stability or instability of the world order is wholly determined by the moral cultivation of the political leader. He maintains that the personal virtue of the leader is the foundation of social order. Hence, he says, "If for one day one can overcome oneself and return to rites, then all under heaven will accept one's benevolent authority."[25] Again, "By cultivating yourself you can bring peace to the common people."[26] Mencius inherited Confucius's analysis at the level of the individual person. He ascribes the presence or absence of world order and the survival of states to whether the ruler has implemented benevolent governance, not simply to the ruler's own moral cultivation. He holds that the reason the first kings of the three dynasties of Xia, Shang, and Zhou rose to leadership of their states whereas the three last kings of the same dynasties lost their positions was that the former governed benevolently and the latter did not: "The three dynasties acquired all under heaven by benevolence and they lost it through lack of benevolence. This is the reason why states decline or flourish, rise or fall."[27]

Xunzi's analysis is largely at the individual level. In analyzing the nature of international society, Xunzi regards the nature of the ruler of the leading state and his ministers as an independent variable—that is, whether international society is that of a sage king or a hegemon is determined by the nature of the ruler of the leading state and his ministers: "Those who follow the principle of humane authority and work with subordinates of humane authority can then attain humane authority; those who follow the principle of hegemony and work with subordinates of hegemony can then exert hegemony."[28]

Sometimes Xunzi also injects analysis from the perspective of the social system. He sometimes argues that human society is communal; hence, unless there are hierarchical norms, conflict will inevitably arise. To uphold interstate order it is necessary to establish hierarchical norms: "The life of human beings cannot be without communities. If there are communities without distinctions, then there will be conflict, and if conflict then disorder, and if disorder then poverty. Hence, the failure to distinguish is the bane of human life, whereas having distinctions is the basic good of all under heaven."[29]

Materialist Determinism and Conceptual Determinism

In stressing the standard of the role of matter or that of concepts, we can separate these seven philosophers into three groups. Hanfeizi is a committed materialist determinist; Guanzi and Xunzi are material and conceptual dualists; and Laozi, Confucius, Mozi, and Mencius are conceptual determinists.

In his examination of the causes of social conflict and recognition of state relations, Hanfeizi is always a materialist. He holds that because times change, material resources cannot satisfy needs, and hence conflict arises within humankind, and rewards and punishments are not able to eliminate it; hence, conflict between states cannot but rely on material forces: "Therefore, when the population increases and goods grow scarce, the energy expended to get by is taxing but the rewards reaped are paltry, so the people strive against one another. Even if you increase rewards and lay on punishments you will not prevent disorder. . . . Thus I say that as circumstances change so the means of dealing with them vary. In the remote past, conflict was decided by morals; in the recent past, it was decided by clever stratagems; today, conflict is decided by strength."[30]

Guanzi is a material and conceptual dualist. Guanzi holds that international order and interstate relations are determined both by relations between human beings' material interests and by conceptual thought.

He holds that to maintain a stable international order both material power and moral thought are necessary. Either one alone is insufficient: "If virtue does not extend to the weak and small, if authority does not overawe the strong and great, if military expeditions cannot bring all under heaven to submission, then it is unrealistic to seek to be hegemon over the feudal lords. If one's own authority is matched by like authority in another state, if one's control of the military is challenged by others, if one's virtue cannot embrace distant states, if one's commands cannot unify the feudal lords, then it is unrealistic to seek to reign over all under heaven."[31]

Xunzi is a moderate conceptual determinist. He sees the ideas of the ruler and chief ministers as the driving force behind state conduct, and therefore the cause of change in a state's status is dependent on the ideas of the ruler and chief ministers. He thinks that the ruler's ideas lead him to choose chief ministers, and this causes changes in a state's status: "By practicing the norms of humane authority and employing humane people, one may attain humane authority. By practicing the norms of hegemony and by employing hegemonic people, one may attain hegemony. By practicing the norms of a dying state and employing people of a dying state, one will perish."[32] Nevertheless, Xunzi's analysis of the cause of conflict resembles that of a dualist. He sees both human desires and material scarcity as the roots of conflict between states: "When people desire the same goods, their desire will be for more than the goods, and then a scarcity of goods will bring about rivalry."[33] At the same time, he sees a class system as an intervening variable in determining the possibility of conflict between states. He holds that if there are no norms for class distinctions, then people will fight over everything. He says, "The life of human beings cannot be without communities. If there are communities without distinctions, then there will be conflict."[34]

Mozi, Confucius, and Mencius all analyze interstate relations in terms of concepts, but they frequently link concepts to the system. Mozi holds that what leads to interstate conflict is that people have failed to love others, and at the same time he holds that there is no system such that people's thought can be unified to meet in a correct point of view. He says, "Examine where disorder comes from. It comes from failing to love each other."[35] And, "It is clear that all under heaven is disordered when there is no political leader to unify everyone's thoughts with a correct view."[36] Confucius and Mencius believe that the basic influence on state relations is the moral outlook of the ruler. Morality as a variable has two values: benevolence and nonbenevolence. Confucius believes that the leader may rely on morality to bring distant peoples to submission: "If distant people do not submit, then cultivate benevolent virtue so as to attract them."[37] Mencius says, "If the Son of Heaven is not benevolent, he cannot retain what is within the four seas. If the feudal lords are not benevolent, they cannot retain their state altars of grain. If ministers are not benevolent, they cannot retain their ancestral temples. If the officials and ordinary folk are not benevolent, they cannot retain their arms or legs."[38] Confucius and Mencius both affirm the role of the system (rites), but they believe that benevolence is the foundation of rites—that is, that a concept is the foundation of the system.

Laozi is perhaps the purest conceptual determinist. He ascribes interstate conflict to people's attitude to, and idea of, life. He says, "There is no greater disaster than not knowing how to be satisfied; no greater misfortune than wanting more."[39] He holds that if at the level of thought people can reduce their desires and be satisfied with the simple life of a small state, and if they fear death and therefore do not dare to travel far, the boats and weapons that could have been used in war will no longer be of use and thus there will be no more violent conflict: "In a small state with few people let there be weapons for tens and hundreds but they shall not be used; let the people so fear death that they shall not travel far. If then there be boats and carriages, yet no one will ride in them; if then there be armor and weapons, yet none will display them."[40]

INTERSTATE ORDER

In the works of the pre-Qin masters there is much about the causes of war and the ways to implement peace. Since their understanding of the nature of war differed, their views of whether it was just and the role of morality in upholding interstate order also differed. On this issue of war

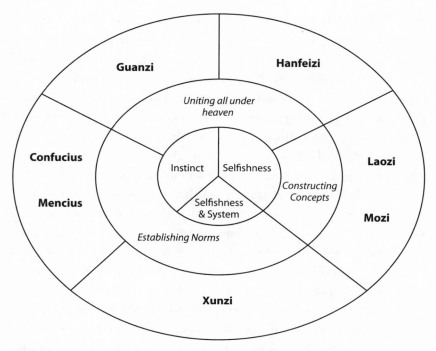

Figure 1.1 The causes of war and maintenance of peace

and peace I group the seven thinkers according to figure 1.1. In the inner circle are the causes of war, in the middle circle are the paths to peace, and in the outermost circle are the masters themselves. From this figure we discover that there is no necessary connection between the causes to which the masters ascribe the outbreak of war and the paths to peace.

Interstate Conflict and War

The seven thinkers discussed in this essay can be grouped into three categories as regards their views of human conflict and war. Laozi, Mozi, and Hanfeizi believe that the cause of human conflict is the selfishness of original human nature; Xunzi believes that the cause lies in selfishness itself and in a lack of order; Guanzi, Confucius, and Mencius believe that it arises from human beings' animal survival instinct.

Laozi, Mozi, and Hanfeizi believe that the cause of conflict is the self-ishness of original human nature. Laozi holds that the greatest sin is the rapacious mind and this mind is what leads men to fall into war. He says, "When all under heaven is without the Way, warhorses must give birth outside the city. There is no greater disaster than not knowing how to be satisfied; no greater misfortune than wanting more."[41] Since he sees war as the result of a rapacious mind, he views war as a crime: "Weapons are inauspicious instruments. Things like these are such that there are those who detest them. Hence one who has the Way does not touch them."[42] Mozi also looks at the cause of war from the point of view of the selfish human mind. He attributes war to people loving only their particular states rather than the world as a whole: "Each prince loves his own state and does not love others' states; hence they attack other states so as to benefit their own."[43] Hanfeizi also attributes violent conflict to the selfish nature of humankind. But he explains conflict from the failure of material goods to meet demand: "Therefore, when the population increases and goods grow scarce, the energy expended to get by is taxing but the re-wards reaped are paltry, so the people strive against one another."[44] He maintains that private interest is the basic motive for state behavior and a state's greatest private interest is to possess hegemonic power. He says, "to be a hegemonic king is a great benefit for the lord of men."[45] Human selfishness is, for him, the reason why interstate war is unavoidable. Some people claim that Laozi and Hanfeizi differentiate between just and unjust wars.[46] In fact, however, neither of them is concerned about whether wars are just or unjust. Laozi disapproves of all war, believing that all wars are bad; hence his saying, "One with the Way does not touch them."[47] Because all wars are bad, he does not judge their justice or injustice. In contrast, Hanfeizi does not ask if the purpose of a war is just or not; he is only concerned to know if it is victorious or not:

> To make war and be victorious is to bring peace to the state and stability to one's own royal person; the army will be strong and your awe-inspiring reputation established. Even if later you have more opportunities, none will be as great as this one. What gains of ten thousand generations should you worry about after winning the

war? To make war and not be victorious is to annihilate the state and weaken the army, you are slain and your reputation extinguished. Even if you want to avoid the present defeat, you will not have a chance to do so, still less can you hope for the gains of ten thousand generations.[48]

Xunzi does not deny that selfishness is the cause of human conflict, but he thinks that if there are the constraints of a social system, then conflict can be avoided. There are scholars who hold that Xunzi sees the pursuit of material gain as the source of conflict, but in fact Xunzi sees human selfishness and the lack of systematic hierarchical norms as the joint causes of war.[49] He says, "when the powers exercised by two people are equal and their desires are the same, then since goods cannot satisfy them there will be conflict."[50] Both Xunzi and Hanfeizi concur in believing that human nature is basically bad and the violent conflict inspired by profit seeking is an inevitable feature of society. Xunzi says, "Now the nature of man is such that from birth he tends toward gain. He follows this inclination, and hence competition and rapacity ensue, while deference and yielding are discarded. . . . Now to follow human nature and go along with human inclinations must lead to competition and rapacity, and be concordant with opposition to distinctions and to disrupting principles and so lead to violence."[51] Xunzi's theory that human nature is bad and Mencius's rival theory that it is good rely on different logics. When Xunzi speaks of selfishness, he means desire for material goods, unlike Mozi. Mozi's "lack of mutual love" is an abstract kind of selfishness. The difference between Xunzi and Laozi, Mozi, and Hanfeizi lies in Xunzi's belief that some wars are just and some are unjust. He says that the purpose of a just war is to stop violence and uproot evil; hence, "the armies of the benevolent circulate under heaven."[52]

Neither Guanzi, nor Confucius, nor Mencius directly tackles the issue of the origins of violent conflict among human beings, but they all see war as an instrument. We may assume that they think that the cause of violent conflict is the struggle for human survival itself. Moreover, this struggle for survival is not equivalent to selfishness. It is part of man's animal nature whereas selfishness is a matter of his social nature. Neither

Guanzi nor Confucius discusses whether human nature is selfish. While acknowledging that war is not a moral instrument, Guanzi nonetheless accepts that it can serve various political ends. He says, "One who plots for military victories will attain hegemonic authority. Now, although arms are not up to the Way or virtue, yet they can assist a sage king and bring success to a hegemon."[53] Confucius holds that war and humankind have always been present together, and he takes the example of the aggressive nature of wasps and scorpions to explain how human beings use weapons in self-preservation, this being part of their survival kit. When Duke Ai of Lu asked Confucius how war came about in ancient times, Confucius said, "The origins of wounding lie far back. It was born along with mankind. . . . Wasps and scorpions are born with a sting. When they see danger they make use of it so as to protect their bodies. Human beings are born with joy and anger; hence, weapons arise, and they came into being at the same time human beings did."[54] Some claim that Confucius and Mencius advocate "no war" and are opposed to all war.[55] In fact, they are not opposed to all war, only to unjust wars. They support just wars. Confucius assesses the justness of a war by its purpose: "The sage uses troops to put down inhumanity and stop violence under heaven, but later generations of rapacious persons use troops to kill the ordinary people and put states in danger."[56] Mencius asserts the goodness of human nature and therefore does not ascribe the cause of war to human selfishness. He uses the terms *punishment* and *attack* to distinguish between just and unjust war: "The Son of Heaven decrees punishment but does not inflict it; the feudal lords inflict punishment but do not decree it."[57] And, "In the Spring and Autumn Period there were no just wars."[58] Mencius also differentiates between just and unjust wars, showing that he believes that war is an instrument designed to implement justice or injustice and that it is a tool humans use to realize their goals.

Interstate Order and Peace

The pre-Qin masters' understanding of the causes of war and their preference for implementing the ways of peace are not wholly uniform. Laozi and Mozi believe that peace can be realized by constructing concepts;

Confucius, Xunzi, and Mencius believe that human behavior can be re-strained by systematic norms and by this means peace can be achieved; Guanzi and Hanfeizi think that it is necessary to increase strength so as to attain peace for one's own state.

Laozi and Mozi both think that it is possible to avoid war by changing people's ideas, but the ideas each seeks to change are quite different. Some people think that Laozi advocated small states with small popula-tions, because if the world were composed only of small states there would be no large states desirous of making war on small states.[59] In fact, Laozi attributes the cause of conflict to human selfishness and believes that this selfishness cannot be eliminated; he thinks that forcing people to fear death and enjoy life will cause them not to wish to go out, thereby reducing interaction between groups of people and, hence, reducing conflict:

> In a small state with few people let there be weapons for tens and hundreds, but they shall not be used; let the people so fear death that they shall not travel far. If then there be boats and carriages, yet no one will ride in them; if then there be armor and weapons, yet none will display them. Let the people tie knots and use them, enjoy their food, embellish their dress, repose in their homes, rejoice in their customs. Neighboring states will look across at one another, calls of chickens and dogs will reply to one another. The people will reach old age and die, but not communicate with others.[60]

He believes that forcing people not to seek progress will help in prevent-ing conflict: "In governing human beings, empty their minds, fill their bellies, weaken their will, strengthen their bones, always make it such that the people know nothing and desire nothing, so that the knowledge-able will not dare to act."[61] Laozi's thought reminds one of Francis Fukuy-ama, who claims that the better conditions of life in developed countries are such that young people have no great passions and, hence, developed countries do not think of going to war.[62]

The stress Mozi puts on the human fear of death and demand for no progress is the exact opposite of what Laozi says. Mozi advocates diminishing human beings' selfish psychology and replacing it with an altruism of loving one's neighbor as oneself and thereby avoiding war. Mozi believes that human selfishness is a necessary condition for war and so by changing human beings' selfish nature—such that they love others as themselves—peace will be realized. Mozi says, "Look at the state of others as one's own. . . . Therefore, if the feudal lords love one another there will be no savage wars."[63] Mozi thinks that to bring about this idea of loving one's neighbor as oneself one must establish a structural system, that is, a system that can unify people's way of thinking. In this way the government's advocacy of the spirit of loving one's neighbor as oneself can be transformed into an idea of the whole society. He thinks that when there is a system by which "the superiors affirm something, then everyone will affirm it, and if they deny something, then everyone will deny it."[64] In such a system, it would be possible to construct a universal idea of loving one's neighbor as oneself. Hence, he says, "Examine how all under heaven is governed. If the Son of Heaven can but unify the thoughts of all under heaven, then all under heaven is governed."[65]

The Confucians—Xunzi, Confucius, and Mencius—think that only by establishing norms (rites) for class distinctions can social order be upheld, but the norms that each proposes differ. Xunzi ascribes the cause of war to human selfish desires and to a lack of norms for class distinctions. He thinks that there is no way to eliminate selfish desires and hence one must rely on authoritative norms that allocate resources to each class: "Hence failure to make distinctions is the bane of human life, whereas having distinctions is the basic good of all under heaven. The ruler is the key to the management of distinctions."[66] The norms that Xunzi speaks of are the authoritative norms that allocate resources to each class. He says, "The early sage kings hated disorder and so they determined the distinctions of rites and norms, so that there were the grades of rich and poor, high and low status, sufficient so that there could be mutual oversight. This is the root for fostering all under heaven."[67] Xunzi thought that norms for classes would ensure the rightful authority of the feudal lords but would also set limits to that authority. Hence, by having norms the princes could check on one another and each be at peace with the others.

Confucius thought that the conduct of the feudal lords could be restrained by the moral norm of benevolence and in this way interstate order could be upheld: "If the superior likes rites then the people will easily go along with him."[68] And, "To overcome oneself and return to rites is benevolence. If for one day one can overcome oneself and return to rites then all under heaven will accept one's benevolent authority."[69] The rites that Confucius refers to are the moral norms to uphold benevolence and justice. This is different from Xunzi's understanding. Mencius has no discussion of how to uphold peace but we can assume that his ideas on this are similar to those of Confucius.

Guanzi and Hanfeizi think that long-lasting peace is impossible; they merely discuss how to strengthen a state so as to uphold its own peace. They differ in their views on the causes of war. Guanzi ascribes it to human survival instinct whereas Hanfeizi attributes it to human selfishness, but they both see war as an instrument for realizing the good of the state and both hold that the peace of the state comes from exerting military power over other states. Guanzi says, "If war is not won and defense is not firm, then the state will not be secure."[70] Hanfeizi thinks that the cause of conflict is that material goods cannot satisfy demand, but he does not think that systematic norms are able to prevent conflict. He says, "Even if you increase rewards and lay on punishments you will not prevent disorder."[71] He thinks that force is the only thing that can preserve a state's peace. He says, "Hence when a state has greater force, then no one under heaven will be able to invade it."[72] Since force is the basis of peace, neither Guanzi nor Hanfeizi can avoid the conclusion that the stronger will constantly make war on the weaker. Guanzi thinks that the strong state will use war to enhance its international status. He says, "The importance of a state will depend on the victories of its armies; only then will the state be firm."[73] Hanfeizi puts it even more plainly: "A small state must listen to the demands of a large state; weak troops must submit to the advances of strong troops."[74] Following the logic of Guanzi and Hanfeizi, it is only by using military force to unify everything under a world government that it is possible to realize universal peace. Neither Guanzi nor Hanfeizi discusses whether it is possible to prevent war when two states are evenly balanced in power.

Morality and Interstate Order

In general, the pre-Qin thinkers hold that morality and the interstate order are directly related, especially at the level of the personal morality of the leader and its role in determining the stability of interstate order. If morality and violent force are taken as two functions by which international order is upheld, then we may divide the seven thinkers considered in this essay into three groups. Hanfeizi believes that only in special circumstances does morality play a role in upholding interstate order, whereas normally violent force is the sole factor in play. Guanzi, Laozi, Confucius, Xunzi, and Mencius believe that morality is a necessary condition for upholding interstate order, but they are not opposed to the use of violent force to maintain order. Mozi, by contrast, holds that morality alone is sufficient to maintain interstate order because, to him, morality implies a rejection of violence.

Hanfeizi has been held as denying the role of morality and his observation, "In the remote past, conflict was decided by morals; in the recent past, it was decided by clever stratagems; today, it is decided by strength," has been quoted as proof. Yet he does not unconditionally reject the role of morality in upholding interstate order; rather, he thinks that the role of morality is founded on two presuppositions: first, that the main threat facing humankind is not from other human beings but from wild animals and illnesses, and second, that basic needs for clothing and food are met:

In the remote past, people were few but birds and beasts were many. People could not overcome the birds, beasts, insects, or snakes. A sage arose who fashioned wood into nests so as to avoid the many ills and the people liked this and made him reign over all under heaven, calling him "nest-builder." The people ate fruit, gourds, mussels, and clams; the stink hurt their stomachs and the people suffered many illnesses. A sage arose who struck a flint in tinder and made fire so as to transform the putrid foods, and the people liked this and made him reign over all under heaven, calling him "tinder man." . . . In the remote past men did not plow, the fruit of plants and trees sufficing for their food; women did not weave, skins of birds and beasts sufficing for their clothing. Because they did not exert any force and yet were fed and clothed sufficiently, people were few in number and goods were more than enough; hence, people did not fight. Therefore rich presents were not distributed nor were heavy punishments administered, and the people regulated themselves.[75]

He thinks that when threats to security come from human beings themselves and the basic requirements of food and clothing are not met sufficiently, then morality loses its role in maintaining order.

Guanzi, Laozi, Confucius, Xunzi, and Mencius believe that morality is the key factor in upholding interstate order. For Guanzi, morality is quite simply a necessary condition for international leaders. Only when a leader exercises morality toward other states can interstate order be upheld: "One who wants to employ the political authority of all under heaven must first extend virtue to the feudal lords."[76] Confucius thinks that raising the moral standing of the leaders will result in distant states that had not submitted to their rule coming to heel: "If distant people do not submit, then cultivate benevolent virtue so as to attract them."[77] Xunzi thinks that if the morality of the leaders of the leading states in the world is high, then all under heaven will avoid disorder. The reason for all under heaven being disordered is that the leaders are not up to scratch: "Let morality be whole and attain the highest peak; cultivate civilized principles and unify all under heaven. If you then but touch the tip of a hair there is no one under heaven who will not submit. This is the business of the heavenly king. . . . If all under heaven is not united and the desires of the feudal lords are opposed, then the heavenly king is not the appropriate person for the post."[78] Mencius believes even more that morality is the key to maintaining interstate order: "Should you make people submit to force rather to the heart, force will never suffice; should you make people submit to virtue, they will heartily rejoice and sincerely follow as the seventy disciples followed Confucius."[79]

Laozi distinguishes between the roles the Way and virtue play in upholding interstate order. Laozi thinks that the Way is the foundation of peace: "When the Way exists under heaven, then running horses are kept for their manure."[80] By this he means that when the world has the Way, then horses are detached from their war chariots and taken to the fields to provide manure and there is no need to go to war anymore. He interprets "virtue" as an application of the Way. As he puts it, "The Way generates them [the myriad things]; virtue nourishes them."[81] He thinks that the higher the "virtue" of the Way a political leader implements, the larger the group of people the "virtue" will reach and the more broadly it will extend. He says, "when practicing it [virtue] in the state, one's virtue is abundant; when practicing it in all under heaven, one's virtue is universal."[82] Given the relationship between the Way and virtue that Laozi sees, a political leader who has virtue can realize the Way and thereby uphold interstate order.

Even though these five thinkers all believe that morality is the key to maintaining order between states, they also hold that to speak of morality does not imply a total rejection of violent force to uphold order. Guanzi holds that the morality of world leaders includes gentleness toward the obedient and punishment of the recalcitrant. In other words, to fail to punish someone who disrupts interstate order is immoral. He says, "The double-faced were punished by war; the obedient were sheltered by civil ways. When both war and civil conduct were implemented there was virtue."[83] Confucius thinks that reliance on preaching to uphold the norms of benevolence and justice is inadequate. Hence he thinks that the way of war should be employed to punish the princes who go against benevolence and justice. For example, he recommends that Duke Ai should militarily punish the state of Qi for undertaking a political revolution.[84] Xunzi even goes so far as to think that talking about morality does not exclude using military force to annex other states. He says, "A humane authority militarily punishes only those who are unjust and never lays siege to others unjustly. . . . Thus people in disordered states dislike their own governments but like the humane authority's governance and welcome his military occupation."[85] Mencius thinks that using just war to uphold the norms of benevolence and justice between states is lawful. He says, "It is permissible for the minister of heaven to punish those without the Way."[86] The idea of these four philosophers that just war can be used to uphold international order still has a great influence today. The fifth master, Laozi, thinks that only when it is unavoidable should war be used to uphold order between states, although war itself cannot be said to be just. Hence he says, "Weapons are inauspicious instruments, not the instruments of the gentleman. They may be used only when unavoidable; calm restraint is superior."[87]

Mozi affirms that morality can be an effective way of maintaining order among states. Moreover, he thinks that the mention of morality should preclude resort to violence as a means of upholding that order. He is astonished that policy makers do not know what morality is. Policy makers do not apply the domestic norms of morality to interstate matters; hence, interstate order is unable to attain the degree of stability that is found within a state. Mozi notes that people generally look on individual thieves, brigands, and murderers as unjust, but when it comes to the invasion of states, annexation, and war, these phenomena are paradoxically designated as just. It is a failure to apply morality to interstate issues that causes disorder at this level: "Now what is small and wrong is said to be wrong and this is known to be so. Hence it is condemned. What is big and wrong—such as attacking states—is not known to be wrong and so people go along with it and praise it, saying that it is just. Can this be said to be knowledge of the difference between what is just and what is unjust? Therefore it is known that exemplary persons under heaven are confused in their distinction between just and unjust."[88]

LEADERSHIP AMONG STATES

The pre-Qin masters generally thought that order among states was determined by the nature of their leaders, and therefore they regularly invoked the concepts of "all under heaven" and "to reign as a sage king." Moreover, these two concepts are often joined into one: "to reign over all under heaven." Pre-Qin people did not have the idea of the Earth as a globe; they thought the Earth was square and flat. They did not know that there were lands not joined to the mainland, nor did they know that in other lands there were other people and civilizations. Hence, conceptually speaking, the "all under heaven" of pre-Qin people and today's "world" have two points in common: one is that the Earth is understood to include

TABLE 1.2

The Nature of All under Heaven and the Basis of Humane Authority

	Nature of All under Heaven			
Basis of Humane Authority	*Like State Authority*	*Unlike State Authority*	*Moral Authority*	*Transsecular Authority*
Increasing force	Hanfeizi			
Seeking good for the people	Mozi			
Increasing moral force		Guanzi		
Promoting benevolence and justice			Mencius	
Speaking of morality			Xunzi	
Cultivating morality			Confucius	
Suffering for the people				Laozi

the whole surface of the land beneath heaven; the other is that it is limited to the totality of social relationships among human beings. The pre-Qin expression "to reign over all under heaven" and our modern expression "to attain hegemony over the world" have both similarities and differences. Moreover, like today's thinkers, pre-Qin people had many different notions of what "all under heaven" or the "world" was and they also differed in their understanding of "humane authority" and "hegemonic authority." With respect to their attitudes to all under heaven and to humane authority, we may classify the differences among the seven thinkers according to table 1.2.

The Nature of All under Heaven

We can classify the pre-Qin thinkers discussed in this essay into four groups depending on their answer to the question whether all under heaven and the state share the same nature. Mozi and Hanfeizi think that the authority of the state and all under heaven share a common nature;

Guanzi holds that they are dissimilar; Confucius, Mencius, and Xunzi think that the state is a matter of power and all under heaven is a moral authority, and hence they are different in nature; Laozi thinks that the difference between state and all under heaven lies in the former being secular and the later being transsecular.

Hanfeizi and Mozi both think that all under heaven is the state writ large and so power over them is the same in nature. They think that there are four progressively larger social organizations—family, feudal town, state, and all under heaven—and these four are similar in nature. It is only the scale that differs. Hanfeizi looks at the state and all under heaven as issues of political power and believes that power alone suffices to annex all the states existing in all under heaven into one. In addressing King Zhao of Qin, he talks about the advantages of terrain, saying, "The commands and ordinances, rewards and punishments of Qin, the advantages of its terrain are unlike any [other state] of those under heaven. By relying on these to gain all under heaven, it can easily be annexed and possessed."[89] Mozi believes that power over the state and power over all under heaven are similar in nature, and by using the same methods of governance they can obtain the same results. He says, "Governing the states under heaven is like governing a household,"[90] and again, "When a sage governs a state, then its income is doubled; when he governs something as big as all under heaven, all under heaven's income is doubled."[91]

Guanzi thinks that all under heaven and the state both have to do with political power, but different kinds of political power, and so they cannot be grasped in the same way. Guanzi holds that family, local community, the state, and all under heaven are different levels of the social unit and they are essentially different and hence the method of governing each is distinct: "Trying to run the district like a household, the district cannot be run. Trying to run the state like a district, the state cannot be run. Trying to run all under heaven like a state, all under heaven cannot be run."[92] Guanzi believes that acquiring all under heaven is not equivalent to unifying all under heaven, but rather is to allow each feudal state to willingly obey, and so acquiring all under heaven relies not only on power but especially on exercising morality toward the feudal states. He says, "One who wants to employ the political authority of all under heaven must first extend virtue to the feudal lords. In this way, the first sage kings were able to gain and to give, to retract and to win trust, and thus they could employ the political authority of all under heaven."[93] And, "It was political skill by which the first sage kings acquired all under heaven, political skill that amounted to great virtue."[94]

Confucius, Xunzi, and Mencius think that there is an essential difference between the state and all under heaven: the former has to do with political power whereas the latter has to do with moral authority. Confucius thinks that all under heaven is composed of many states and that all under heaven and the state are different concepts: "Hence sages used rites to show them; hence all under heaven and states could be acquired and ruled correctly."[95] This statement shows that Confucius sees all under heaven and the state as two different political units. He thinks that all under heaven is owned by all humankind: "The working of the great Way is for all under heaven to be owned by all."[96] Because the Son of Heaven is the representative of heaven:

> Under heaven's canopy there is nowhere that is not the
> sage king's land;
> Up to the sea's shores there are none who are not the
> sage king's servants.[97]

Confucius thinks that all under heaven should be seen as having to do with moral authority, and so the rulers of states may not do what the Son of Heaven—who represents heaven—can do: "None but the Son of Heaven may determine rituals, fix measurements, and decree the form of writing."[98] He even thinks that whoever carries out inspections—whether it is the Son of Heaven or the feudal states—to enforce interstate norms and undertake military expeditions, is an indicator of whether there is moral authority under heaven: "When all under heaven has the Way, then rites, music, and punitive expeditions proceed from the Son of Heaven; when all under heaven is without the Way, then rites, music, and punitive expeditions proceed from the feudal lords."[99]

Xunzi thinks that the state is a matter of political power and hence both moral and immoral persons may strive to obtain it and use it, but all under heaven is a matter of moral authority and only the sage may enjoy it and use it: "The state is a small thing and a small-minded person may possess it. A person little gifted with the Way can obtain it and it can be held by little force. All under heaven is a huge thing. It cannot be possessed by the small person nor can it be obtained by a person little gifted with the Way, nor held by only a little force. A state can be held by a small-minded person but it cannot exist forever. All under heaven is the greatest and no one but a sage can hold it."[100] He particularly stresses that because the state is a matter of power, people who strive may be able to gain hold of it, whereas because all under heaven is a matter of authority, it cannot be acquired by striving for it. The authority of all under heaven is automatically reserved for the sage: "Tang and Wu did not seize all under heaven . . . all under heaven accrued to them. Jie and Zhòu did not lose all under heaven . . . all under heaven left them."[101] Hence, Xunzi says, "It is possible for a state to be stolen from others; it is not possible for all under heaven to be stolen from others. It is possible for states to be annexed but it is not possible for all under heaven to be annexed."[102] Mencius argues in a similar vein: "There are those lacking benevolence who have acquired states; but there has never been anyone lacking benevolence who acquired all under heaven."[103] We can compare the authority of the Pope in the Vatican and that of the military junta in Myanmar to understand the distinction Xunzi and Mencius make between 'all under heaven' and 'states.'

Laozi thinks that all under heaven has to do with transsecular authority and hence is totally different from the secular state. Acquiring state power and acquiring all under heaven cannot be achieved in the same way. All under heaven naturally accrues to one. In this Laozi shares the view of Xunzi. Laozi says, "Govern the state by orthodox methods; use troops in unorthodox ways; acquire all under heaven by undertaking nothing."[104] He even holds that not only can human striving not acquire all under heaven, but no one can hold it: "I have seen that it is not possible to acquire all under heaven by striving. All under heaven is a spiritual vessel and cannot be run or grasped. To try and run it ends in failure; to try and grasp it leads to losing it."[105]

The Foundations of Interstate Leadership

Pre-Qin thinkers generally believed that there were two kinds of inter-state leadership, humane authority and hegemonic authority. Among the seven pre-Qin thinkers discussed in this essay, Hanfeizi and Mozi thought that there was no great difference in substance between humane author-ity and hegemonic authority; Guanzi, Mencius, and Xunzi thought that there was a difference; and Confucius, and Laozi have no discussion of whether the two differed.

Hanfeizi thought that hegemonic authority and humane authority were alike in nature. In his exposition, he often links the terms *hegemon* and *sage king* as in "the titles of hegemons and sage kings," "the Way of hegemons and sage kings," "one who is a hegemon or sage king." This shows that he does not think there is any difference in nature between the two. Unlike the other pre-Qin thinkers, he does not think that the foundation of hu-mane authority is morality. He holds that in ancient times humane au-thority was upheld by morality, but with changes of the times the system of humane authority now no longer relies on morality for support: "Of old King Wen practiced benevolence and justice and reigned over all under heaven; King Yan practiced benevolence and justice and lost his state, which goes to show that benevolence and justice were of use in the past but are of no use today."[106] He thinks that the kernel of humane au-thority and hegemonic authority is to bring the states of the feudal lords to submit: "If the feudal lords round about do not submit, then the title of hegemon or sage king is unfulfilled."[107] Because of this, he thinks that humane authority is also dependent on military might and a legal system. He says, "A sage king is able to attack others."[108] "Hence making the law is the basic task of a sage king."[109]

Mozi uses the term *sage king* more than the term *hegemon*, but he does not indicate whether there is any distinction between them. Rather, he uses historical examples of humane authority and hegemonic authority to explain the same principle. Mozi's understanding of humane authority is very secular. He sees humane authority as a matter of social accumula-tion, a form of social prestige, and he thinks that this prestige is born from the government's carrying out policies that are beneficial to the people. He thinks that the sages established the institution of humane authority because it is of benefit to the people and hence it exists for their good. He says, "Of old the enlightened kings and sages were able to reign over all under heaven, and direct the feudal lords because their love for the people was sincere. Loyalty joined together with trust and led to benefits. Therefore, throughout their lives no one hated them, and up to their deaths no one tired of them."[110] Mozi thinks that Shun, Yu, Tang of the Shang Dynasty, and King Wu of the Zhou exercised humane authority whereas Duke Huan of Qi, Duke Wen of Jin, King Zhuang of Chu, King Helü of Wu, and King Goujian of Yue exercised hegemonic authority, but he does not say what the difference between them was. He thinks that what the two have in common is that they are founded on a policy of employing worthy and capable persons: "What the former four kings were influenced by was correct, and hence they reigned over all under heaven. . . . What these five princes were influenced by was correct and so they held hegemony over the feudal lords."[111] This says that the four sage kings and the five hegemonic lords were all influenced by worthy people and hence able to reign or become hegemons. Mozi ascribes the establishment of humane authority and hegemonic authority to the exclusive use of worthy people and the standard of worthiness is that they bring benefits to the people.

Guanzi thinks that the core difference between hegemonic and humane authority lies in the presence or absence of moral ability in the leading state. He thinks that what royal and hegemonic authority have in common is powerful material power and where they differ is that humane authority has the ability to correct the errors of other states whereas hegemonic authority lacks this. He thinks that humane authority can correct the errors of other states becomes it comes from a superior moral status, not because of any material power. He says, "One who enriches his own state is called a 'hegemon.' One who unifies and corrects other states is called a 'sage king.' The sage king is gifted with clear vision. He does not take over states of like virtue; he does not reign over those who go the same Way. Among those who contend for all under heaven, a sage king usually conquers violent states with authority."[112] He also says, "One who is conversant with virtue will attain humane authority; one who plots for military victories will attain hegemonic authority."[113] He thinks that humane authority and hegemonic authority can be attained by making an effort, but because the moral prestige of humane authority is high, it can attract the majority of states to follow it, whereas, given that the moral prestige of hegemonic authority is correspondingly less, only half of the states will submit to it: "The one who wins over the majority of all under heaven enjoys humane authority; the one who wins over only a half enjoys hegemonic authority."[114]

Mencius thinks that the root difference between humane authority and hegemonic authority is that the former relies on morality and the latter on power to uphold interstate order. He thinks that hegemonic authority relies on power whereas humane authority relies on a stronger form of morality for its maintenance and can survive without a particularly large material force. He thinks that the standard for differentiating between humane and hegemonic authority lies in the purpose for which the ruler upholds his power, not in the amount of his strength. Hegemonic authority borrows the slogan of benevolence and justice to uphold its power whereas humane authority uses power to implement a policy of benevolence and justice. He says, "Using force and pretending to benevolence is the hegemon. The hegemon will certainly have a large state. Using virtue and practicing benevolence is the sage king. The sage king does not rely on having a large territory."[115]

Xunzi thinks that both royal and hegemonic authority need the twin forces of power and morality, but that humane authority relies more on morality and hegemonic authority more on power. Xunzi uses the examples of King Tang of the Shang and King Wu of the Zhou, who reigned over states of a hundred square kilometers and upheld the order of all under heaven, to explain that morality is more important than material power in upholding the system of humane authority: "By practicing justice in their states, their fame spread in a day. Such were Tang and Wu. Tang had Bo as a capital, King Wu had Hao as a capital; each state was only ten thousand square kilometers, yet both kinds unified all under heaven and the feudal lords were their ministers; among those who received their summons, there were none who did not obey. There was no other reason for this but that they implemented norms. This is what is called 'establishing norms and attaining humane authority.'"[116] He thinks that the use of morality to uphold humane authority is a sign of a sage king, who chooses to act by moral norms and judges affairs by legal rules. He says, "The sage king acts according to rites and justice and makes clear judgments according to the applicable norms."[117] Xunzi thinks that, even though hegemonic authority relies mainly on material force for support, without the most basic political credibility it cannot be maintained:

> Although virtue may not be up to the mark nor norms fully realized, yet when the principle of all under heaven is somewhat gathered together, punishments and rewards are already trusted by all under heaven; all below the ministers know what they can expect. Once administrative commands are made plain, even if one sees one's chance for gain defeated, yet there is no cheating the people; contracts are already sealed, even if one sees one's chance for gain defeated, yet there is no cheating one's partners. If it is so, then the troops will be strong and the town will be firm and enemy states will tremble in fear. Once it is clear the state stands united, your allies will trust you. Even if you have a remote border state, your reputation will cause all under heaven to quiver. Such were the Five Lords. . . . This is to attain hegemony by establishing strategic reliability.[118]

In other words, even if the moral level of hegemonic authority is not high, at least one should speak the truth and be trusted by the people of one's own state and by one's allies. In those years, the five hegemons were all able to achieve this and thus they established their hegemony.

In the writings of Confucius and Laozi there is no clear discussion of the distinction between humane and hegemonic authority, but their attitudes to humane and hegemonic authority are very different. Confucius has a discussion of hegemonic authority but nothing about humane authority. From his affirmation of the role of Guan Zhong in establishing the hegemony of Duke Huan of Qi, we see two points about his understanding of hegemony. First, he thinks that hegemonic authority also needs morality; a mild use of military power to successfully rule as hegemon is benevolence. He says, "He gathered the feudal lords from the nine directions not by troops and chariots but by the strength of Guan Zhong. Oh! who has his benevolence! Who has his benevolence!"[119] Second, Confucius thinks that hegemonic authority has the ability to determine the norms of the world. Subjectively one holds the hegemonic position while objectively the mass of the people benefit: "Guan Zhong served Duke Huan, who was hegemon over the feudal lords and unified all under heaven. The people have bene-fited from his grace up until today."[120] Confucius exalts the ancient sage kings, Yao and Shun, believing that they established their humane authority by their own moral cultivation. He says, "By cultivating themselves they could bring peace to the common people. Were Yao and Shun not con-cerned about not being up to this?"[121] This is to say, by raising one's own virtue and cultivation to comfort the ordinary people, even great moral leaders such as Yao and Shun were concerned lest they had not done enough. Since he thinks that humane authority is based on self-cultivation, Confucius thinks that Shun ruled all under heaven by nonaction. He says, "using nonaction to rule, was that not Shun?"[122]

Laozi discusses humane authority but not hegemonic authority. Laozi thinks that humane authority is a form of prestige that makes all under heaven submit and obey. Its foundation is the moral spirit of willingness to suffer for the people. He uses the example of the sea becoming the king of the rivers—because it is lower than any river—to explain that humane authority requires a willingness to put oneself at the bottom: "Rivers and seas are able to be the king of the hundred valley streams because they are good at choosing the low place and so they can be king over the hundred valleys."[123] He thinks that anyone in the world can attain royal power because he can accept the greatest disaster of a state. He says, "To accept disaster for the state is called being the lord of the altars of soil and grain; to accept destruction for the state is to be the sage king over all under heaven."[124] Because Laozi thinks that only by being willing to suffer on behalf of the multitude is it possible to attain humane authority, his logic is that to contend for humane authority betrays a selfish mind and a selfish person will not think of accepting suffering, so the people who think of contending for humane authority will not achieve it. He thinks that to attain humane authority one must rely on "not striving, for none under heaven may contend with him."[125]

In this section, we have discovered that there is a very close correlation between how the pre-Qin thinkers understand the concept of all under heaven and how they understand humane authority (see table 1.2). Hanfeizi and Mozi think that all under heaven and the state belong to the same secular power; hence, they believe that increasing state power or increasing the benefits given to the people are the foundations of humane authority. Guanzi thinks that all under heaven differs from the secular power of the state and hence he sees the basis of humane authority as lying in the moral force that corrects states' mistakes. Confucius, Xunzi, and Mencius think that all under heaven is a matter of moral authority and hence they talk about moral cultivation and implementation of benevolent government as the foundation of humane authority. Laozi thinks that all under heaven is a transsecular authority; hence he believes that the foundation of humane authority is the willingness to suffer on behalf of the people.

SHIFTS OF HEGEMONIC POWER

Shifts in hegemonic power are a constant topic in international politics. Pre-Qin thinkers also have something to say about the rise and fall of hegemons. Basically, they look at the rise and fall of hegemonic power in terms of state leadership and universally attribute it to political causes. It is very rare for pre-Qin masters to attribute it to economic causes, and no one ascribes it to the level of production. Yet, although they all speak in terms of political causes, they differ in their understanding of exactly which political factors are decisive.

The Power-Base of Interstate Leadership

The pre-Qin masters generally think that the power base of leadership among states is comprehensive and that elements of state power are not convertible. The classic position is outlined by Sima Cuo: "Someone who wants to enrich a state must enlarge its territory; someone who wants to strengthen the army must enrich the people; someone who wants to be a sage king must extend his virtue."[126] Pre-Qin thinkers generally believe that political, economic, and military factors are all important, but they also generally believe that political capability is the foundation that integrates comprehensive state power.

The pre-Qin thinkers discussed in this essay all believe that politics is the decisive factor in integrating state power. Guanzi says, "If a state is large and its governance small, the state will follow the governance. If a state is small yet the governance big, the state becomes large."[127] Laozi says, "By giving priority to the accumulation of virtue [you find that] there is nothing that cannot be overcome; when there is nothing that cannot be overcome, then none will know your limits; when none know your limits, then you can possess the state; when you possess the key to the state, then your state can last for a long time."[128] Mencius says, "If today, O King, you expand your governance and implement benevolence . . . who then can resist?"[129] Xunzi says, "Hence those implementing the rites will attain humane authority and those stressing governance will be strong."[130] Hanfeizi says, "That by which a state is strong is politics."[131] Mozi thinks that the wealth or poverty and rise or fall of a state all depend on whether the employment of people in politics is appropriate. He sets out all the reasons why a state is not able to become rich and strong: "It is because in governing their states the kings, dukes, and great officials have not bothered to appoint the worthy and use the capable in their administration."[132] In discussing with his disciples what is important in governing a state, Confucius points out that the trust of the people is more important than supplies of food or the army.[133]

Even though the pre-Qin masters generally agree that politics is the basis for the strength or weakness of state power, they have different views as to what constitutes the core factor of political power. Laozi and Confucius both think this core factor is the ruler's morality. Laozi thinks that accumulation of virtue by the leader is the key to survival of the state. He sees accumulation of virtue as "the way of being deeply rooted, firmly grounded, long-lived, and forever caring."[134] Confucius says, "Using virtue for governance is to be like the North Star: it holds its position and all the stars circle around it."[135]

Mencius thinks that the core factor for political power is to implement a policy of benevolence and justice. He thinks that, on the basis of the leader's own cultivation of virtue, it is also necessary to implement a policy of benevolence and justice. He thinks that benevolent governance means a reduction in the use of punishment and a reduction in extortionate taxes so that the ordinary people may carry on their business in peace and calm, leaving families and society harmonious. If a state is harmonious domestically then its army, even though it be weak, will nonetheless be victorious over strong enemies. He tells King Hui of Liang, "O King, if you should implement benevolent governance for the people, reduce punishments, lighten taxes and duties, allowing for deeper plowing and ensuring that weeding is done well, then the fit will spend their holidays practicing filial piety, brotherly affection, loyalty, and constancy. At home they will serve their parents and elders; outside they will serve their masters; then they can but take wooden staves in hand and attack the armored troops of Qin [in the northwest] and Chu [in the south]. . . . Thus it is said, 'the benevolent has no enemies.'"[136]

Xunzi thinks that the core factor of political power is the political guidelines of the state. He holds that the political line can determine the future of the government. There are three political lines to choose from—morality, strategic reliability, and political scheming—which lead to attaining humane authority, attaining hegemonic authority, and losing the state, respectively. He warns princes to choose their political line with care: "Hence in matters of state, norms being established, one can attain humane authority; reliability being established, one can attain hegemony; political scheming being established, the state will perish. These three choices are to be carefully considered by the enlightened lords, and they are something that benevolent people cannot fail to understand."[137]

Mozi thinks that the core factor of political power is a policy of employing only those who are morally worthy. He thinks that the historical experience of establishing humane authority always hinges on the employment of people and whether the prince is in a favorable or difficult situation: "Under favorable conditions it is necessary to appoint the worthy. In difficult times, it is necessary to appoint the worthy. If you want to honor the way of Yao, Shun, Yü, and Tang, you cannot not appoint the worthy. Appointing the worthy is the root of governance."[138]

Hanfeizi, in contrast, thinks that the core of politics is to implement a legal system: "If the one who enacts the law is strong, then the state is strong; if the one who enacts the law is weak, then the state is weak."[139] He thinks that the number of reliable, worthy people is small and inadequate to supply the needs of the state. Hence one must rely on the law to manage the officials so that they complete their tasks and undertake their responsibilities:

> The number of reliable officials today does not exceed ten, but there are several hundred posts in the state. If it is necessary to employ only reliable persons, then there will not be enough for the posts available. If the posts are left unfilled, then those who do keep order will be few while the disorderly will be numerous. Hence, the way of the enlightened lord is to single-mindedly enact the law and not seek out the wise; to let techniques of governance be firm and not yearn for the reliable. Now when the law does not fail, then the various officials have no room for deceit or trickery.[140]

He thinks that to fail to rely on the law and to trust merely the morality of the leader is to court disaster: "By relaxing the law and techniques of governance and turning to governing by the heart, even Yao could not hold the state together on the correct path."[141] This is to say that even a virtuous prince like Yao could not have ruled a state without the use of law.

Guanzi thinks that the core factor in political power is to integrate the means of governing the state. Guanzi thinks that the morality of the leader, the employment of worthy officials, a legal system, unified thinking, and diplomatic initiatives are all related to the rise and fall of states:

> A state does not fall merely because it is small or has bad luck. It is rather because the moral conduct of the lord and great ministers is not up to scratch, because official posts, a legal system, and political education are lacking in the state while externally there is plotting

by the feudal lords. Because of this the territory is whittled away and the state imperiled. A state is not successful only owing to its large size or because of good luck. It is rather because the lord and his great ministers practice their virtue, because official posts, a legal system, and political education are maintained within the state and the plotting by the feudal lords without is under control. After all this, one's efforts are crowned with success and one's reputation established.[142]

Guanzi sums up all these political factors in the phrase "the techniques of doing" and goes on to say, "Those called sage kings by people in the world know the techniques of doing. . . . [Those] who are not esteemed by people in the world do not know the techniques of doing. For one who is capable of doing, a small [state] becomes great, a weak [state] powerful. For one who is not capable of doing, then even if he were the Son of Heaven, he could be dethroned by others."[143] He also says,

If a state's territory is large but not well run, this situation is called being replete with land; if a state's population is numerous but not well governed, this situation is called being replete with people; if its army is awesome but not kept in control, this situation is called being replete with troops. When the three are all replete and continue to increase, then the state is no longer one's own state. When land is broad but not cultivated, then it is not one's land; when ministers are honored but not subordinate as servants, then they are not one's ministers; when the population is numerous but they are not supportive, then they are not one's people.[144]

Power Shifts among the Leaders of States

Pre-Qin thinkers hold that power shifts among the leaders of states are inevitable: as Hanfeizi says, "Among states none are always strong; none are always weak."[145] But this is simply a judgment about the inevitability of shifts in leadership among states and does not explain the cause of these shifts. Following on the examination of the foundations of state power by the seven pre-Qin thinkers analyzed in the preceding section, we may present the similarities and differences in their views of power shifts among states as in figure 1.2.

First, we notice that, despite the diversity of views regarding the identity of the core factor of political strength, all of the thinkers ascribe the ultimate cause of shifts in interstate leadership to the ruler himself. This is the first independent variable to the left in figure 1.2. The move from the success or failure of state governance to shifts in leadership among states is but a process of moving from quantitative to qualitative change. In other words, from the success or failure of state governance to the power gap between the two sides is a shift from a change of degree to a change of nature and then to a shift in leadership among states. As Guanzi puts it, "Having perfected their own states while neighboring states are without the Way is a major asset for becoming a hegemon or sage king. . . . The early sage kings were able to reign as sage kings because the neighboring states made wrong decisions."[146]

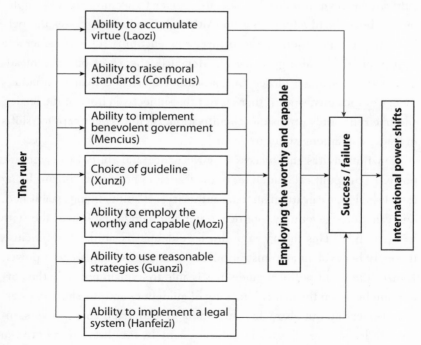

Figure 1.2 Political strength and shifts of international power

The seven pre-Qin thinkers had different views on the causes for the success and failure of the prince's administration of the state, as reflected in figure 1.2. Confucius takes the personal moral cultivation of the leader as the cause of the success or failure of governance. This view is shared by all the other thinkers discussed except Hanfeizi (see table 1.2). We can see that, apart from Hanfeizi, the other six thinkers all believe that the basis of humane authority belongs to the category of morality, but they differ in their view as to what constitutes the core of the leader's morality.

Mencius ascribes the success of the state and the shift of leadership among states to whether the ruler implements a benevolent government: "The three dynasties acquired all under heaven by benevolence and they lost it through lack of benevolence. This is the reason why states decline or flourish, rise or fall."[147] His theory of benevolent government, even more than Confucius's theory of personal morality, challenges the activities and initiatives of the government; that is, the prince must not only cultivate his own morality but also use power to accumulate and implement a benevolent administration. Although Confucius stresses the personal moral cultivation of the prince, this encompasses a considerable degree of laissez-faire governance. Mencius's theory of benevolent administration is much closer to historical experience than Confucius's theory of morality, since if there is not the subjective effort of the leader, and one relies only on his moral cultivation, then it is very rare for shifts in leadership among states to occur.

Xunzi attributes the success of governance and shifts in hegemonic power to the political guidelines of the leader, as he puts it: "norms being established, one can attain humane authority; reliability being established, one can attain hegemony; political scheming being established, the state will perish."[148] This theory of political guidelines is similar to Mencius's theory of benevolent administration, but it has deeper explanatory power. Xunzi's theory of political guidelines is able to explain not only the correlation between the prince's making of guidelines and the shifts in interstate leadership but also why, after shifts in leadership among states, interstate leadership changes in nature—namely, the distinction between humane and hegemonic authority. Xunzi thinks that once the political guideline is confirmed it will guide the ruler's policy and his choice of men to serve in the government: "Those who follow the principle of humane authority and work with subordinates of humane authority can then attain humane authority; those who follow the principle of hegemony and work with subordinates of hegemony can then exert hegemony; those who follow the principle of a failed state and work with subordinates of a failed state will fail."[149]

Mozi attributes the success of governance and shifts in leadership among states to whether one employs worthy people. Regarding the successful reigns of Shun, Yü, Tang of the Shang, and Wu of the Zhou and the failure of Jie of the Xia, Zhòu of the Yin (i.e., the Shang), and Li and You of the Zhou, he notes, "What the former four kings were influenced by was correct; hence, they reigned over all under heaven and were established as Son of Heaven; their efforts and reputation covered heaven and earth. . . . [T]he latter four kings were influenced by what was incorrect and hence their states were destroyed and they were killed, becoming the shame of all under heaven."[150]

Guanzi ascribes the success of state governance to having reasonable strategies. He says,

> Though now great, yet if one does not work on it, it will revert to small; though now strong, if one does not manage it well, it will revert to weakness; though it has now a large population, if one does not manage it well, its population will revert to a small one; though it is now honored, if it is lacking the rites, it will revert to being slighted; though it is now important, if one is not temperate about it, it will revert to being treated lightly; though it is now rich, if one is overly proud about it, it will revert to poverty.[151]

Guanzi's theory of reasonable strategies is very inclusive. He opts for a multivariable analysis. The strategies for governing a state he mentions include morality, political strategies, guidelines, employment of officials, and the rule of law, including the core viewpoints of the other thinkers. Although Guanzi's theory of strategy is complete and easy to put into practice, a multivariable explanation prevents one from grasping the core factor of his theory.

Confucius, Mencius, Xunzi, Mozi, and Guanzi all explain shifts in hegemonic power through the one mediating variable of the need to employ worthy people; that is, all of them think that employing worthy and capable persons is a necessary, even the crucial, condition for successful governance. As Guanzi says, "one who contends for all under heaven must first contend for men."[152] Confucius thinks that only if one employs worthy and capable persons will the people in general trust the government: "If you appoint the upright and dismiss all the crooked, then the people will submit; if you appoint the crooked and dismiss the upright, then the people will not submit."[153] Mencius says, "When you honor the worthy and employ the capable, then outstanding people will be at their posts and then all exemplary persons under heaven will be happy and will want to serve in your court. . . . In this way you will have no enemies under heaven to compete with you."[154] Xunzi says, "Hence one who honors sages may attain humane authority; one who honors the worthy may attain hegemony; one who respects the worthy will survive, whereas one who slights the worthy will perish. From of old until now it has always been the same."[155] Mozi puts even more weight on elevating the worthy as the basis for good governance.

Laozi thinks that the accumulation of virtue is the way to run a state and attain all under heaven, but he does not think that employment of the worthy and capable is a good thing. In this he differs from the five other thinkers discussed so far in this section (see figure 1.2). Laozi thinks that to refuse to compete is a virtue and, hence, the way from accumulating virtue to attaining to all under heaven passes by the policy of doing nothing. As he puts it, "Acquire all under heaven by undertaking nothing."[156] He thinks that appointing the worthy and capable increases opportunities for competition between people and, thus, to avoid conflict it is better not to appoint such people. He says, "Do not appoint the worthy, lest the people compete with one another."[157]

Hanfeizi thinks that the legal system is the first cause of the rise of a state. His theory of the legal system is quite different from the theories of the other thinkers. It differs, first, in that he denies any role to morality in the rise and fall of states or in shifts of interstate power (see table 1.2): "Hence King Yan was benevolent and just and the state of Xu fell; Zi Gong was eloquent and wise and the state of Lu split. Clearly then, benevolence, justice, eloquence, and wisdom are not the means by which to maintain a state."[158] The second difference is that he ascribes the cause of shifts of power to the system, not to the employment of persons. He thinks that a stern system of officials will make a state strong, whether one employs the worthy and capable or not (see figure 1.2): "When officials are ruled, then the state is rich; when the state is rich, then the army is strong and all the business of being a hegemon or sage king is accomplished."[159]

THEORY AND STRATEGY

Theory of Diplomacy for a Harmonious World

Most of the pre-Qin thinkers discussed in this essay were conceptual determinists—apart from Hanfeizi, who was a strong materialist determinist (see table 1.1). This phenomenon makes us realize that ancient Chinese thinkers had a deep understanding of the role of concepts. Their thought can enrich present-day international relations theory. In today's international relations theory, the two well-developed theories are realism and liberalism, and both of these schools look at international relations from the point of view of material benefit and material force. The theories of these two schools are tending to converge and they are widely used in practical international politics. Since the end of the twentieth century, international relations theory has begun to hold the role of concepts and thought in mind, such that constructivism and international political psychology have emerged. These two theories are not yet mature, however, and they are stuck at the academic level, having not yet entered into the political sphere. What pre-Qin thinkers have to say about international relations is all grounded in policy; their thought is oriented toward practical political policies. Therefore, to hold up what the pre-Qin thinkers say about the role of concepts in international relations as a mirror may help constructivism and international political psychology achieve success in the field of political policy. At the same time, it may enrich the theories of realism and liberalism.

That the pre-Qin thinkers analyze interstate relations on the basis of concepts sheds light on the construction of China's theory of harmonious world diplomacy. What emerges is that a theory of harmonious world diplomacy will have difficulty in attaining any great influence on international relations or in acquiring historical vitality unless it presents a universal vision. Among the views of the pre-Qin masters, Confucius's idea of benevolence and justice most easily finds points in common, since its universal nature is strong, its influence and vitality are correspondingly great. Mao Zedong's theory of perpetual revolution is a theory of the weak overcoming the strong, which has very strong universal potential and may be used for military conflict by many weak groups resisting powerful ones; hence, it has been studied and applied by many weak and small nations and states throughout the world. On the one hand, if China's harmonious world diplomacy can be universalized, then its international influence will be very great. On the other hand, if harmonious world diplomacy proposes ideas on the basis of China's special characteristics, then it can be used only in China or in a very limited number of other countries. In that case, it would have difficulty in attaining international influence and the number of countries that would accept it would be small.

Theory of Security Cooperation

The pre-Qin thinkers analyzed in this essay generally believe that the cause of war lies in human nature or selfishness (see figure 1.1). This point is the same as the basic understanding of modern international security theory. On a theoretical level, this tells us that using violence to defend a state's survival is natural: a point that is already accepted as an axiom of international security studies. In enriching contemporary international relations theory, with this axiom as a basic premise, we may avoid many unnecessary disputes and quarrels. Although the pre-Qin thinkers all think that human nature or selfishness is a cause of war, they differ greatly in their understandings of how to implement peace (see figure 1.1). On a theoretical level, this tells us that there may be several ways to implement peace. Improving humankind's idea of a morality of peace, increasing material strength to uphold peace, and erecting a system and norms for upholding peace can all be of use in implementing the possibility of peace for all. This is like being in a windowless room: there is only one cause of darkness, but there are many ways to bring in light. A candle, a flaming brand, a light, or an electric flashlight could all dispel the darkness in the room. Now, the research in contemporary international security theory seeks the most practical and most effective means of realizing universal international peace. This resembles the time—before there was modern science—when people could study how to increase the illuminating power only of candles or fire.

Hanfeizi thinks that, in facing nonhuman security threats, the role of morality is greater than it is when facing human threats. This understanding is theoretically revealing. It shows that, with today's rise of nontraditional threats to security and the decline of traditional threats to security, morality may play a greater role in international security cooperation than in the Cold War period of security attained between two opposing military blocs. Apart from terrorism, nontraditional security threats are basically nonhuman threats to security, such as the financial crisis, the energy crisis, environmental pollution, and climate change. Climate change especially is seen as an increasingly grave threat to international security. Reducing carbon dioxide emissions has become a moral issue. Research on security theory may have to take a moral angle to analyze conflict, cooperation, success or failure, and position shifts in the area of nontraditional security. During the Cold War, Europe was always a follower of international security cooperation. After the attacks of September 11, 2001, Europe did not change its position as a follower in international cooperation against terrorism. Since 2006, climate change has been seen as a practical security threat and Europe has become a leading force in security cooperation in this field.

The three basic ways of understanding how to maintain peace advocated by the pre-Qin thinkers carry two messages for China's international security policy. First, China should mainly rely on its own military construction to maintain its own peaceful environment. Given that the concept of peace cannot yet become the external security policy of all states, and given that international order and norms are not yet able to effectively prevent war breaking out, China has no option but to increase its military capacity to maintain its own peaceful environment. Second, China should press for the establishment of an international security system and norms, and promote the realization of universal world peace. Since the United Nations Charter of 1945 provided legitimacy for each nation to achieve independence, the number of countries in the world has not ceased to grow and this tendency has not diminished even today. This implies that it is not possible to implement world peace by establishing a world government. More than two thousand years ago, Mozi and Laozi thought of realizing peace by constructing human concepts, but human nature and selfishness have not changed in the past two thousand years. Yet the international security system and norms are already very different from what they were two thousand years ago. Hence, the policy orientation in which China promotes world peace should concentrate on the international security system and norms, rather than on constructing human concepts of peace.

Theory of the Stability and Rise of Hegemonic Power

The pre-Qin thinkers' understanding of all under heaven informs us that if international leadership relies solely on the strength of hard power, it is difficult to maintain. The distinction pre-Qin thinkers made between state power and international authority makes us realize that contemporary international relations theory lacks a distinction between power and authority. Furthermore, it lacks any research into the issue of authority. The former is the strength of enforcement and is mainly built on force, whereas the latter is the strength of legitimacy and is mainly built on trust. Police and doctors may be said to represent power and authority, respectively. Given the absence of world government, the nature of international leadership is one of authority rather than power. This implies that research into issues of international authority may lead to a breakthrough in the development of international relations theory.

Apart from Hanfeizi, the other pre-Qin thinkers analyzed in this essay all think that the basis of humane authority is the moral level of the leading state (see table 1.1). This understanding provides our theory with the insight that the theory of hegemonic stability in contemporary international relations theory has overlooked the relationship between the nature of hegemonic power and the stability of the international order. After the Cold War, American neoconservatism proposed a theory of the United States of America as a "benevolent empire" (hegemon).[160] But this theory was unable to propose a concept of international benevolent authority corresponding to hegemonic power, hence, it was thought to be cosmetic propaganda and was unable to go deeper and provide an understanding of how hegemonic power could be beneficial to international order. Not only did the pre-Qin thinkers provide a concept corresponding to hegemonic power—namely, humane authority—but they also recognized that the core difference between the two was in morality. According to their way of thinking, we can suppose that the level of morality of the hegemon is related to the degree of stability of the international system and the length of time of its endurance. In the Clinton years after the Cold War, the United States adopted a policy of multilateralism that stressed international norms. During his first term in office, George W. Bush adopted a policy of unilateralism that rejected international norms. The result was that the degree of stability in the international order was higher during the Clinton period than during the Bush period. Or again, throughout history, Great Britain and France, respectively, adopted policies of indirect and direct administration of their colonies. Great Britain's colonial policy was gentler than France's, with the result that violent opposition movements were less frequent in British than in French colonies. This sort of observation may be extended to say that within a given region, the moral level of the leading state has an influence on regional stability and the durability of regional cooperation.

The pre-Qin thinkers developed two ideas, namely that "all under heaven is an authority" and that "humane authority is based on morality." These two ideas have implications for China's rise: only when the international community believes that China is a more responsible state than the United States will China be able to replace the United States as the world's leading state. Whether a state is a responsible major power is not something that the state itself can decide; it is a matter of judgment by other states. Should China increase its material power without at the same time increasing its political power, China will have difficulty being

accepted by the international community as a major power that is more
responsible than the United States. Examples of the irresponsibility of the
United States in the international community are many, but even these
are not such as to lead most countries in the world to think that China is
more responsible than the United States. If it is said that in contemporary
history there is no state that comes up to the moral level of humane authority, nonetheless there is a difference in the moral levels of the hegemonic states. After World War II, the United States replaced Great Britain
as the world hegemon not only because it had more economic and military power than Britain but especially because the U.S. Army liberated
states occupied by the totalitarian Axis powers and gave economic assistance to the nations destroyed in the war. If China's foreign policy cannot
improve the nation's standing as a great and responsible state, China may
follow in the dust of 1980s Japan, unable to replace the United States as
the leading state in the world.

Theory of International Power Shifts

Pre-Qin thinkers ascribe the basic cause of shifts in international power
to various aspects of the political leader. What this phenomenon implies
for our theory is that the basic cause of shifts in international power lies
in the thought of the leaders rather than in material force. The theory of
imperial overstretch[161] and the coalition politics theory[162] both explain
the fall of hegemonic power in terms of excessive consumption of the
hegemon's material strength, and both overlook the fact that under different leaders the same state's power may rise or fall. For instance, in the
Reagan era of the 1980s and again in the opening years of the twenty-first
century under Bush, American academia discussed the relative decline of
the United States' hegemonic power, whereas in the 1960s under Kennedy and in the 1990s under Clinton, academic discussion focused instead on the increase of U.S. hegemonic power. In fact, newly rising powers also exhibit increases and decreases in strength under different leaders.
For instance, under Stalin and Khrushchev, the Soviet Union's power increased rapidly, whereas under Andropov and Gorbachev the Soviet
Union's power decreased until eventually it disintegrated. By reflecting

on the pre-Qin thinkers' understanding of the role of leaders, in the field of international relations theory we may further investigate types of leaders and research correlations between the continuity of leadership capability and shifts in international power.

Although pre-Qin thinkers have different views of what aspects of political leadership influence shifts in international power, yet for the most part they think that it has to do with whether worthy people are employed. This observation makes two contributions to China's personnel strategy for its ascent. First, the greatest talent is the foundation of competitiveness for a large state. Guanzi says, "One who competes for all under heaven must first compete for men."[163] If competitiveness among large states more than two thousand years ago and competitiveness among large states in the contemporary globalized world both involve competition for talent, this implies that competition for talent is not a phenomenon peculiar to the era of the knowledge economy but rather is the essence of competition among great powers. If China's ascent strategy cannot attract more first-class people than the United States can, then it will be difficult to realize a national resurgence. At present, China's immigration policy is less tolerant than that of the United States. Moreover, there are many limitations imposed on foreigners assuming posts in China. Second, the core aspect of great power competition lies in the talent of potential leaders. Pre-Qin thinkers considered smart policymaking by talented leaders as much more important to strengthening a state than technical inventions by talented scientists and engineers. For instance, the strategies of recruiting one first-class university president or one first-class professor to a university so as to win status as a first-class university are essentially quite different. Hence, China's strategy for attracting talent must consider if it is to emphasize people of leadership quality or merely technicians. The degree of openness of a state's personnel policy is often related to the confidence of its government.

Theory of the Construction of International Concepts

Having analyzed the seven pre-Qin thinkers discussed in this essay, we have found that they share one thing in common, namely, that the leader's political preference is the important issue (see figure 1.2). What this phenomenon contributes to our theory is that internationalization of a concept may be based on strong states' export of that concept to weak states. Constructivism holds that international concepts are formed in the process of interaction among states, and it even notices that following the suit of great powers is a path of interaction, but constructivism has not said anything about the direction of that interaction.[164] Constructivism's understanding of international interaction has a flaw similar to one found in early interdependence theory, namely, that it fails to notice that relations between states are not equal. Seen in terms of economic interdependence, there is a difference in who relies more on others. In conceptual terms, the pre-Qin thinkers failed to consider whose concept has greater influence and who learns more from others. They noted that the construction of concepts began with the leaders and then trickled down to lower classes of society. In other words, the interaction of concepts is initiated by the leader, whereas the lower levels of society receive the concepts passively. That means the lower levels of society imitate the higher. In international society, strong states play the lead in pressing ideas, which then proliferate in weaker states. The post–Cold War political currents of democratization and marketization are classic examples illustrating how developed countries have constructed concepts in developing countries.

Pre-Qin thinkers' notion of the construction of ideas is from top to bottom, from strong to weak. This has two implications for China's rise. First, the ideas that China promotes abroad should be ones that it has practiced domestically, if they are to be accepted by the international community. In the mid-1990s, China proposed a new security concept for international security cooperation. This idea was accepted by southeast Asian countries because China was not involved in military alliances against a third party. China's proposal for democratization of international relations has not been easily accepted by the international community because China could not abandon its special veto power in the United Nations Security Council. Second, the new ideas that China proposes require that China have a powerful position in that area or else they will not prevail in the international community. For example, China's idea that economic reform should come before political reform has been universally accepted by developing nations. This idea has challenged the Western notion that democracy is a precondition for successful development. This idea has become popular in developing countries because China's economic development is the most successful in the world and has won supreme status in the world in the area of reform.

There is still great scope for looking at the pre-Qin philosophers' interstate political philosophy and seeing how this can enrich contemporary international relations theory—and using it to develop a more effective strategy for China's rise. This essay seeks to arouse fellow scholars' interest in studying at pre-Qin interstate political thought from various points of view.

2

Xunzi's Interstate Political Philosophy and Its Message for Today

Yan Xuetong

Xunzi (ca. 313–238 BCE) was a famous thinker from the Warring States Period. There have been many in-depth studies of his philosophy in the light of the history of thought in China, but in the political arena the majority of such studies examine his view of domestic administration; very few scholars have examined Xunzi's ideas from the perspective of international politics.[1] What Xunzi has to say about international politics is found scattered throughout his writings but is largely concentrated in three chapters: "Humane Governance," "Humane Authority and Hegemony," and "Correcting: A Discussion."[2] Although what Xunzi has to say about international politics cannot strictly be called a theory in the full sense of that term, yet from the ideas he set out more than two thousand years ago it is possible to explain aspects of modern international politics.[3] This implies that some of his ideas must be quite reasonable. This essay looks at Xunzi's interstate political philosophy from the perspectives of methodology, the basic concepts of international politics, and the strategy for China's rise.

METHOD OF ANALYSIS

Analysis of Individual Entities and on the Level of the Individual

International actor and international system are two important analytical variables in contemporary international relations theory. To explain the phenomenon of international politics by means of changes of actor is called "individualistic analysis"; to explain the same phenomenon by means of changes in the international system is called "holistic analysis." Although Xunzi does discuss interstate norms (rites) and the system of Five Services as a means of preventing international conflict, yet since his thought is grounded in the premise of the unity of the whole world, he discusses how to implement a stable international order from the viewpoint of the policy of major powers. Xunzi thinks that major powers are the cause of the success or failure of stability in the international system but the international system cannot change the behavior of major powers. He begins by analyzing the conditions under which states rise, fall, and collapse, and then brings together the causes of change in the international order. In his analysis, order and disorder serve as the two values of the dependent variable, interstate order. Sage king (or humane authority), hegemon (or hegemony), and tyrant (or tyranny) serve as the three values of the independent variable, the nature of the state.[4] In the *Xunzi*, as verbs *wang* (to be a sage king) means "to lead the world"; *ba* (to be a hegemon) means "to dominate the world," and *qiang* (to be a tyrant) means "to be stronger than other states." As nouns, the three terms refer to states or their leaders who undertake these respective actions. Xunzi sees the character of the state, the type of ruler, and the nature of policy as three aspects of the same thing, holding that these three are all of a piece. The degree of stability of international order is determined by the nature of the world's major powers. He concludes that if the world's major powers are ruled by sage kings or hegemons, then the international order is stable; if by tyrants, then it is unstable. If the great power is a hegemon, then even though it enjoys stable relationships with its allies there is instability in relations with countries outside the alliances (see table 2.1).

An established methodology for studying international relations theory is what is known as the levels of analysis. The three levels of analysis in international studies are: system, organization and individual. Xunzi's analysis belongs to that of the individual. In his analysis, the state is a mediating variable and the ruler is the most basic independent variable. He thinks that the state is a tool with which the ruler can administer society.

TABLE 2.1
International Order in Relation to the Nature of Major Powers

International Order	Type of Major Power		
	Humane Authority	Hegemony	Tyranny
Stable			
Unstable			

Differences in the ruler's morality and beliefs result in different principles and policies in running the state and hence in different types of state. The differences in morality of the rulers of the world's major powers lead to a difference in the nature of their states, and this in turn determines whether the international order is stable. He says, "The state is the most important instrument for ruling all under heaven. The ruler holds the most important position under heaven. If you find the way to hold it, then there is great peace and great glory, and the source of all that is praiseworthy. If you do not learn the way to hold it, then there is great danger, and a great accumulation of such dangers means that it would be better not to have the state than to have it."[5]

Xunzi's analysis of individuals is not limited to the ruler alone; he also emphasizes the role of the chief ministers. In his analysis, the chief ministers and the nature of the state are equally important mediating variables. The chief ministers are a mediating variable coming between the ruler and the nature of the state (figure 2.1). He believes that the core role of the ruler is not to administer the state himself but to choose chief ministers who will do this. He says, "One who holds the state must not administer it alone, since strength and weakness, glory and shame lie in choosing chief ministers. An able person with able chief ministers may be a sage king. Someone who is not able but knows and is fearful because of it yet seeks able persons may be a powerful ruler. Someone who is not able and who does not know that he should be fearful and does not seek able

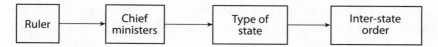

Figure 2.1 Policy makers and interstate order

persons, but surrounds himself with flatterers, hangers-on, and favorites, is in such danger that, at its most intense, the state falls."[6]

In comparing the two variables of the ruler and the chief ministers, Xunzi thinks that the role of the ruler is decisive because the mediating variable of the chief ministers changes along with changes in the type of ruler. Xunzi thinks that worthy ministers are not rare, but the important question is whether the ruler is able to use them. There are many kinds of chief ministers, but the decisive factor is what type the ruler employs:

> Hence, King Cheng, with regard to the duke of Zhou, was such that the king went along with whatever the duke suggested since he knew the duke was of value. With regard to Guan Zhong, Duke Huan employed him in all the affairs of state, since he knew he was of benefit. The state of Wu had Wu Zixu, but he was not used and the state was brought to its knees, losing the Way and losing the worthy. Therefore, one who honors sages may attain humane authority; one who honors the worthy may attain hegemony; one who respects the worthy will survive, whereas one who slights the worthy will perish. From old times until now it has always been the same.[7]

Conceptual Determinism and Internal Causal Determinism

International political theory may be categorized into three groups: materialist determinism, conceptual determinism, and a combination of the two. In general, realist theory is materialist determinism, seeing the hard power of a state as the determining factor; constructivist theory is classical conceptual determinism, seeing human ideas as the determining factor. Institutionalist theory adapts from both of these, holding that material strength and organizational norms are of equal importance. Xunzi does not deny the importance of material power but his method of analysis is the same as that of constructivist theory, seeing concepts as the original

motivation for all conduct. The difference between him and the construc-
tivists is that his independent variable is the personal concept of the ruler
and the chief ministers, whereas constructivism stresses that the independent variable is the concept of society as a collective. In discussing norms
of action, Xunzi uses the three terms *humane authority / sage king, hegemony /
hegemon,* and *tyranny / tyrant.* These are somewhat similar to Alexander
Wendt's use of *Kantian culture, Lockean culture,* and *Hobbesian culture.* Xunzi
says, "Humane authority wins over the people; hegemony wins over allies; tyranny wins over territory."[8] This means that emperors and kings
compete for talented people, hegemons compete for neighboring allies,
and the rulers of great powers compete for territory. Xunzi thinks that to
win over talented people requires morality; to win over allies requires
sincerity and credibility; to win over territory requires strength. Wendt
thinks that the three different types of cultural structure—Kantian, Lockean, and Hobbesian—are international norms that differ, being grounded
in legitimacy, cost, and power.[9] If we compare these two sets of concepts
we find that humane authority and tyranny are similar to Kantian and
Hobbesian culture, respectively, but hegemony is not very much like
Lockean culture.

Xunzi sees the cause of change in a state's status as dependent not on
the ability of the ruler and chief ministers but on their ideas. He thinks
that the various ideas of the ruler lead him to choose chief ministers who
reflect the new political principles leading to different results and hence
changes in a state's status: "Those who follow the principle of humane
authority and work with subordinates of humane authority can then attain humane authority; those who follow the principle of hegemony and
work with subordinates of hegemony can then exert hegemony; those
who follow the principle of a failed state and work with subordinates of a
failed state will fail."[10]

Since Xunzi sees the ideas of the ruler and chief ministers as the original driving force for state conduct, his method of analysis is that of internal causal determinism. "One suitably prepared will be a sage king; one
suitably prepared will be a hegemon; one suitably prepared will survive;
one suitably prepared will perish. In the use of a state of ten thousand

chariots, the wherewithal to establish its authority, the wherewithal to embellish its renown, the wherewithal to overcome its enemies, and the wherewithal to determine security or danger for the state all depend on oneself, not on others. To be a sage king or a hegemon, to be secure or in peril and perish, all are determined by oneself, not by others."[11] This means that the ruler's type of political achievements depends on the conditions he has prepared.

Rigorous Analysis and Comparative Analysis

All international political phenomena are the result of many factors coming together. Depending on the number of independent variables that are chosen for the analysis, analytical methods may be separated into rigorous analysis or comprehensive analysis. Comprehensive analysis involves joining together several variables to explain the changes of the dependent variable, but not examining the relationships among the joined variables. Unlike comprehensive analysis, rigorous analysis refers to the use of a single variable to explain the logical causal relationship between independent and dependent variables. For instance, Kenneth N. Waltz explains the presence or absence of war in the international system in terms of the independent variable of the power structure of major states. This is an example of rigorous analysis. Hans J. Morgenthau explains the changes in the international system according to many independent variables such as power, military strength, economic profit, culture, law, morality, and diplomatic strategies. This is an example of comprehensive analysis.

Xunzi's method of analysis is rigorous rather than comprehensive. He treats the ideas of the ruler as the most basic independent variable and explains this as determining the type of chief ministers who will implement state policies; he uses the type of chief minister to explain the type of state, and then uses the type of state to explain whether there is international stability (see figure 2.1). If we refine his analytical logic, we arrive at figure 2.2. We can add policy direction as a mediating variable between the chief ministers and the type of state, and state power and foreign relations between type of state and interstate order. In Xunzi's

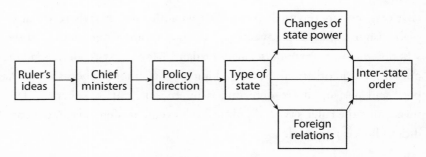

Figure 2.2 Relationships of variables at different levels

thought, variables at different levels have clear logical relationships and these logical relationships are consistent.

Comparative analysis contrasts with case analysis. Single-case analysis refers to giving arguments in support of a thesis based on a particular case, whereas comparative analysis relies on using different cases to illustrate the pros and cons of an argument. Xunzi habitually uses cases from each side to discuss a point, and thus his method is that of comparative analysis. The examples he quotes most often in support of his thesis are King Tang of the Shang, the duke of Zhou, and King Wen of Zhou. The counterexamples he chooses are Jie of the Xia and Zhòu of the Shang. For example, in discussing whether humane authority is seized or naturally accrues to its incumbent, he says,

> Tang and Wu did not seize all under heaven. They practiced the Way, carried out justice, worked for the common good of all under heaven, and removed the common ills of all under heaven so all under heaven accrued to them. Jie and Zhòu lost all under heaven. They acted contrary to the virtue of Yü and Tang, muddled the distinctions of rites and norms, acted like birds and beasts, accumulated evil, and gave full rein to wickedness and all under heaven left them. That to which all under heaven accrues is called "humane authority"; that which all under heaven deserts is called "death."[12]

This means that no ruler can seize world leadership. World leadership will automatically come to those who do sufficient good for people and depart from those who commit evil.

Although Xunzi's understanding of interstate politics is quite markedly logical, according to the standard of modern science his analytical method is not scientific. His way of quoting examples to justify his arguments is not done well according to scientific positivism. Many of the examples he chooses come from historical legends. They lack any time for the events, background, or basic account and there is no way of ascertaining their authenticity. Moreover, his examples lack the necessary variable control and his way of using examples is by simple case-selection. Although this method is frequently used in modern international relations theory, its scientific value is poor. It is weak in terms of his powers of confirmation and persuasion.

STATE POWER

The Dual Nature of the State as Actor and Tool

In Xunzi's writings the term *state* sometimes refers to a political unit and sometimes indicates a tool of the ruler. This usage is basically the same as in contemporary politics. From the perspective of international politics, the state is an international actor, but from the perspective of domestic politics, the state is the tool by which the ruler rules the people.[13]

Xunzi distinguishes between the state of the Son of Heaven and those of the feudal lords, depending on the greatness of their power: "Of old, the Son of Heaven had a thousand officials whereas the feudal lords had a hundred. One who employed these thousand officials to make his writ run among the states of the feudal lords was called 'sage king'; one who employed those hundred officials to make his writ run within his own boundaries—even though the state was not secure, yet at least it would not change hands and be abolished—was called 'prince.'"[14] In this passage the term *state* refers to a political unit. The state of the Son of Heaven was a royal state, however, and its territory and strength far exceeded those of the feudal states; thus, its power was greater than that of the feudal states.

From the point of view of function, Xunzi thinks that the state is a political tool: "The state is a big instrument under heaven and entails heavy responsibility. One may not but carefully choose people to deal with it and then run it. Placing it in risky hands will only lead to danger."[15]

The Relationship of Political Strength to Military and Economic Strength

Xunzi's view of the roles of political strength, military strength, and economic strength and the relationships among them is rather unlike that held nowadays. Today it is generally held that economic strength is the basis of political strength, but Xunzi holds the opposite view. He thinks that political strength plays a role as the basis for economic and military strength. He believes that whatever the strength of one's economic or military might, they are meaningless without the foundation of political strength. This idea of Xunzi is similar to that of the former CIA chief analyst Ray S. Cline (1932–2009), who formulated the equation that expresses the relationships among the components of comprehensive national power. According to Cline's equation, $Pp = (C + E + M) \times (S + W)$.[16] Comprehensive national power is the product of both soft and hard power, so if soft power is zero, then comprehensive national power will also be zero and hard power will be unable to play any role. Xunzi says,

> King Wen obtained the Way and with a territory of less than a hundred square kilometers he united all under heaven. Jie and Zhòu lost the Way. They held power over all under heaven but could not enable an ordinary person to live till old age. Hence, for one who is good at using the Way, even if he has a state of less than a hundred square kilometers, that suffices to be independent. For one who is not good at using the Way, even if had a country like Chu of three thousand square kilometers, he would be put into servitude by his enemies.[17]

The history of the breakup of the Soviet Union in 1991 can help us to understand why Xunzi thinks that political strength is the foundation of military and economic strength. When the Soviet Union broke up, its military strength was equal to that of the United States and its economy ranked third in the world. But when the Soviet government lost people of ability because of its internal and external politics, its hard power was unable to exercise any role in ensuring the survival of the nation.

Xunzi also thinks that political strength is the basis for the growth of hard power. Xunzi holds to moral determinism; hence, he believes that the key to the success or failure of a state is whether the state's policy is correct. When the policy is correct, state power will increase, but when it is incorrect, it will diminish:

> If the top leader does not value the rites, then the army will weaken; if the top leader does not love the people, then the army will weaken; if one is not faithful in what one has promised, then the army will weaken; if rewards and payments are not plentiful, then the army will weaken; if the generals and commanders are incapable, then the army will weaken. If the top leader has a penchant for exploitation, then the state will be impoverished; if the top leader has a penchant for profit, then the state will be impoverished; if the officials and great ministers are numerous, then the state will be impoverished; if craftsmen and merchants are numerous, then the state will be impoverished; if there are no constraints on undertakings, then the state will be impoverished. . . . Thus, in the time of Yü there was a decade of floods and in the time of Tang seven years of drought but there was no famine under heaven. After ten years the harvest was plentiful again and there was more than enough. There was no other reason for this but that they understood the beginning and end and the origin and course of events.[18]

The tripartite separation of powers in the United States, the Meiji Restoration in Japan, and the socialist system of the Soviet Union are all political factors that resulted in a rapid increase of national power for the nations concerned. This modern history helps us to understand Xunzi's idea that political strength is the basis for a growth in hard power.

Xunzi thinks that a state's political system is the basis that ensures whether a state's economy can develop rapidly. This idea is the exact opposite of that which holds that the economic level is the basis for a political system. He says, "Hence, one who restores the rites attains humane authority; one who works at politics becomes strong; one who wins over the people is secure; one who hordes wealth perishes. Thus the one who is a sage king enriches the people; the one who is a hegemon enriches the officials; a state that will survive enriches the great ministers; a dying state enriches its coffers and fills its storerooms."[19] In 1978, China adopted the policy of reform and opening to replace the previous political guideline based on class struggle, and its economy developed rapidly. This part of history helps us to understand Xunzi's idea that political policy is the basis for growth of economic strength.

Xunzi also thinks that the political principle of foreign policy is the basis for guaranteeing state security. He thinks that state security is not wholly dependent on the size of military force, but is also determined by whether at the political level a state is able to maintain reasonable relationships with others:

> If you want to deal with the norms between small and large, strong and weak states to uphold them prudently, then rites and customs must be especially diplomatic, the jade disks should be especially bright, and the diplomatic gifts particularly rich, the spokespersons sent should be gentlemen who write elegantly and speak wisely. If they keep the people's interests at heart, who will be angry with them? If they are so, then the furious will not attack. One who seeks his reputation is not so. One who seeks profit is not so. One who acts out of anger is not so. The state will be at peace, as if built on a rock, and it will last long like the stars.[20]

In the 1960s, China adopted a policy of opposition to the two hegemonic powers, the Soviet Union and the United States. But in the early twenty-first century, China has adopted the policy of living harmoniously with its neighbors. In the 1960s, China fought with the United States in Vietnam in the south, and in the north the Soviet army put pressure on the border, whereas in the early twenty-first century China maintains normal relations with major powers such as the United States and Russia (which is the successor after the breakup of the Soviet Union in 1991). China's security today is much better than it was in the 1960s. This historical comparison helps us to understand Xunzi's idea that the principle of foreign policy is the basis for state security.

Xunzi thinks that political strength plays a greater role than economic strength in diplomatic conflicts. He thinks a policy of economic bribery is ineffective in interstate relations. Rather, the most effective means is to use proper conduct to win over other states:

> If you serve them with wealth and treasure, then wealth and trea-sure will run out and your relations with them will still not be nor-malized. If agreements are sealed and alliances confirmed by oath, then though the agreements be fixed yet they will not last a day. If you cut off borderland to bribe them, then after it is cut off they will be avaricious for yet more. The more you pander to them, the more they will advance on you until you have used up your resources and the state has been given over and then there is nothing left. . . . Thus the intelligent prince does not do so. He must restore rites so as to unify his court, correct law so as to unify his officials, be even in governing so as to unify his people, and then customs will be unified in court, the various affairs will be unified under the officials; the mass of ordinary people will be unified along with him. If you do so, then those close by will compete for affection and those far away will want to draw near. The whole country will be of one mind. The three armies will join their strength together. Your reputation will be such as to overawe them and your authority strong enough to goad them. They will come and bow down to you and accept your direc-tion. No strong or violent state will not send ambassadors to you, like in the fight between Wu Huo [a giant] and Jiao Yao [a dwarf].[21]

In 2005, in order to gain a permanent seat on the United Nations Se-curity Council, the Japanese government spent sixteen billion U.S. dol-lars buying votes from developing countries but still failed to win a seat.[22] In 1971, the United States opposed the United Nations granting China's seat to the People's Republic of China (PRC). At the time, American aid to third world countries far exceeded Chinese aid. Nevertheless, with the help of friendly countries in Africa, the PRC successfully acceded to the China seat at the United Nations that year. These two historical examples help us to understand Xunzi's idea that in foreign affairs political strength is more useful than economic strength.

The Principle of Uneven Development of Power

Xunzi thinks that an important reason why one's own state can be strong is that the administration of other states is a failure: "Others accumulate faults daily; we become more perfect every day. Others become poorer daily; we become richer every day; others are overloaded with work daily; we have more and more leisure every day. In the relations between prince and ministers, people of high and low status, others draw daily further and further apart while we grow closer and closer every day. One acts correctly while others make mistakes. One who makes his own state act correctly will attain hegemony."[23] This view of Xunzi is very similar to the idea of relative power in contemporary international relations theory. Because the power status of a state in terms of strength is relative to that of other states, a state's relative advantage relies on its increasing the gap between its own strength and that of others. Nevertheless, an important factor accounting for the increasing gap is the decline of the other state. If the increase in strength of all states was equal, then their relative strengths would not change.

Xunzi also says, "The states of others are all in a mess and my state alone is well-ordered. Others are in danger and I alone am safe. Others have lost their states; I arise and administer them. Therefore, in using the state the benevolent person does not rely only on his own state; he must also conquer the will of people in other states."[24] Xunzi is not opposed to annexation but he thinks that different kinds of annexation yield different results. He thinks that morally correct annexation can increase strength whereas immoral annexation will decrease strength: "One who uses virtue to annex others will attain humane authority; one who uses might to annex others will become weak; one who uses riches to annex others will become poor. From of old until now it has always been the same."[25]

Guided by conceptual determinism, Xunzi attributes the cause of uneven development of state power to different ideas on the part of the rulers. He says, "Speaking of ministers, there are flattering ministers, usurping ministers, efficient ministers, and sagacious ministers. . . . [T]hus by using sagacious ministers one can attain humane authority, by using efficient ministers one can be strong, by using usurping ministers

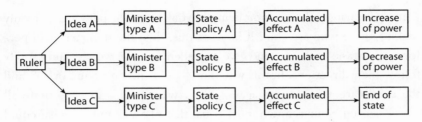

Figure 2.3 Causes of uneven development of power

one is in danger, and by using flattering ministers one will perish."[26] Based on this statement, we can extrapolate the logic of the relationship between rulers and ministers. Changes in the status of state power arise from state policy, which is formulated by high-ranking officials. Choice of these ministers is determined by the ideas of the ruler (see figure 2.3).

Xunzi says, "There is no lord of men who does not want to be strong and does not hate weakness, who does not want to be secure and does not hate danger, who does not want renown and does not hate shame. This is what Yü and Jie held in common. To fulfill these three desires and avoid the three ills, what way is the most appropriate? I say: 'prudently choose your prime minister; there is no other way than this.'"[27] Xunzi also summarizes the experience of the extinction of states in history: "In the past there were ten thousand states, and now there are fewer than a hundred. There is no other explanation for this; they did but fall away from this [a careful choice of ministers]."[28]

Because Xunzi thinks that the choice of the type of officials employed is directly related to the rise and fall of state power, he sees the choice of people as the core of a strong state's strategy: "If you wish to harmonize all under heaven and restrain Qin and Chu, there is nothing better than employing intelligent and exemplary persons. They easily use their knowledge and wisdom. They do not overwork themselves at their tasks but their accomplishments and fame are very great. They work easily and happily; hence the perspicacious prince treats them as a treasure, whereas the foolish one finds them difficult."[29] Xunzi also proposes the principle of talent, which does not distinguish between noble and mean in choosing worthy people: "Why can the lord not open positions to talent broadly, neither favoring relatives nor being partial to noble persons, but only seeking those who are able? If he does this, then the ministers will perform their tasks with ease and give precedence to the worthy and happily follow their directions. In this way there could still be a Shun or a Yü and the royal career could rise again. If you want your efforts to unite all under heaven, your renown must equal that of Shun and Yü; what could be more joyful or more praiseworthy than this?"[30]

Xunzi's understanding of shifts in state power is a classic case of having an intelligent prince and worthy aides. It is this understanding that leads him to the conclusion that political talent is the key to a state's strength. On this point his view is basically the same as that of China's ancient political philosophy, which sees regulations as determined solely by human beings and does not see the system of democratic election as having the inherent capacity to remove unsuitable people. In Xunzi's time, people had not yet realized that political system creativity is a basic factor affecting changes of status in state power.

Since Xunzi makes unifying the world the highest political goal of the prince, he is not unconditionally opposed to states pursuing a policy of annexation. He assesses the correctness of annexation according to the nature of the annexation. This idea is manifestly incompatible with international norms since World War II. He rather exaggerates the role of political power with regard to state security. Even if a small state upholds a moral foreign policy, it will be hard to avoid large states having ambitions to invade it. In 1990, Iraq invaded Kuwait, which is a typical example of this.

INTERNATIONAL POWER PERSPECTIVE

Contemporary international relations theory discusses three aspects of international power: first, the nature of power relationships, that is, whether relationships among states are cooperative, competitive, or confrontational; second, the grade of power, that is, whether it is dominant, subordinate, or participatory; and third, the content of power, that is, to which area a state's power belongs: political, economic, or military.

Xunzi's discussion of state power concentrates mainly on the character of power, a topic that is very seldom addressed in contemporary international relations theory.

Definitions of "All under Heaven" and "Possessing All under Heaven"

The idea of "all under heaven" is the basis for Xunzi's analysis of the nature of state power. Clarifying this concept is helpful for understanding his ideas of the three types of international power: humane authority, hegemony, and tyranny.

He thinks that "all under heaven" is the whole world and that "possessing all under heaven" amounts to having world leadership. This kind of power is the result of the masses and the various feudal states willingly accepting the leadership of the sage. It is not a status that the ruler can win by violence: "All under heaven is the heaviest burden there is; unless one is very strong one cannot bear it. It is huge; unless one is very clever one cannot administer it. Its people are many; unless one is very perspicacious one cannot keep them in harmony. None but a sage can manage to perform these three tasks properly. Hence none but a sage can be a sage king. . . . All under heaven is so huge that none but a sage may possess it."[31] Xunzi rejects the idea that Jie and Zhòu possessed world leadership: "A popular saying goes that 'Jie and Zhòu possessed all under heaven; Tang and Wu usurped and took it.' It is not so. That Jie and Zhòu had the title of Son of Heaven and that the title of Son of Heaven was theirs is correct, but to say that all under heaven was Jie's and Zhòu's is not correct."[32] Here he denies the popular saying that the kings Tang and Wu usurped world leadership from Jie and Zhòu, respectively. He thinks that it is correct to say that Jie and Zhòu had the *title* of leader of the world, but it is wrong to say that they possessed world leadership.

Xunzi holds that the title of world leadership and world leadership itself are two different things:

> The sons of a sage king are his children. They have the legitimacy
> to inherit the position of a sage king after his death as well as the

ancestral house of all under heaven. If they are incompetent or improper, however, then internally the ordinary people will detest them and externally the feudal lords will rebel against them; close at hand there will be no unity within the domain and far away the feudal lords will not obey. Commands will not run within the domain. Furthermore, the feudal lords will invade and attack them. If it is like that, then even if they do not perish, I say that they do not possess all under heaven.[33]

Between 2002 and 2010, the Afghan government ruled Afghanistan in name, but in practice its authority was restricted to the capital, Kabul. Even though this example is not one of world leadership, it can help us to understand what Xunzi has to say about "possessing all under heaven."

Xunzi thinks that state power and world leadership are different. He holds that state power can be seized but world leadership may not be; rather, it automatically accrues to the appropriate person: "It is possible for a state be stolen from others, but it is not possible for all under heaven to be stolen from others. It is possible for states to be annexed, but it is not possible for all under heaven to be annexed."[34] At the beginning of World War II, the military and economic power of Nazi Germany rose considerably and the expansion of its armies outward increased Germany's power over world affairs, but Germany was not able to rely on this to gain international leadership; instead, it increasingly became the enemy of many countries. This experience from history can help us to understand Xunzi's distinction between the ruling power of a state and leadership of the world (all under heaven).

Humane Authority Founded on Political Morality

Xunzi thinks that humane authority is the highest form of world power. Its foundation is the morality of the ruler of a kingdom (the Son of Heaven): "Thus it is said: by practicing justice in their states, their fame spread in a day. Such were Tang and Wu. Tang had Bo as his capital, King Wu had Hao as his capital; both were only a hundred square kilometers, yet they unified all under heaven and the feudal lords were their ministers; among those who received their summons there were none who did not obey. There was no other reason for this but that they implemented norms. This is what is called 'establishing norms and attaining humane authority.'"[35] This is to say that the superior morality of King Tang of the Shang and King Wu of the Zhou were such that they could attain leadership of all under heaven based on the small cities of Bo and Hao, respectively. The religious authority of the Vatican is rather like what Xunzi says about humane authority. The territory of the Vatican is even smaller than that of Singapore and its economic might is not up as great as Singapore's. Moreover, it has no army. Nevertheless, the Vatican's authority in world affairs is far beyond Singapore's. This example can help us to understand why Xunzi thinks that morality is the foundation for attaining leadership under heaven.

Xunzi thinks that people who possess humane authority do so because they implement moral norms. Speaking of the sage king, he says,

> Unlike others, his benevolence stretches to all under heaven; his justice to all under heaven; his authority to all under heaven. Since his benevolence stretches to all under heaven, there is no one in all under heaven who does not love him. Since his justice stretches to all under heaven, there is no one in all under heaven who does not respect him. Since his authority stretches to all under heaven, there is no one in all under heaven who dares oppose him. Relying on the authority of invincibility and a policy of winning people's support, one can win victories without wars, acquire without attacking. Troops in armor are not sent out and yet all under heaven submits. This is the man who knows the humane way of leadership.[36]

Since Xunzi thinks that humane authority is founded on the superior morality of the ruler himself, he thinks that only a sage can possess humane authority: "The sage is someone who possesses the Way and is perfect all round and who is the standard for judging the authority under heaven."[37] We would have difficulty finding a political leader who meets Xunzi's standard, but if one compares Franklin Delano Roosevelt as president of the United States during World War II and the recent George W. Bush, we can see what Xunzi means about the moral power of the leader playing a role in establishing international norms and changing the international system. Roosevelt's belief in world peace was the impetus for the foundation of the United Nations after World War II, whereas Bush's Christian fundamentalist beliefs led to the United States continually flouting international norms, which resulted in a decline of the international nonproliferation regime.

Hegemony Based on Hard Power and Strategic Reliability

Xunzi thinks that hegemony is a lower form of international power than humane authority. Humane authority is something that other states are willing to accept as their leadership under heaven, whereas hegemony is interstate domination when the ruler's moral level falls short of that required for humane authority and when he attains interstate leadership by great force and strategic reliability. Humane authority naturally accrues to a sage but hegemony can be gained only by the ruler's striving for it.

Xunzi thinks that even though hegemony is a lesser form of interstate power than humane authority yet attaining hegemony is not easy. Even though the moral level of the hegemon is not as high as that of humane authority yet it must at least reach the level of being strategically reliable. In other words, one cannot attain hegemony by trusting to hard power while lacking strategic reliability. When describing hegemony, Xunzi says,

> Although virtue may not be up to the mark, nor were norms fully realized, yet when the principle of all under heaven is somewhat gathered together, punishments and rewards are already trusted by all under heaven, all below the ministers know what they can expect. Once administrative commands are made plain, even if one sees one's chance for gain defeated, yet there is no cheating the people; contracts are already sealed, even if one sees one's chance for gain defeated, yet there is no cheating one's partners. If it is so, then the troops will be strong and the town will be firm and enemy states will tremble in fear. Once it is clear the state stands united,

your allies will trust you. Even if you have a remote border state, your reputation will cause all under heaven to quiver. Such were the Five Lords. Hence, Huan of Qi, Wen of Jin, Zhuang of Chu, Helü of Wu, and Goujian of Yue all had states that were on the margins, yet they overawed all under heaven and their strength overpowered the central states. There was no other reason for this but that they had strategic reliability. This is to attain hegemony by establishing strategic reliability. [38]

Xunzi thinks that strategic reliability is a necessary but not sufficient condition for hegemony. Strategic reliability alone cannot ensure that one attains hegemony; one also needs a basis in hard power. The ruler of a hegemonic state must win the trust of his allies and must also strengthen his hard power. Only in that way will the allies respect him as a hegemonic lord. When Xunzi describes the hegemons, he says,

They open up wasteland for cultivation, fill their barns and storehouses, make all their preparations, carefully recruit, select, and accept officials of talent and skill, and then reflect on congratulating and rewarding them to advance them, and strictly punishing them to correct them. They save dying states and ensure an inheritance to lines that are dying out. They uphold the weak and forbid the violent, and, since they have no mind for annexation, the feudal lords love them. They practice the way of turning enemies into friends so as to draw closer to the feudal lords and the feudal lords delight in them. . . . Thus by clarifying their conduct as lacking all desire for annexation, and relying on their way of turning enemies into friends, even when there is no sage king or hegemon, they can always win. These are the men who know the way of hegemony. [39]

Tyranny Based on Military Force and Stratagems

Xunzi thinks that tyranny is a lesser form of international power than hegemony. This kind of power relies on military force and stratagems. Since the only way for an expanding tyranny to invade the territory of other states is by military force, a state ruled by tyranny will inevitably have many enemies. This implies that tyranny will easily be weakened. Xunzi says,

> One who uses brute force will face the defended cities of others and fight with the troops of others, and we will use force to overcome them; hence, injuries to the other's people will inevitably be serious. When injuries to the other's people are serious, then the hate of the people of other states against us will inevitably be great. When the hate of the people of other states against us is great, then they will want to fight us every day. Their defended cities fighting with their troops, and our using force to overcome them will all inevitably result in serious injuries to our people. When injuries to our people are serious, then the hatred of our people against us will inevitably be great. When the hatred of our people against us is great, then they will increasingly not want to fight for us. When the people of other states increasingly want to fight us and our people increasingly do not want to fight for us, this is why the formerly strong become weak. Territory will be taken but the people flee, troubles will mount and achievements diminish; even if the land defended increases, the defenders will decrease. This is why the formerly great will be weakened.[40]

This passage says that the rule of tyranny relies only on force and lacks morality. This type of power inevitably turns everyone else into an enemy; thus it is doomed to perish.

According to what Xunzi has set out about the three forms of interstate power—humane authority, hegemony, and tyranny—we may illustrate their nature and basis as in table 2.2.

In his analysis of the foundations of the three forms of interstate power, Xunzi overlooks the importance of hard power for humane authority. Even if the territories of Bo and Hao ruled by the kings Tang and Wu, respectively, were small, the states of the feudal lords of that time may have been even smaller and weaker. By the Spring and Autumn Period, the scale of states had generally increased in size. Both Qi and Qin were once larger than Chu, and so Chu was not the strongest state at the time. Therefore, when Xunzi uses the example of Chu's being larger than the lands of the kings Tang and Wu and yet not being able to attain all under

TABLE 2.2
The Foundations of Different Types of Power

	Type		
Foundation	Humane Authority	Hegemony	Tyranny
Moral standing	Strong moral standing	Some morality, reliability	No moral standing
Power	Strong/weak	Strong	Strong

heaven to prove that power is not important for humane authority, his argument is less persuasive.

The international moral authority of the U.S. president Woodrow Wilson at the end of World War I was very high, and he proposed the very moral Fourteen Point plan and proposed the founding of the League of Nations. But within America, isolationism prevented Wilson from fully participating in international affairs, with the result that after World War I the United States could not attain world leadership. This shows that the moral standing of a leader, though a necessary condition for attaining world leadership, is not a sufficient condition. Lacking strong power or failing to play a full part in international affairs and having only moral authority is not sufficient to enable a state to attain world leadership. Hard power may in fact be equally important for both humane authority and hegemony. Morgenthau notes that the moral norms that restrain savage conflict domestically are invalid in international society. International society and domestic society have two different kinds of moral norms.[41] Clearly, Xunzi did not think about any difference in nature between interstate and domestic society and so he held that the norms of domestic society are wholly applicable to the interstate social system.

INTERNATIONAL ORDER

Although Xunzi's understanding of the role of concepts is like that of constructivist theory, his understanding of interstate conflict and stability is like that of contemporary realist theory. His ideas for preventing interstate conflict and upholding interstate order, however, are like neo-liberal theory.

The Human Origin of Conflict

Xunzi holds that human nature is evil. That people strive for gain is a natural social phenomenon. Competition inevitably leads to violent conflict: "Now, the nature of man is such that from birth he tends toward gain. He follows this inclination, and hence competition and rapacity ensue while deference and yielding are discarded. . . . Now, to follow human nature and go along with human inclinations must lead to competition and rapacity and be concordant with opposition to distinctions and to disrupting principles and so lead to violence."[42] The first principle of Morgenthau's summary of the six principles of political realism is objective law rooted in human nature: "Political realism believes that politics, like society in general, is governed by objective laws, that have their roots in human nature. . . . Human nature, in which the laws of politics have their roots, has not changed since the classical philosophies of China, India, and Greece endeavored to discover these laws."[43]

Xunzi wrote a special chapter to discuss human nature. He criticizes Mencius's theory that human nature is good for failing to understand what human nature is:

Mencius says, "Man learns because his nature is good." I say, "It is not so. Rather it is that he did not yet know human nature, nor did he examine the distinction between human nature and custom. Whatever nature is, is given by heaven and need not be learned or worked for. Rites and norms are produced by the sage and it is possible for men to learn them and they can be accomplished through working. What need not be learned or worked for by man is called human nature; what can be learned or accomplished through working is called custom. This is the distinction between nature and custom."[44]

Xunzi thinks that the evil of human nature is the basic cause of interstate conflict, because since human desires are unlimited there is no way to fulfill them with material goods: "When man is born he has desires. Though desires are unfulfilled yet he cannot but seek. If he seeks, and has no limits set, then he cannot but conflict with others. If he conflicts with others there will be disorder, and if there is disorder there will be poverty."[45]

The Restraining Role of Social Norms

Xunzi holds that increasing a society's material wealth cannot solve the problem of conflict among people. He looks to restraining human desires as the way to avoid social conflict. He defines human desires as a reflection of human emotions. He says, "Nature is what heaven provides; emotions are the essence of nature; desires are the reflection of emotions."[46] Based on this understanding of desire, Xunzi thinks that by reinforcing rationality, the "mind," it is possible to restrain the desires, which are a reflection of emotions, and thus social disorder can be avoided:

> Man's desire for life is strong; man's hatred of death is strong. Yet people follow life and still choose to die, not because they do not want to live or because they want to die, but because they are not able to live and they are able to die. Therefore, when one's desires aim to cross the limit and action does not reach the point it is because the mind stops the action. What the mind is able to do is to aim for principle and then, no matter how many the desires are, they will not harm order! If desires are not over the mark and action goes over it, this is the work of the mind. If the mind loses principle, then even if desires are few they will only stop at chaos! Hence, ordering chaos lies in what the mind can do rather than in the desires of the emotions.[47]

Xunzi thinks that the way to reinforce the rationality in the mind is to establish social norms (rites). He wrote a special chapter discussing what "rites" are: "Rites are what direct the administration. To administer without rites is for administration to fail to run. . . . Rites are to directing a state as scales are to light and heavy, as the inked cord is to crooked and straight. Hence, without rites human beings cannot live and without rites affairs cannot be accomplished and a state without rites is not at peace."[48] This is to say that rites are the norm for directing politics. If one does not deal with political affairs according to norms, then they will not be settled. Since he believes that the norms are present in the human mind, Xunzi holds that it is possible to restrain human nature via the norms in the mind: "Now, human nature is evil and it must be corrected by teachers and the model. Once rites and norms are obtained, then it can be ordered. Today people have no teachers or models and they incline to wrongdoing and are not correct. They have no rites or norms and so they are recalcitrant and disordered."[49] This means that human behavior is conditional on the mind being educated or constrained by social norms.

Xunzi explains how interstate norms can restrain state behavior from the perspective of a balance of supply and demand and how violent conflict can then be avoided and international order upheld. He thinks that norms in the mind can rationalize human desires and also increase the level of satisfaction. In other words, when human desires decrease and the capacity for satisfaction increases, then it is easier to attain a balance between them. Xunzi says, "The early kings hated disorder and so established rites and justice to distinguish people, to cultivate human desires, and to provide for what human beings sought, such that desires would not outstrip things and things not fall short of desires. The two together supported each other and grew up, and this is whence rites arose."[50]

Xunzi's ideas about how to use norms to prevent interstate violent conflict has points in common with contemporary neoliberalism, since both hold that norms are to be found in the human mind and that the norms in the human mind can control people's selfish pursuit of their own interests. Referring to agreements relating to trade and nuclear weapons, Robert O. Keohane and Joseph S. Nye say, "All these regimes were designed to resolve common problems in which the uncontrolled pursuit of individual self-interest by some governments could adversely affect the national interest of all the rest."[51] And, "Over time, governments develop reputations for compliance, not just to the letter of the law but to the spirit as well. These reputations constitute one of their most important assets."[52]

Hierarchical Basis for Social Norms

Xunzi thinks that social norms have two roles that help to prevent interstate violent conflict. The first is what has just been outlined in the preceding section, that norms can adjust the balance between desires and levels of satisfaction. The second is to determine classes in society so that people's conduct will be determined by the class to which they belong and so violent conflict will be avoided. He says, "The life of human beings cannot be without communities. If there are communities without distinctions, then there will be conflict, and if conflict, then disorder, and if disorder, then poverty. Hence, the failure to make distinctions is the bane of human life, whereas having distinctions is the basic good of all under heaven. The ruler is the key to the management of distinctions."[53] When explaining how hierarchical norms are able to prevent disorder in society, he says, "The early kings hated disorder and so they determined the distinctions of rites and norms so that there were classes of rich and poor, high and low status, sufficient so that there could be mutual oversight. This is the root of fostering all under heaven."[54] Norms for distinguishing social classes are the basic way to maintain the stability of all under heaven.

Xunzi thinks that if there were no social classes to repress human beings' natural desire to seek material goods, then interstate violent conflict could not be avoided. He says,

> When distinctions are equal, then there is no sequence. When one grasps hold of equality, then there is no unity. When the mass of people are all equal, then no one can be sent on commission. There is heaven and there is earth and hence up and down are to be distinguished. As soon as an enlightened king holds power, he runs his state with regulations. Two nobles cannot obey each other; two commoners cannot commission each other. This is the setup of heaven. When the powers exercised by two people are equal and their desires are the same, then since goods cannot satisfy them there will be conflict. If there is conflict, there will inevitably be disorder. And if there is disorder, there will be poverty.[55]

According to the historical experience of the Five Services of the Western Zhou, Xunzi thinks that by relying on the relationship of near and far to establish interstate norms of different grades it is possible to repress interstate violent conflict.[56] He thinks that the system of Five Services established by the Zhou was able to uphold the stability of the interstate system under the Western Zhou because this system involves different grades of state undertaking different areas of responsibility and hence this system of norms was effective: "The norms of humane authority are to observe the circumstances so as to produce the tools to work thereon, to weigh the distance and determine the tribute due. How could it then all be equal!"[57] This is to say, interstate norms should be designed according to the differences between states rather than be the same for each state. In fact, modern international norms still share this characteristic. The members of the United Nations are classified into three grades: permanent members of the Security Council, nonpermanent members of the Security Council, and ordinary members. The International Monetary Fund allocates the number of votes according to the size of contributions. The World Trade Organization determines the level of tariffs to be paid according to whether one is a developed or developing country. These examples help us to understand how Xunzi sees hierarchical distinctions as a basis for the effectiveness of interstate norms. See figure 2.4, which sets out the logical relationships in Xunzi's view of human nature, social grades, social norms, and interstate order.

Xunzi describes the Five Services of the Western Zhou as follows:

> Therefore, the various Chinese states had the same service and the same customs, whereas the states of the Man, Yi, Di, and Rong had the same service but different regulations. Within the pale was the domain service and outside the pale the feudal service. The feudal areas up to the border area were the tributary service; the Man and Yi were in the formal service; the Rong and Di were in the wasteland service. The domain service sacrificed to the king's father, the feudal service sacrificed to the king's grandparents, the tributary service sacrificed to the king's ancestors, the formal service presented tribute, and the wasteland service honored the king's accession. The

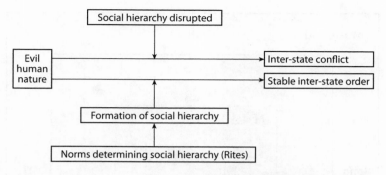

Figure 2.4 The influence of evil human nature and social hierarchy on interstate order

sacrifices to the father were carried out daily, to the grandfather monthly, to the ancestors by season. Tribute was offered once a year. This is what is called observing the circumstances so as to produce the tools to work thereon, weighing the distance, and determining the tribute due. This is the system of humane authority.[58]

The modern understanding of the system of Five Services is as follows. The states of central China gave the same kind of service to the Son of Heaven and were governed by the same rites and institutions, while the states of other nationalities, though still owing the same service to the Son of Heaven, were governed by different institutions. The feudal lords surrounding the royal capital offered agricultural service. The feudal lords at a distance of 250 kilometers offered service as border guards. The feudal lords from the feudal area to the border area gave tribute at fixed seasons. The task of the minority tribes of the south and east was to pacify the local population. The minority people of the north and west merely had to give tribute at irregular intervals to show that they accepted the leadership of the Son of Heaven. Those responsible for agriculture had to provide offerings for sacrifice every day. Those responsible for security had to provide sacrificial offerings every month. Those responsible for tributary goods had to provide sacrificial offerings every season. Those responsible for keeping their own peace gave sacrificial offerings once a year. Those who merely showed their acceptance of the leadership could

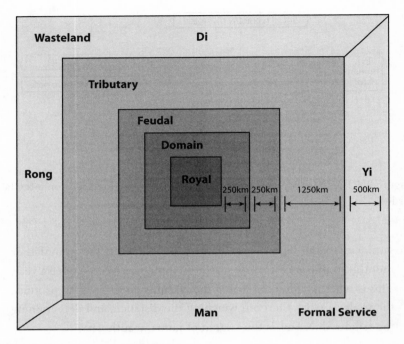

Figure 2.5 The system of Five Services

give offerings irregularly. The norm of providing offerings at different frequencies was made according to geographic distance from the throne. This is the method of the kings. In figure 2.5, the formal and wasteland services are interpreted as geographically distinct areas rather than as sequential concentric regions. The ancient Chinese believed that the earth is quadrate and covered by a round heaven.

Xunzi's understanding of the causes of war is basically the same as that of realist theory, namely, that international war comes from social anarchy. Xunzi considers only how a hierarchical system can help in reducing interstate conflict, however, and does not consider how changes in the balance of power among states may also alter the hierarchical relationships in the interstate system. When the balance of power changes and the status of a state is not adjusted, then war may break out. The main reason Xunzi fails to discuss how to adjust hierarchical norms so as to adapt to changes in the relative power of states is that he is an internal causal determinist. He considers only how state policy can influence changes in state power and does not consider what impact changes in the balance of power have on the conduct of states.

CONCLUSION AND FINDINGS

My main purpose in reinterpreting Xunzi's interstate political philosophy is less to introduce an ancient author's view of interstate relations than to learn something relevant to the strategy of China's present rise.

The Goal of the Strategy of China's Rise

Xunzi thinks that humane authority is a form of interstate leadership that is higher than hegemony. All under heaven accrues to the sage king by itself and is not seized. This view merits reflection. What kind of superpower does China want to become? A superpower may be a humane state or a hegemonic state. The difference between the two lies not in the greatness of their power but in their moral standings. If China wants to become a state of humane authority, this would be different from the contemporary United States. The goal of our strategy must be not only to reduce the power gap with the United States but also to provide a better model for society than that given by the United States.

The international community increasingly focuses on what kind of superpower China will become. International society clearly does not want China to become like the Nazi Germany or fascist Japan. At the same time, it does not want to see China become another United States. If China becomes another United States, two things could follow: the world could be divided between two hegemonies and there would be a return to the Cold War, or China would replace the United States and the world order would remain unchanged. The international system of humane authority is not perfect, but compared with the present hegemonic system it allows for more cooperation and greater security.

For China to become a superpower modeled on humane authority, it must first become a model from which other states are willing to learn. Scholars have coined the terms *Beijing Consensus* and *Washington Consensus*.

In fact, these are two competing models of society. As long as China can build itself up as a country worthy of imitation by others, it will then naturally become a humane state. Since China undertook its policy of reform and opening in 1978, the Chinese government has made economic growth the core of its strategy. An increase in wealth can raise China's power status but it does not necessarily enable China to become a country respected by others, because a political superpower that puts wealth as its highest national interest may bring disaster rather than blessings to other countries. In September 2005, the Chinese government proposed a foreign policy of a harmonious world and set the goal of building friendships with other countries.[59] But in August 2008, the report at the Foreign Affairs Meeting of the Party Central Committee again said that "the work of foreign affairs should uphold economic growth at its core."[60] Two months later, the October meeting of the Tenth Plenary Session of the Central Committee of the Sixteenth Party Congress of the Chinese Communist Party again set the building of a harmonious society as the long-term historical task of the socialist state, and proposed social fairness and justice as the basis of social harmony.[61] The lack of coordination of these announcements shows that the Chinese government does want to replace accumulation of economic wealth with the building of a harmonious society as its highest political goal but, owing to political inertia formed over the long period during which economic growth has been the core, the Chinese government has not yet been able consciously to make building a humane authority the goal of its strategy for ascent.

The Power Basis of the Strategy for China's Rise

The Chinese government has already proposed the strategic principle of the road of peaceful development,[62] yet whether this strategic principle has as its core increasing resource power or increasing operating power—that is, political power—is not yet clear. At present, the most popular idea in China is that of the basic path of increasing comprehensive national power by developing the economy. If we use Xunzi's view of political power as the basis for hard power, however, and apply it to the question of comprehensive national power, we find that, since 1949, China first underwent political change before there was an increase in economic development or military power. In 1949, the Chinese Communist Party founded a completely new political system in China and, hence, there was a great increase in comprehensive national power from 1949 to 1956. In 1978, the Chinese government implemented reform and opening-up and so created the historical economic boom of the past thirty years. In 2002, the Chinese government began to implement the policy of balanced development of military buildup and economic construction, with the result that national defense capability rapidly increased.[63] In contrast, when the government adopted mistaken political guidelines, such as during the Great Leap Forward or the Cultural Revolution, the national economy and military force were seriously diminished.

Xunzi's idea of justice and the current popular notion of soft power are different. The notion of soft power does not differentiate between cultural power and political power, whereas Xunzi's idea of justice refers to the leader's ideology and is a matter of political power. He sees political power as the basic factor in comprehensive state power. This is very revealing for us today. If we take soft power as being made up of both cultural and political power, then we find that political power plays an enabling role as the basis for other elements of power to play a role. For instance, the United States' military power, economic power, and cultural power grew during the period 2003 to 2006, but because the Iraq war launched by the Bush administration in 2003 lacked international legitimacy, U.S. capability in terms of political mobilization both at home and abroad—that is, political power—went into serious decline. Thus, the United States' comprehensive national power shrank and its international status declined during those three years. This example, as well as that of the collapse of the Soviet Union, proves that political power is the resource power for operating power, military power, economic power, and cultural power. Without the former the latter cannot play their roles. On this basis, we can depict the relationships among the various factors of power as in figure 2.6.

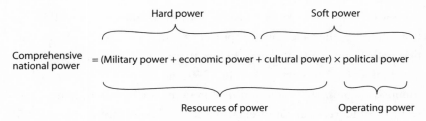

Figure 2.6 Relationships among the various factors of power

If CP stands for comprehensive state power, M for military power, E for economic power, C for cultural power, and P for political power, then figure 2.6 may be rewritten according to the following formula:

$$CP = (M + E + C) \times P$$

According to this formula, given no change in China's current military, economic, or cultural power, it is only if China can greatly increase its political power—at least its strategic reliability—that China can greatly increase its comprehensive national power and international status. We may take the 2006 China-Africa Summit as an example. The total of China's aid to African countries over the previous three years had not exceeded that of Europe or the United States, but the positive reaction to China's aid from African countries vastly exceeded that to aid from Europe and the United States. The reason was not that the sum of aid offered by China was greater than that given by Europe or the United States, but rather that China's aid to Africa has no political conditions attached, whereas European and American aid comes with political conditions. China's sincerity in its economic aid has increased its political influence. What this tells us is that although the work of increasing China's soft power includes both political and cultural power, the key lies in political power.

Strategy of Ascent

If the basis for China's strategy of ascent is based on increasing political power, then the current versions of strategy popular in academia do not apply to China's situation. The idea of economic construction as the core made materialism the dominant social belief in China. This had a strong influence on the discussion of the rise of a great state. Academia discusses four kinds of important strategies: the strategy of change (multipolar or confrontational), the strategy of avoidance (independent autonomy or isolationism), the strategy of merging (free rider or following the strongest), and the strategy of following the crowd (multilateral cooperation). Apart from the strategy of change, the other three strategies are all based on the logic of increasing China's economic wealth.

Unlike the materialist strategy, the strategy Xunzi recommends for a rising power stresses human talent, that is, it focuses on competition for talent. Xunzi attributes changes in international politics to the political ideas of the leader and makes the choice and employment of talented persons the basic strategy for strengthening a state. In 1935, Joseph Stalin proposed the slogan "Cadres determine everything." In 1938, Mao Zedong proposed a similar view that "once the political line is determined, the cadres are the decisive factor."[64] Their views are like Xunzi's. At present, China's strategy of seeking talent is still mainly used for developing enterprises and has not yet been applied to raising the nation as a whole. Talent is still understood as having to do with technicians rather than politicians or high-ranking officials. What Xunzi's ideas about talent tell us is that the strategy of seeking talent should not be one of enterprise development. Rather, it has always been the strategy for the rise of a great power. The personnel requirements for the rise of a great power are not for technicians but for politicians and officials who have the ability to invent systems or regulations, because a pronounced ability to invent systems and regulations is the key to ensuring the rise of a great power.

If in the agricultural era of two thousand years ago the success or failure of the rise of a great state was determined by human talent, then, two thousand years later, the economic development of today's knowledge economy is also determined by human talent; hence, we can suppose that the factor determining the success or failure of a rising power today is also human talent. Xunzi thinks that there are many talented people with both morality and ability, and the key is whether the ruler will choose them. This tells us that the strategy of finding talent to ensure the rise of a great power has several aspects. One is that the degree of openness is high: choosing officials from the whole world who meet the requisite standards of morality and ability, so as to improve the capability of the government to formulate correct policies. For example, in ancient times, the Tang Dynasty in China and the Umayyad Empire in North Africa, Spain, and the Middle East, in the course of their rise, employed a great number of foreigners as officials. It is said that at its peak more than 70 percent of officials in the Umayyad Empire were foreigners.[65] The United States has attained its present hegemonic status also by its policy of attracting talented and outstanding foreigners. A second point is that the speed of correction was rapid. Unsuitable government officials could be speedily removed, reducing the probability of erroneous decisions. This applied to all politicians and officials if they lost their ability to make correct decisions for any reason, such as being corrupted by power, being out-of-date in knowledge, decaying in thought, suffering a decline in their ability to reflect, or experiencing deterioration in health. Establishing a system by which officials can be removed in a timely fashion provides opportunities for talented people and can reduce errors of policy and ultimately increase political power.

Equitable International Norms

After the Treaty of Westphalia of 1648, equality of state sovereignty gradually developed to become a universal international norm. Xunzi's thought is the exact opposite of equality of sovereignty. He thinks that norms for an unequal hierarchy are a help in preventing interstate conflict. Some countries are concerned that China's rise will result in a return to the tribute system of East Asia. The tribute system once played a role in maintaining regional order but it is outdated for the modern world. In fact, any effort to restore the tribute system will weaken China's capability for international political mobilization. Furthermore, the objective power status of large and small states is not equal. Establishing hierarchical norms is a help in maintaining a balance between a state's power and its international responsibility and is a help in reducing international conflict and improving international cooperation

In current political discourse, *hierarchy* is a pejorative term, implying inequality. Objectively, however, not all states are alike in power, and therefore hierarchical norms are the only way to ensure equity. The norm of equality cannot maintain equity. Boxing competitions are carried out according to different grades of weight. This is one kind of hierarchical norm and it serves to guarantee the equity of the competition. To fail to distinguish grades of weight and to rely only on norms of equality to determine the winner would be to fail to uphold equity. According to Xunzi's interpretation of the system of Five Services, distinctions in international norms should be decided according to a state's status in international society. Large states with a central power status in the world should be subject to more stringent international norms, whereas marginalized states that lie farther away from the center of world power should be subject to more relaxed international norms. This is an unequal international norm that helps to uphold international equity. In the cooperation of the 10 + 1—the Association of Southeast Asian Nations (ASEAN) and China—China is required to implement the norm of zero tariffs in agricultural trade before the ASEAN states do. This unequal norm enabled the economic cooperation of the 10 + 1 to develop more rapidly than that between Japan and ASEAN. Japan's demand for equal tariffs slowed the progress of its economic cooperation with the ASEAN states, which lags far behind that of China and ASEAN.

Historically, neither hierarchical norms nor norms for equality have been able to prevent large-scale international war from breaking out, but if we examine recent international history, we can see that in those areas that implemented hierarchical norms, international peace was better maintained than it was in areas that had norms for equality. During the Cold War, the equal status of the United States and the Soviet Union was such that they undertook many proxy wars in order to compete for hegemony, while their special status in NATO and in the Warsaw Pact, respectively, enabled them to prevent the members of these alliances from engaging in military conflict with one another. China's rise cannot avoid influencing the international security system. Now, what kind of international norms should China propose to uphold international peace? To maintain world peace requires great capability, and none but a super-power has that kind of capability. Based on Xunzi's understanding that hierarchical norms are beneficial in preventing conflict, China should propose that large states and small states should have different international responsibilities, and that different states should respect different security norms. For instance, in upholding international peace, small and large states with different security responsibilities have different rights. If nuclear weapons do not proliferate, then nuclear states must strictly adhere to nonproliferation while providing security guarantees to nonnuclear states.

I personally think that a phrase of Xunzi's can summarize his interstate political philosophy: "Hence, in matters of state, norms being established, one can attain humane authority; reliability being established, one can attain hegemony; political scheming being established, the state will perish."[66] When applied to the strategy of China's rise, this means that by making political power the foundation and constantly renovating the political system, China will rise to become the world's leading power; if it develops political, military, and economic power on an equal footing, then it can become a great power. If it makes economic construction the core, then it will gradually become a medium-level developed country. If political strife is the guideline, then it will decline. Xunzi's thought is but one of many schools of interstate political philosophy that were current in ancient China. If we can rediscover more interstate political ideas of ancient Chinese philosophers and use them to enrich contemporary international relations theory, this will provide the guideline for a strategy for China's rise. There are also defects in Xunzi's thought; hence, in borrowing ideas from him we need to exercise caution.

Hegemony in *The Stratagems*
of the Warring States

Yan Xuetong and Huang Yuxing

*T*he Stratagems of the Warring States records the history of the Warring
States.[1] Most academics have denied that the book contains any philosophy as such. One scholar who believes that the book lacks any philosophy says, "The riches of *The Stratagems of the Warring States* from the
literary point of view cannot conceal its poverty from a philosophical
point of view."[2] As a historical record *The Stratagems of the Warring States*
clearly cannot have a complete philosophical system, but if we read it
carefully we can discover many illuminating points of philosophical interest nonetheless. Contending for hegemony was a key theme of interstate
politics during the Warring States Period; hence, this book has many pas-
sages that discuss issues of hegemony. The book was compiled at least
1,900 years ago, yet its understanding of hegemonic issues can still be
used to explain the phenomenon of great power hegemonic struggles
today. This indicates that some of its views may reflect the essence and
laws of international relations. This essay looks at three topics: the power
base of hegemony, the role that norms play in hegemony, and the principles of the strategies used to gain hegemony. It then draws together the
lessons about hegemony of the book and looks at their relevance for developing contemporary international relations theory.

ANALYTICAL POINT OF VIEW

There are basically three kinds of research related to *The Stratagems of the Warring States*: (1) language and literary studies, (2) textual criticism, and (3) philosophical study. The first area, language and literature, is not particularly related to the topic discussed here. Textual criticism falls into two kinds—textual criticism as such and historical criticism—both of which provide historical and literary background for understanding the interstate political philosophy of *The Stratagems of the Warring States*, but they lack philosophical considerations. Although the philosophical studies lack any input on interstate political philosophy, some scholars have analyzed the thought of the horizontalists and verticalists[3] (or the strategists of alliances) of the Warring States Period in four areas: political philosophy, principles for the employment of personnel, philosophy of life, and policies for managing affairs. Some scholars think that *The Stratagems of the Warring States* suggests that in strategy the strategists' aims are the deciding factor and that the book stresses thought about diplomacy.[4] There are scholars who analyze the way of thinking of the horizontalists and verticalists from the point of view of their dialectic and who note that the configuration of the world in the twentieth century had points in common with the Warring States Period of more than two thousand years ago.[5] The focal point of these studies, however, is not the interstate political philosophy of *The Stratagems of the Warring States* and, furthermore, they lack any study of the theme of hegemony.

This essay thus focuses on an analysis of the interstate political philosophy of *The Stratagems of the Warring States*. Hence, it looks at the ideas expressed in *The Stratagems of the Warring States*. Given that ideas are mainly expressed through language, this essay analyzes the ideas expressed by the discourses of the personalities in the book. Many of these discourses are aimed at canvassing support and, hence, what is said is not necessarily in conformity with facts, displaying tendencies to exaggeration or understatement. The purpose of this essay's analysis, however, is to examine how people in the past thought about the question of hegemony as expressed by the masters discussed in this book; it does not matter for our analysis whether the facts recorded actually took place or what the speakers' aims were. Since this essay focuses on what *The Stratagems of the Warring States* has to say about hegemony, the review of literature will focus on what scholars have said that is directly relevant to the three themes of hegemonic power, norms, and strategy.

Although there are no studies that analyze *The Stratagems of the Warring States* from the point of view of hegemonic power, in their studies of the book many scholars have noticed that competition for talented personnel and actions to gain hegemony are very closely related in the Warring States Period. For instance, some scholars think that "the idea of talent in *The Stratagems of the Warring States* would not seem to be particularly manifest, yet once it is considered in relation to planning for military strategy, then it assumes special significance."[6] This kind of analysis highlights the importance of talented personnel in the struggle for hegemony but it overlooks the fact that *The Stratagems of the Warring States* sees talented personnel as important to the survival of a state. In other words, talented persons are important to the struggle for hegemony and are equally important to a state that does not struggle for hegemony but simply seeks to survive. Some scholars think that *The Stratagems of the Warring States* is of the view that state competition is competition for personnel, but hold that soliciting talent is a stratagem of power politics.[7] This opinion acknowledges the significance of talent for raising the status of a state's power, but viewing the recruitment of talent as a stratagem of power politics implies that the author does not realize that *The Stratagems of the Warring States* sees talent as the core of the state's political power. One scholar with a much more thoughtful view thinks that in *The Stratagems of the Warring States*, "Rulers who are politically wise generally see the competition for talent as more important than the struggle for towns and often make the possession of talent the primary decisive condition for the possession of towns and the seizing of wealth."[8] This analysis sees political talent as the basis for strengthening material power in all states, but its inadequacy is that it overlooks what is said in the book about the role talent plays in deciding the nature of hegemony. Political talent can not only increase a state's material power but also determine the nature of its hegemony.

Many scholars think that the transition from the Spring and Autumn era to the Warring States Period was one in which the role of moral norms

in foreign policy went into decline.[9] For instance some scholars say, "in
The Stratagems of the Warring States, the authors advocate a philosophy of
life that pursues advantages by any means, completely disregarding rites,
justice, sincerity and faithfulness, loyalty and filial piety, restraint and
shame. There would seem to be no standards for normative human conduct." And again, "the strategists of the Warring States deny rites and justice; they disparage traditional values and standards of conduct. What
they respect is power play and insouciance with regard to breaking faith
and discarding justice."[10] There are scholars who point out, "in the Spring
and Autumn Period, the way of the hegemons 'aped justice as its claim
and relied on correctness for its successes.' In the Warring States Period
the feudal lords of the states did not even lay claim to the appearances of
justice or correctness to cloak over the way of hegemony."[11] This point of
view holds that the struggles for hegemony described by *The Stratagems of
the Warring States* lack restraining norms between states and that hegemony itself does not need to follow interstate norms and does not need a
basis of legitimacy. If we read *The Stratagems of the Warring States* carefully,
however, we discover that the discourses of many strategists stress the
importance of respect for interstate norms in attaining or maintaining
hegemony. Some scholars have noticed this point but they think that the
strategists of the Warring States Period stress benevolence and justice and
morality simply as a cloak for their struggle for hegemony. For instance,
one scholar says, "The benevolence and justice on the lips of Su Qin and
Zhang Yi is quite different from the concept of benevolence and justice in
the Confucian tradition. Its roots can be traced to a service in favor of
gain and power politics. What is said is one thing; what is meant is another. In fact, they reject and criticize the benevolence and justice, morality and grades of respect that flourished in the Spring and Autumn
Period."[12] This analysis affirms the positive role played by the practice of
interstate norms in *The Stratagems of the Warring States* as a means of realizing hegemony, but it fails to fully understand the reason why the strategists stress norms. If we examine the question from the point of view of
international relations theory then norms are an important component of
a hegemonic system, the source of the legitimacy of a hegemonic state,
and the basis for upholding the hegemonic order. Without the support of

norms and relying only on power, the strategists of the Warring States Period could not have attained hegemony; hence, their emphasis on interstate norms is genuine and not primarily intended as a cloak for a profit motive.

Most that is written about the struggle for hegemony in *The Stratagems of the Warring States* focuses on the level of strategy and fails to analyze the logic and principles of the strategies of hegemonic struggle. Some scholars focus on what *The Stratagems of the Warring States* says about "stratagems," and summarize the stratagems in the book as

> political stratagems: strategies for reform and strengthening, strategies for employing the worthy and rejecting flatterers; strategies for reinforcing territory and uniting the people, strategies for internal struggle amongst the ruling group; foreign policy stratagems: strategies for a united front, strategies for division and disintegration, strategies for psychological deterrence, strategies for calculated concessions, strategies for overcoming others by eloquence; military stratagems: strategies for "wait and see," strategies for military cooperation, strategies for first weakening and then destroying, strategies for seizing the opportunity, strategies for making the enemy his own enemy, strategies for getting spies to act as double agents. Plans by which the strong may advance, schemes by which the weak may survive; strategies also for alliances of two strong states to create a win-win situation or for their falling out with each other and attacking each other. Victors have ways of being victors and losers ways to lose; spectators have schemes of "a third party steals the spoils," while those who incite others have their ideas of "pouncing on the unsuspecting from behind."[13]

This summary enables us to see the great variety of strategies in *The Stratagems of the Warring States*, but it does not help us to understand what the main factors in the overriding strategy of gaining hegemony are, or what the basic principles of the strategy to gain hegemony are. There are even scholars who think that the horizontal and vertical policies of Su Qin, Zhang Yi, and others like them are simply to satisfy the short-term needs of the princes. They are "short-term schemes."[14] This view would not

seem to fit the real political goal by which large states struggled for hegemony in the Warring States Period. Moreover, it will lead people to overlook the relevance of what *The Stratagems of the Warring States* has to say
to about the strategies in the struggle for hegemony, and about research
into the strategy for the rise of a major power today.

THE POWER BASE OF HEGEMONY

There is much discussion in *The Stratagems of the Warring States* of the
power base of hegemony. The discussions touch on the factors leading to
the formation of comprehensive national power; the relationship between the factors of political and other forms of power; political leadership; and geographical conditions. Although the views presented in the
book reflect the context of an agricultural economy with "cold" weapons
as opposed to firearms, the message transcends its time.

Comprehensive National Power Is the Power Base of Hegemony

In their discussion of hegemonic power, the strategists of *The Stratagems of
the Warring States* mostly analyze the components of comprehensive national power. Moreover, the factors of national power they analyze are of
different kinds. Unlike some scholars today, they do not see comprehensive national power as composed only of economic aspects. Among the
factors of national power, they frequently mention four: political, military, economic, and geographic. For instance, in analyzing the power base
that enabled Chu to attain hegemony, Su Qin tells King Wei of Chu that
there are only these four factors. He thinks that the reason Chu was able
to attain hegemony was that it relied on the wisdom of its leader, the advantages of its terrain, the strength of its army, and the resources of its
economy. He says,

> Chu is a great state under heaven. Great King, you are a wise king
> under heaven. In the west of Chu are Qianzhong [Northwest
> Hunan, East Guizhou] and Wuqun [East Sichuan], to the east Xiazhou

[Hanyang] and Haiyang [Southeast Chu, formerly Wu and Yue], to the south are Dongting [Hunan: Lake Dongting] and Cangwu [Guangxi: Cangwu County], to the north Fen [Fenqiu], Xing [Henan: Xingshan], and Xunyang [Shaanxi], an area of five thousand square kilometers. There are a million troops in armor, a thousand four-horse chariots, ten thousand horses, and ten years' supply of grain. These are the resources of a hegemon.[15]

The personages in the book have many arguments supporting the idea that comprehensive national power is the basis for hegemony. Some think that there are different ways to strengthen different factors of power. Although this understanding cannot be equated with the principle that factors of power are not interchangeable, as proposed by contemporary international relations theory, it implies that different factors of national power realize different ends for the state. Sima Cuo tells King Hui of Qin, "Someone who wants to enrich a state must enlarge its territory; someone who wants to strengthen the army must enrich the people; someone who wants to be a sage king must extend his virtue. With these three resources in place, humane authority will follow."[16] Sima Cuo's summary of the contribution of the three factors of national power to comprehensive power includes three levels of awareness. The first is that strengthening economic, military, and political power must rely on expanding land, improving the livelihood of the people, and implementing virtuous government. The second is that only states that expand these three factors of power can attain world leadership. The third is that political power is a necessary condition for attaining world leadership and that it is more important than military or economic power.

Although the strategists in the book generally think that a struggle for hegemony requires comprehensive national power, they fail to measure comprehensive national power by a common standard. Reflecting their own political needs, they continually stress the great qualities of one state and portray the flaws in the power of opposing states as extremely serious. Today we are still hampered by this lack of a common standard by which to measure state power. Contemporary international relations theorists have not yet resolved it. Although the personages in the book frequently resort to arbitrary assessments of a state's comprehensive power, their analysis of hegemonic power from the angle of many factors of power shows that they realize that a state of single-factor power cannot attain hegemony.

Political Power Is the Core Factor in Hegemonic Power

The politicians of *The Stratagems of the Warring States* all agree that political, military, economic, and geographical factors together comprise the comprehensive state power of a hegemon, but they differ on which of the four is most important. Normally people say that *The Stratagems of the Warring States* stresses the importance of military power. For instance, although Su Qin and Zhang Yi differ in their political views, in talking separately to King Hui of Qin they both say that to become a hegemon one must rely on military power. Su Qin draws on the experience of becoming a king or a hegemon in history to come to the conclusion that it is necessary to use armed force to attain hegemony. He tells King Hui of Qin,

> In ancient times, the Divine Farmer punished Busui; the Yellow Emperor fought at Zhuolu and captured Chi You; Yao punished Huandou; Shun punished the Three Miao tribes; Yü punished Gong Gong; Tang punished the Xia King; King Wen punished the state of Chong [Shaanxi: Huxian]; King Wu punished Zhòu; Huan of Qi fought wars and became chief lord under heaven. From this it can be seen, when was there no war? . . . If today you want to annex all under heaven, defeat states of ten thousand four-horse chariots, make enemy states submit, rule all within the seas, love the ordinary people, and make feudal lords subordinate, it cannot be done without the military.[17]

Zhang Yi tells the king that the state of Qi fought five wars to gain hegemony and so if Qin is to become a hegemon it must fight and use war to overcome Chu. He says, "Qi is a state that fought five wars. It would not have survived had it lost any one of the five. From this it can be seen that war decides the survival or demise of a state of ten thousand four-horse chariots. . . . In the east you should fight Qi and Yan; in the center you should battle the three Jin states [Zhao, Wei, and Han]. And then with one move you will win the title of sage king of sage kings, and the feudal lords of all four sides will come to pay you homage."[18]

In *The Stratagems of the Warring States* there are also many discussions that stress that political power is decisive. The term *political power* is modern; its corresponding terms in the ancient period are *virtue, benevolence, the Way, justice, law, worthies*, and *sages*. For instance, although Su Qin thinks that it is necessary to wage war to become a hegemon, he also says that, compared to population, territory, and military power, politics is even more decisive for attaining hegemony. He takes the examples of Yao having few people, Shun having a territory that was not large, Yü coming from a small village, and Tang of the Shang and Wu of the Zhou having armies that were not powerful to show that, even with these disadvantages, one can still become a sage king or hegemon, and thereby he illustrates that politics is indeed the key to becoming a hegemon. He says to King Huiwen of Zhao: "I, your minister, have heard that Yao did not even have three acres of land, Shun did not have even a yard of land, and yet they acquired all under heaven. Yü did not have a village of even a hundred people to become a sage king over the feudal lords. The armies of Tang and Wu did not exceed three thousand men and their chariots were not more than three hundred four-horsers, yet they were established as Son of Heaven. Reliability won them their Way."[19] These words of Su Qin do not deny the importance of other forms of power for becoming a hegemon. Rather they show that to realize the concrete goal of becoming a hegemon, the political power of an ability to marshal and manipulate resources is the primary factor. The strategist of the prince of Chun Shen in Chu holds a similar view. He too thinks that if the ruler is worthy and intelligent he may become a hegemon even if he is somewhat weak in resources. The strategist takes the example of the kings Tang of the Shang and Wu of the Zhou having small territories and yet attaining hegemony over all under heaven to prove this point. The strategist says to the prince of Chun Shen, "Tang had Bo [Henan: Nan Qiu] and King Wu had Hao [Shaanxi: Xi'an], which were neither a hundred square kilometers and yet they acquired all under heaven."[20]

The book seems not to include discussion of the relative importance of political and economic power but there are discussions of the relative importance of political and geographical factors. In these debates, those who argue in favor of political power have greater plausibility. For instance, Wang Zhong thinks that Jin's great strength lies in its geographical advantages, and by improving these it can attain hegemony. When Prince Wu of Wei points out the significance of strategic places, Wang replies, "This is that whereby Jin is strong. If you maintain them well then you have all you need for attaining hegemony or humane authority."[21] Wu Qi thinks that geographical advantages are not the foundation for restoring hegemony, however. He takes the examples of the three Miao tribes, Jie of the Xia, and Zhòu of the Yin [Shang], who all had advantages of terrain but, owing to political mistakes, were destroyed, to prove that surefooted politics is the key to attaining hegemony. Moreover, a state that makes political mistakes, even if it has geographical advantages, will nonetheless go to ruin. He says,

> To trust in the strategic value of rivers and mountains does not guarantee your holding on to them. The business of the chief king does not take this path.
>
> Of old, the territory of the three Miao had Pengli [Lake Poyang] on the east, Lake Dongting on the west, to the south Mount Wen [Sichuan Mount Min], to the north Mount Heng [in Hunan]. Since they relied on these strategic areas, yet governed badly, Yü sent them into exile.
>
> The state of King Jie of the Xia had the *yin* of the Gate of Heaven on the east [Tianjing Pass in Shanxi: Jincheng County], the Valley of Heaven on the west [Hangu Pass], Mount Lu and Mount Gu to the north, and the Yi and Luo rivers to the south [Henan]. Since he relied on these strategic areas yet governed badly, Tang punished him.
>
> The state of King Zhòu of the Yin [Shang] had Meng Gate [Mount Taihang Pass] on the east, and on the west the Zhang and Fu rivers. On the south it was surrounded by the Yellow River and on the north it rested against Mount Taihang. Since he relied on these strategic areas yet governed badly, King Wu punished him.

Meanwhile, you, O Prince, personally joined me, your minister, in overcoming and defeating our enemy's city. It is not that the city wall was not high or that the population was not large, yet you could annex and possess them. Rather it was a result of government. Seen from this angle, how can the strategic advantages of terrain suffice to attain hegemonic or humane authority?[22]

He points out that it is dangerous to think one can rely on geographical advantages to attain hegemony and criticizes Prince Wu of Wei for over-valuing them: "My prince's words are the path of a state at risk."[23]

The Core of Hegemonic Political Power Is the Employment of Worthy and Able Ministers

Contemporary scholars think that political power comprises the character of the state, political system, political organization, the leader of the state, and organizational and policymaking ability.[24] In *The Stratagems of the Warring States* nothing is said about the factors that comprise political power, yet in this book the merits and leadership of the ruler and the chief ministers are frequently seen as the core factors in hegemonic political power—as the well-known saying puts it, "an intelligent king and worthy prime minister." The notion of the intelligent prince stresses the importance of the leadership of the ruler, whereas that of the worthy prime minister stresses the importance of the collective leadership of the policy makers. Many personages in *The Stratagems of the Warring States* take the employment of worthy and capable persons as the standard by which to assess the intelligence of the ruler. They think that there are many worthy and capable persons in the world; the key lies in whether the ruler employs them. They attribute the attainment of hegemony by Duke Huan of Qi to his employment of worthy and capable people. For instance, when Wang Dou is discussing with King Xuan of Qi why the king cannot become a hegemon and why Duke Huan of Qi was able to do so, he explains that Duke Huan was good at employing worthy and capable persons, whereas King Xuan is incapable of doing so. He says, "The former prince valued his ministers; but you, O King, do not value your ministers."[25]

Lu Zhong goes on to say that Duke Huan of Qi not only valued worthy and capable persons, he was even able in his choice of talent to overlook small failings. He explains this point with the example of Duke Huan's not dwelling on Guan Zhong's three mistakes but still entrusting great responsibilities to him, which enabled the duke to become the hegemon of all under heaven. He says, "Guanzi made three mistakes but was still put in charge of the government of Qi. He corrected all under heaven and gathered together the feudal lords so that the duke became the foremost of the Five Hegemons. His fame spread through all under heaven and his light illumined the neighboring states."[26] Su Dai thinks that Duke Huan's intelligent leadership shows in his trust in the ministers who form his policies. When King Hui of Yan asks Su Dai why he thinks that King Xuan of Qi will not become hegemon, he says it is because King Xuan "does not trust his ministers."[27] Even though Su Dai's purpose here is to persuade King Hui to reemploy Zi Zhi as his chief minister, afterward people understood what he said to have general significance and therefore believed what he said.

The strategists of the Warring States Period thought that the leadership of the rulers could be graded as high or low based on their employment of the worthy and capable, and this distinction not only decided whether a state could establish hegemony, it even affected the type of hegemony that was established. In ancient China, people distinguished four grades of hegemon: sovereign, emperor, king, and hegemon. For instance, the *Guanzi* speaks of "understanding the One is the sovereign; inspecting the Way is the emperor; penetrating virtue is the king; planning for military victories is the hegemon."[28] Guo Wei of Yan thinks that a ruler who employs a worthy and capable person as his teacher can establish an empire, one who makes him his friend can establish humane authority, one who treats him as his minister can establish a hegemony, whereas one who treats him as a servant will find that his state falls. He says to King Zhao of Yan, "An emperor deals with a teacher; a sage king deals with a friend; a hegemon deals with a minister; a falling state deals with a servant."[29]

There are also personages in the book who think that a worthy minister and an intelligent ruler are both equally important to the political power of a hegemon. This way of seeing things always leads to treating the importance of the role of prime minister as equal to that of the ruler. For instance, a strategist of Chu thinks that if a key worthy leaves, then a ruler who once had all under heaven will lose it. The strategist proves his point with the examples of the Xia Dynasty, which lost Yi Yin, and the state of Lu, which lost Guan Zhong, and then both fell into decline. He tells the prince of Chun Shen, "Of old, Yi Yin left the state of Xia to go to the state of Yin; Yin attained humane authority and the Xia perished. Guan Zhong left the state of Lu and went to the state of Qi; Lu became weak and Qi became strong. Regarding the presence of a worthy, should his prince not respect him, then the state will not attain glory."[30] The assessment of *The Stratagems of the Warring States* is that Su Qin himself is the decisive person in determining hegemony in the Warring States Period. By employing Su Qin alone one can bring all under heaven to submit to one. The book declares, "At that time, all under heaven was huge and the peoples many, the sway of the kings and princes, the power of the politicking ministers all sought to decide according to the strategies of Su Qin. Without spending a bushel of grain, without bothering one soldier, without fighting a single battle, without breaking a single bowstring, without shooting a single arrow, the feudal lords loved one another even more than they loved their own brothers."[31]

Some personages do not concentrate on just one particular worthy minister as important to attaining hegemony but rather think that the whole group of ministers is the key factor. For instance, Zhang Yi thinks that if conditions for the resources of power hold, then the loyalty of all ministers is of decisive significance for attaining hegemony. He thinks that Qin has not yet been able to attain hegemony despite its supreme geographical, military, and economic advantages because the politicking ministers of Qin are not loyal to the state. He tells King Hui of Qin, "The feudal lords on all four sides do not submit, and the title of king of kings is not attained, and this is for no other reason than that the politicking ministers do not exert themselves to loyalty."[32] There are also those who think that to acquire hegemony requires may officials who are skilled in debate and able to think up many strategies. For instance, Shixing Qin thinks that if you can find people like the skilled debaters and schemers of the Western and Eastern Zhou then you can attain hegemony. He tells the *da ling zhao* (a high-ranking official) of Qin, "If you want the title of hegemon or sage king, then there is nothing better than to obtain the clever officials of the two Zhou kingdoms."[33]

The Right Geographical Conditions Are Essential for Attaining Hegemony

The strategists of *The Stratagems of the Warring States* already have the idea of geopolitics and lay great stress on the role of geographical advantages in attaining hegemony; they see geography as a necessary condition for attaining hegemony. In their analysis of the conditions of hegemony, the personages in the book frequently begin by referring to the geographical environment of a given state. For instance, when Su Qin analyzes the foundations of power that will enable Qin to gain hegemony for King Hui of Qin, he says,

> Your state, great King, in the west has the agricultural advantages of Ba [West Hubei and East Sichuan], Shu [West Sichuan] and Central Han [South Shaanxi and Northwest Hubei]; in the north you have the war service of the Hu and Mo nomads and of Dai and Ma; in the south there are the limits of Mount Wu and the Qian Plain [formerly the state of Chu]; in the east there are the protections of Mount Xiao and the Han Pass [Henan]. Your fields and pastures are outstanding; your people numerous and rich; your war chariots number ten thousand; your fertile borderlands a thousand square kilometers; your flocks and grain abundant; the lie of your land strategic. This is what is called the palace of heaven and yours is a powerful state under heaven. By relying on your worthiness, Great King, on the multitude of your officials and people, on the use of your chariots and horsemen, on the learning of military methods you can gather the feudal lords and annex all under heaven, become emperor, and rule.[34]

When Fan Sui analyzes the power base of hegemony for King Zhao of Qin, he too begins by mentioning the geography of Qin. He says,

Your state, great King, in the north has Mount Sweet Springs [in Shaanxi] and the Valley Mouth Pass [in Shaanxi], in the south the Jing and Wei rivers [both in Shaanxi], to the east Mount Long and Shu [both in Sichuan], to the west the Han Pass and Mount Ban [Mount Xiao]. Your war-chariots number a thousand, your special forces a million. If with the courage of the Qin army and the huge number of chariots and riders you attack the feudal lords, then it will be like hunting with swift hounds of the state of Han and catching rabbits. The business of a hegemonic king can be attained.[35]

The strategists of those times had already realized the dual role of geographical advantages in the struggle for hegemony, namely, that they could serve as a power resource for the state aspiring to hegemony and could serve as an obstacle to other states pursuing hegemony. For instance, a planner for the state of Zhao, in analyzing for Prime Minister Zhang why Zhao had successfully controlled the strong power of Qi and stopped the forty-year expansion of Qin, says that the reason was Zhao's geographical conditions and military might. He says, "Today Zhao is a strong state of ten thousand four-horse chariots; to the south there are the Zhang and Fu Rivers [Hebei: Handan], to the west Mount Chang [Heng Shan in Shanxi], to the east there is the area between the rivers [Hutuo and Zhang in Hebei], to the north there is the County of Dai [Hebei Weixian and Northeast Shanxi]. It has a million armored troops and once crushed the strength of Qi. For the past forty years, Qin has not been able to expand as it would wish."[36]

In the book, in addition to the personages who analyze the role of natural geographical conditions in the struggle for hegemony, there are also some who notice the role of geopolitical conditions. Zhang Yi starts from the inferiority of the natural geography and geopolitics of Wei and explains to King Xiang of Wei the necessity of making an alliance with Qin. He points out that Wei's territorial size is small and it has no natural defenses. To the east of Wei lies Qi, to the south Chu, to the west Han, and to the north Zhao, and if it has poor relationships with any of them, that state will attack Wei from one direction and Wei will become a battlefield on which the states will fight for hegemony. He tells King Xiang of Wei,

> The territory of Wei is not over a thousand square kilometers and its army has no more than three hundred thousand men. Its land is flat in all directions and the feudal lords can communicate across it from all four directions like the spokes of a wheel. It has no obstacles such as a famous mountain or great river. From Zheng [capital of Han] to Liang [capital of Wei] is not more than a hundred kilometers; from Chen [capital of Chu] to Liang, two hundred kilometers. If horses race and men run without tiring they will come to Liang. In the south it borders Chu, in the west Han, in the north Zhao, in the east Qi, and its only defenses are to have its armies posted on all four sides. Its observation posts and border garrisons are sparsely dotted. Its grain, waterways for transporting it, and open silos are not less than one hundred thousand. The lay of the land of Wei is such that it is a battlefield. If in the south Wei sides with Chu and not with Qi, then Qi will attack it in the east. If in the east it sides with Qi and not with Zhao, then Zhao will attack it in the north. If it does not join with Han, then Han will attack it in the west; if it is not friendly to Chu, then Chu will attack it in the south. This is what is called "a splitting road."[37]

Zhang Yi's geopolitical analysis succeeded in convincing King Xiang to form an alliance with Qin.

THE ROLE OF NORMS IN HEGEMONY

The history of the wars in the Warring States Period and the history of how Qin unified the states by annexing them both lead us to think that the strategists of the Warring States Period were not concerned with the political role of interstate norms. From the dialogues of the personages in *The Stratagems of the Warring States*, however, we find that in fact there are many instances of interstate norms being proposed as the basis for the legitimacy of hegemony. This essay's analysis of the philosophy of the norms in *The Stratagems of the Warring States* is not based on whether these understandings are the real beliefs of the speakers or whether the norms are effective or not, but rather emphasizes the content of these ideas. Hegemony is not only a form of international status; it is also a form of international order. Hence, acquiring and maintaining hegemony are both related to the norms of the international order. In *The Stratagems of the Warring States*, the discussions about social norms and their relation to hegemony are apparent in many places, among which three areas are particularly discussed: the relationship of norms to the legitimacy of hegemony, the relationship between respecting norms and using military force, and the relationship between the establishment of new norms and the preservation of old norms. The focal point of the discussions of international norms by contemporary theorists is the effect of norms and the principles of their evolution, whereas the personages of *The Stratagems of the Warring States* tend rather to discuss the political consequences of obeying or flouting interstate norms.

Respect for Norms Is a Basis for the Legitimacy of Hegemony

In *The Stratagems of the Warring States* two aspects of legitimacy in regard to hegemony are discussed: the form and the substance of legitimacy. In the Warring States Period, acknowledgment by the Zhou Son of Heaven was the formal norm of legitimacy for a hegemon, whereas recognition from most of the feudal states was the substantive norm of its legitimacy. Different people had differing understandings of the importance of both its formal and substantive legitimacy. Zhang Yi was more inclined to stress formal legitimacy and thought that if Qin could send an army to surround the Zhou royal capital, seize the set of nine tripods (the symbol of the king from the Xia Dynasty until it was seized by Qin in 255 BCE) and the map and household register, and control the Son of Heaven, then he could attain legitimacy for his hegemony. He said to King Hui of Qin, "Seize the set of nine tripods, lay hold of the map and household register, force the Son of Heaven to let you lead all under heaven, and then no one under heaven would dare to disobey. This is the king's affair."[38] Sima Cuo prefers to stress substantive legitimacy, however, and thinks that if the way for

Qin to acquire the nine tripods, the map, and the registry is to attack Han and seize the Son of Heaven, then not only will this lead to Qin not acquiring legitimacy for its hegemony but it will also be exceedingly dangerous. He rejects Zhang Yi's view, saying, "If today you attack Han and kidnap the Son of Heaven, well, kidnapping the Son of Heaven will give you a bad reputation and it will not necessarily bring you any good. You will also have a reputation for being without justice and you will attack a state—which is something all under heaven does not want. Both actions are dangerous!"[39]

Some of the strategists in the book think that to win over the majority of states to recognition of one's hegemony, military force is not sufficient. The hegemonic state must also respect interstate norms. One Qin strategist thinks that the way the state victorious in war treats other states and honors treaties it has signed will affect whether other feudal states willingly accept its hegemony. He thinks that someone who wins and is not arrogant may attain humane authority. One who signs agreements and is not angry or resentful may attain hegemony. The former will bring it about that all states submit, whereas the latter will lead neighboring states to join in an alliance. He tells King Wu of Qin, "The troops of a king are victorious and not arrogant; the chief lord heeds agreements and is not resentful. Thus, being victorious but not arrogant, you can get the world to serve you. Making agreements and not being resentful, you can get the neighbors to follow you."[40] From this passage we can see that in the Warring States Period people had already realized that whether a hegemonic state could lead, or even whether it was conscious of respecting interstate norms, has great influence on its hegemonic status. The unilateralist foreign policy of President George W. Bush weakened the international political mobilizing capacity of the United States, which is an example of the failure to recognize this aspect of legitimacy.

Norms Provide a Hegemon with the Legitimacy to Use Military Force

The strategists of *The Stratagems of the Warring States* are very much concerned with the question of a hegemon's legitimacy to engage in armed conflict. Many of them think that a failure to use troops legitimately will harm the hegemon's legitimacy. For instance, when King Hui of Wei attacks Zhao, Ji Liang thinks that, although the king's purpose is to attain hegemony and to win the trust of all the states, his strategy of using troops to attack the Zhao capital of Handan, expand his territory, and increase his renown is counterproductive. He tells King Hui the story of driving south to get to a northern destination and warns him that the more he relies on strong troops to attack other states, the more he will lose legitimacy to lead other states. He says, "Today the king moves troops to become a hegemonic king and attacks to gain the trust of all under heaven. You rely on the size of the kingdom and the might of your troops and attack Handan so as to expand your territory and win honor for your name. The more numerous your military actions, O King, the further you are far from attaining humane authority."[41]

There are many possible sources of legitimacy for the military actions of a hegemonic state, but the personages in the book refer most often to three. The first is the justness of the war's purpose. For example, in analyzing under what conditions Qin should deploy troops, the great Qin general Bai Qi says that the purpose a state that aspires to hegemony has in deploying troops is to console states that are fearful, to put down arrogant states, or to punish and annihilate states that have lost the Way. Only then may a state give orders to the feudal lords and then bring peace to all under heaven. He says to King Zhao of Qin, "Console those that are fearful; punish those that are arrogant; punish and destroy those without the Way. Thus you can order the feudal lords and all under heaven can be put in order."[42]

The second source of legitimacy is that the state to be punished with military force is evil. For instance, Su Qin thinks that a hegemonic state worthy of the name will certainly want to use military force to destroy violent states, to restructure chaotic states, to obliterate evil states, and to attack states with violent rulers. He says to King Min of Qi, "Today the sage king who takes military action must punish violent states and correct the disordered, intervene in those without the Way, and attack the unjust."[43] Although Su Qin says this in the hope of influencing the king of Qi's foreign policy with a view to helping Yan, his view wins King Min's

approval. Zhang Yi also thinks that starting a war against a just state is illegitimate. Of any two states at war, logic dictates that only one can be
just and so he holds that for a violent, evil, or rebellious state to attack a
benevolent, just, or peaceful state is to sow the seeds of its own defeat.
He tells King Hui of Qin, "The disordered state that attacks the ordered
will perish; the evil state that attacks the just will perish; the rebellious
state that attacks the obedient will perish."[44]

The third source of legitimacy for the use of force is found when one's
adversary is of a lower level of civilization. It is legitimate for a state that
judges itself culturally superior to use military force against a barbarian
state. For instance, in the Warring States Period, Shu did not belong to the
civilization of the central states and was seen as a barbarian state. Hence,
when Sima Cuo tells King Hui of Qin why an attack on Shu is more legitimate than one on Han, he points out that Shu is the leading power among
states led by minority peoples in the west, and it has exhibited brutal
administration like that of Jie and Zhòu. He says, "Shu is a state in the
remote west and is head of the Rong and Di barbarians and it also has
exhibited the disorder of Jie and Zhòu."[45]

The Necessity of, and Risk in, Establishing New Norms for Hegemony

The politicians in *The Stratagems of the Warring States* have already realized
that for a hegemon to establish a new hegemonic system, it is necessary
to change the current interstate norms to adapt to changes in society. For
instance, when the chief ministers of Zhao, Zhao Wenjin, and Zhao Zao
urge King Wuling of Zhao not to adopt nomadic dress and cavalry ar-
chers, the king replies that the three kings Yao, Shun, and Yü as well as
dukes Xiang of Song and Mu of Qin, and King Zhuang of Chu all established their hegemony by inaugurating different social and political norms,
and he uses this to prove the necessity for a newly established hegemon
to change existing norms. The king thinks that it is not necessary to imitate previous hegemonic norms too closely since present and past norms
differ and the difference is not one of right or wrong. He says, "The three
dynasties had different dress and yet all reigned as sage kings; the five

hegemons adopted different political regulations and yet all ruled. . . . A sage's emergence is such that he does not fit into the past and yet he reigns. The Xia and the Yin collapsed because they did not change their rites and so they perished. Hence, imitating the past is not necessarily wrong nor is following rites necessarily worthy of praise."[46] Even though it is not possible to judge from King Wuling's words whether *dress*, *regulations*, and *rites* refer to domestic or interstate norms, from his use of the example of the three kings and five hegemons we can postulate that the norms he refers to must at least include interstate norms.

Some strategists in the book realize that altering interstate norms is necessary for establishing a new hegemony but it is also risky, especially when it means changing the norms that regulate the hierarchical relationship of the feudal lords to the Zhou court. In the Warring States Period there were many kinds of hierarchical norms, the most distinctive being the appellation of the rulers. The Zhou king was called the Son of Heaven and the rulers of the feudal states were called either king or duke. All states that wished to establish a new hegemony faced the choice of calling their rulers either by their old title or by *emperor* instead of *king*. The use of *emperor* indicated equality with the Zhou Son of Heaven. The change in the norm for naming the ruler was one part of establishing a new hegemonic system. To do so entailed violating current interstate norms and ran the risk of provoking opposition from other states. Prudent strategists thought that the establishment of new norms required a trial period before they could be implemented. When Qin sent a letter to King Min of Qi stamped "emperor," Su Qin thought that on the premise that it was not clear if the other feudal lords would accept the king of Qi calling himself emperor, the practice was dangerous. Hence, he suggested that King Min should first see how the states reacted to Qin's calling its king "emperor" and only then come to a decision. If nobody was opposed to Qin adopting the imperial title, then the king of Qi could also call himself "emperor" and he would then win the support of everyone in the world. Su Qin said to King Min of Qi, "If Qin uses the title and everyone accepts it, then the king may also use the title. . . . If Qin uses the title and everyone rejects it, then the king may not use the title for this reason, and you will have won the support of everyone. This is good for you."[47]

THE BASIC STRATEGY FOR ATTAINING HEGEMONY

Many politicians in *The Stratagems of the Warring States* believe that the rightness of a strategy plays a decisive role in determining success in attaining hegemony. For instance, the prime minister of Wei, Hui Shi, thinks that whereas acquiring humane authority requires reliance on law, attaining hegemony requires strategy. He says, "I, your minister, heard that to become a sage king demands knowing rules, whereas to become a hegemon requires knowing strategies."[48] Chen Zhen, a strategist of Chu, sees strategy as the root whereby a state can be called a hegemon. He says, "Strategy is the root of affairs; following it is the key to survival or failure."[49] Chen Zhen's idea that strategy is the decisive factor is very similar to that held by people today. For instance, the Program of International Strategic Studies of the Chinese Academy of Social Sciences says, "The determination and implementation of international strategy is concerned with the future and fate of the nation."[50]

The discussions of the strategies for attaining hegemony in *The Stratagems of the Warring States* do not distinguish between grand strategy and military strategy. The two are always intimately linked. From the point of view of gaining hegemony, the main strategies in *The Stratagems of the Warring States* are those of annexation and alliance.

The Strategy of Annexation

Many events recorded in *The Stratagems of the Warring States* are cases of large states annexing small ones, or of strong states taking over weak ones. These events reflect that the politicians of the time not only generally understood that the strategy of annexation is an effective way to attain hegemony but also advocated strategies of annexation. In an agricultural society, the combination of land and people formed economic power, and a large population could support a large, strong army; hence, annexing the territory of other states would weaken their economic and military power while increasing one's own economic and military power, thus leading to attainment of hegemony. A Qin strategist told King Wu of Qin that he could achieve what the three kings and five hegemons had done before if he could continue to annex other states one by one, so that no state would dare to oppose his invading the states of the feudal lords and putting pressure on the borders of the Zhou court to deter all the princes from going beyond their borders. Han and Chu would also not dare to deploy their armies against him. He said,

> If now, O King, you took over Yiyang [in Henan], occupied the three rivers area [Yellow River, Luo and Yi], and brought it about that no person of intelligence dared to say a word; if you owned the states of all under heaven and walked along the boundaries of the two Zhou [Eastern and Western Zhou], prevented the lords of the world daring to join their troops at mountain passes, and held Huang Ji [in Henan], then the armies of Han and Chu would not dare to invade. If the king is able to carry this through to the end, then the three kings will not lack a fourth, and the five lords not lack a sixth.[51]

To become a hegemon by annexing territory demands forming relationships with distant states and attacking those nearby, a principle that the strategists in the book realize above all else. For instance, when Fan Sui analyzes for King Zhao of Qin why Chu was able to defeat Qi but was still unable to annex a large area of land, he says that it was not because Qi did not want to occupy that land but rather because between Qi and Chu lay other states, so Qi's annexation of the land would be ineffective. Fan Sui says, "Of old, the people of Qi punished Chu and won in battle, destroying their army and killing their general, and opened up 500 square kilometers of land, but they were not able to retain even a tiny piece, not because Qi did not want land, but because the circumstances did not allow it."[52] According to the same principle, Fan Sui recommends that King Zhao adopt the strategy of establishing good relations with those far off and annexing those nearby. Hence, launching an attack on the distant Chu is unreasonable. He notes that Han and Qin share a common border and this is disadvantageous to Qin, so Qin should first annex Han. He tells King Zhao,

> There is nothing better for the king than to form alliances with those far off and annex those nearby. An inch gained will become the king's inch and a foot gained the king's foot. Now, to neglect this

and attack a distant place, is that not foolish? . . . The terrain of Qin and Han is woven together like silk cloth of many colored threads. For Qin to have Han [as a neighbor] is like a tree having a worm eating it from within or a man having a faulty heart. Of all the challenges under heaven, none is more harmful to Qin than that posed by Han. Far better for the king to take over Han.[53]

When Su Qin analyzes for Lord Wen of Yan whether it is better for Yan to form an alliance with Qin or Zhao, he refers to the principle of establishing relations with the distant and attacking the near. He points out that Qin is far from Yan, and Zhao is between them. Qin cannot attack Yan, nor could it hold it if it did so, whereas Yan and Zhao are neighbors; it would be easy for Zhao to attack and hold Yan. For Yan to be concerned about its relationship with the distant Qin and to ignore the neighboring Zhao would be a big mistake. Yan should be allied with Zhao if there is a security guarantee. Su Qin tells Lord Wen of Yan,

> If Qin attacks Yan, it must overrun Yunzhong [in Inner Mongolia] and Jiuyuan, cross Dai [in Hebei and Northeast Shanxi] and Shanggu [West and Central Hebei], covering a distance of more than a thousand kilometers. Even if it captures the capital of Yan, its concern will be that it cannot hold on to it. From this it is clear that Qin cannot harm Yan! Now, if Zhao should attack Yan, it would issue its command and within ten days some hundred thousand troops would be encamped around Dong Yuan [in Hebei]. They would cross the Hutuo River and the Yi River and within four or five days would reach your capital city. Thus I say, "If Qin attacks Yan, it will fight at a distance of more than a thousand kilometers; if Zhao attacks Yan, it will fight at a range within a hundred kilometers. There is no more mistaken plan than to fail to be concerned with the threat within a hundred kilometers while concentrating on one more than a thousand kilometers away. Therefore, may you, O King, form an alliance of friendship with Zhao and all under heaven will be united and the state will certainly have nothing to fear!"[54]

Since the result of annexation is the swallowing up of another state, the strategists in the book also address the thoroughness of annexation. Some

people think that the ultimate success or failure of annexation is determined by whether the population, not simply the land, is annexed. They
think that annexation of a state involves both population and territory and
to annex only the land while not annihilating the inhabitants of the state
runs the risk that the survivors will seek to restore their state and annex
you in turn. The annihilation of a state includes both material and conceptual aspects and the latter is the key. Changing the occupied people's
sense of belonging is decisive to the success of the annexation. A visiting
official from Qin named Zao uses the historical examples of Wu and Yue,
and Qi and Yan, to tell Lord Xiang, the prime minister of Qin, that annexation must be thorough. He says, "Wu did not annihilate Yue and so
Yue annihilated Wu; Qi did not annihilate Yan and so Yan annihilated Qi.
Qi perished under Yan; Wu perished under Yue. This is because the malady
was not thoroughly rooted out."[55]

The Strategy of Alliance Formation

The strategies of annexation and alliance formation to attain hegemony
are ancient, and both have equally great significance in history. After
World War II, the United Nations charter established the norm of respect
for the territorial integrity of the sovereign state. Since then, the strategy
of annexation has become increasingly unsuited to the times, and therefore alliance formation has become the main strategy used in international politics in seeking to attain hegemony. The principle of forming
alliances is that within an international system of mutual alliances, when
one strong state uses the construction of alliances to form a powerful bloc
and that state also serves as the leader of the bloc, then that state has won
hegemonic status within the system. If this bloc is the strongest bloc
within the world system, then the head of the bloc is the biggest hegemonic power. If that state heads the only bloc, then it is the only hegemonic power within the system. In analyzing the foundations of Wei's
hegemony for Duke Xiao of Qin, Wei Yang says, "The achievements of
Wei are great and its commands run throughout all under heaven and
twelve feudal lords follow it to pay court to the Son of Heaven and so its
allies are certainly many."[56]

The Stratagems of the Warring States records the formation of many alliances, the most famous being the Vertical Union proposed by Su Qin and the Horizontal Link espoused by Zhang Yi. The Vertical Union was an alliance of six states—Qi, Chu, Zhao, Wei, Yan, and Han—against Qin. It was described as "uniting the weak vertically against the one strong state." The Horizontal Link was designed to destroy the Vertical Union and allow Qin to become a hegemon. It worked by turning one weak state against another and was referred to as "serving one strong state and attacking many weak ones."

Su Qin had a deep understanding of how to form alliances in order to gain hegemony. He thought that the key to this strategy lay in mutual trust and solidarity among the partners. The main obstacle to collective action arose from one partner repudiating the alliance. Hence, Su Qin suggested that King Huiwen of Zhao should use the method of the union of the princes of Shandong and decree that when an ally was attacked by a third party, they all should provide military support and exchange hostages among themselves as a guarantee that each state would fulfill its pledges, and in this way he could attain hegemony. Su Qin said,

> Thus, in my humble opinion there is no better plan for the king than to unite the six states of Han, Wei, Qi, Yan, Chu, Yan, and Zhao in a vertical alliance to oppose Qin. Give an order to the generals of all under heaven to meet together above the Huan Shui River [in Henan], exchange hostages, and make a covenant in the blood of a white horse.
>
> The oath will read:
>
> "If Qin attacks Chu, Qi and Wei will each send armed troops to assist Chu; Han will cut off [Qin's] supply lines; Zhao will ford the Yellow River and the Zhang; and Yan will defend to the north of Mount Heng.
>
> "If Qin attacks Han or Wei, then Chu will cut it off from the rear; Qi will send armed troops to assist Chu; Zhao will ford the Yellow River and the Zhang; and Yan will defend Yunzhong [in Inner Mongolia].
>
> "If Qin attacks Qi, then Chu will cut it off from the rear; Han will defend Cheng Gao [in Henan]; Wei will block Wu Dao; Zhao will

ford the Yellow River and the Zhang as far as Bo Pass [in Shandong]; and Yan will send armed troops to assist Qi.

"If Qin attacks Yan, then Zhao will defend Mount Heng; Chu will camp at Wu Pass [on the Shaanxi/Henan border]; Qi will cross the Bohai Sea; and Han and Wei will send armed troops to assist Yan.

"If Qin attacks Zhao, then Han will camp at Yiyang; Chu will camp at Wu Pass; Wei will camp beyond the Yellow River [south of the river]; Qi will ford the Bohai Sea; and Yan will send armed troops to assist Zhao.

"If any one of the feudal lords should renounce the alliance, the other five states will jointly attack that one.

"If the six states maintain their alliance against Qin, then Qin will certainly not dare to send its army to Hangu Pass so as to threaten what lies east of the mountain! In this way the business of the chief lord will be accomplished!"[57]

To enable Qin to attain hegemony, Zhang Yi proposed the strategy of a Horizontal Link. The purpose of this strategy was to undermine the alliance of the six states, and its principle was that small states would break faith in their own interest and attach themselves to Qin. King Hui of Qin adopted Zhang Yi's strategy because he believed that the interests of the six states in the alliance were all different and they would find it difficult to cooperate. He told Han Quanzi, "That the feudal lords cannot be united is as obvious as a flock of chickens cannot sit still in the same direction on the same perch."[58]

The principle of the Horizontal Link propounded by Zhang Yi was confirmed in practice. The reasoning Shen Buhai uses to explain to Prince Zhaoxi of Han why Han should conclude an alliance with Qin is an example of opportunist thought on the part of a weak state. He thinks that if Han and Qin made an alliance, Qin could attain humane authority and Han attain hegemony. Han would thus escape the risk of being threatened by Qin should Qin fail. He says,

The first point is that it is beneficial to join an alliance with a strong state. If the strong state can attain humane authority, then we will certainly attain hegemony. Even if the strong state cannot become a humane authority at least we can avoid its armies and it will not attack us. Hence, the goals of the strong state will be accomplished and we will rely on the emperor and be a hegemon. If the goals of the strong state are not accomplished, then it may treat us generously. Hence, if we now join the strong state and the goals of the strong state are accomplished, then there is good fortune, and if they are not accomplished, at least there is no disaster. To first join the strong state is the plan of a wise person.[59]

The logic of this strategy of forming an alliance with a strong state is rather like that of the strategy of following the strong in contemporary international relations theory.[60]

The twin strategies of annexation and alliance formation discussed in *The Stratagems of the Warring States* are not mutually exclusive but rather are mutually supportive and can be used together. The book discusses the question of which strategy should be the main one and which should be secondary. In the history of strategies, Qi attained hegemony by making alliance formation its main strategy and annexation secondary, whereas Qin made annexation its main one and alliance formation secondary. In the book, even the planners who forcefully insist on annexation as the way to hegemony do not reject the strategy of making alliances. For the most part, they adopt annexation as the main and alliance formation as the secondary strategy. Moreover, the choice of partners for alliances is often geared to the needs of annexation. For instance, Zhang Yi recommends that the grand strategy King Hui of Qin should adopt to become a hegemon is to make annexation the main strategy and alliance formation the secondary one. He suggests that King Hui should destroy the Vertical Union by attacking and occupying Zhao and annexing Han, so that Jing and Wei both become subordinate, but he should make alliances with Qi and Yan and thus establish hegemony. Zhang Yi says, "The method by which to attack and destroy the Vertical Union under heaven is to attack Zhao, annihilate Han, make Jing and Wei vassals, be friendly with Qi and Yan, and thus gain the title of sage king of sage kings and the skill of getting the princely states around you to come to your court."[61]

The Opportunity for War

Both annexation and alliance formation rely on military expeditions; hence, *The Stratagems of the Warring States* also discusses the issue of when it is good to go to war, and especially the choice of whether to attack first or wait to be attacked before replying. Many strategists in *The Stratagems of the Warring States* think that the one who waits before acting has more advantages in winning hegemony. For instance, Su Qin uses a syllogism to present to King Min of Qin the advantages of waiting. Su Qin thinks that the first aggressor will run into many problems later, whereas one who responds later can rely on more allies, and the more allies one has the greater one's strength. A greater number of men and more power can put down one who has little assistance and can lead to victory in war. Doing things in such a way as to win people's minds is necessarily advantageous. For a large state to adopt the strategy of waiting to be attacked means that it can become the hegemonic lord without wasting its force. Su Qin says, "I, your minister, have heard that using troops and happily doing so before everyone else is disastrous. . . . The one who mobilizes later should react to the moment."[62] He also says, "The one who mobilizes later in response has many allies and strong armies. Hence, to gather all your strength and respond to the weak and small will certainly bring you victory in battle. This will not go against everyone's feelings and so gains will certainly follow. If a great state acts thus, then its fame and honor will be won without a struggle and the title of the king of sage kings established without your having done anything."[63]

The strategy of mobilizing later led to the development of the idea of "sitting on the mountain and watching the tigers fight." When Qi and Chu were contending for hegemony, Chen Zhen sought to prevent Qin from helping Qi in its attack on Chu, and so he told King Hui of Qin the story of sitting on the mountain and watching the tigers fight and showed how this would help Qin in gaining hegemony. He first related how Guan Yu urged Guan Zhuangzi to wait for the two tigers to wound each other before stepping in to catch them both, and then recommended that King Hui should wait for Qi to be defeated in its war with Chu before moving to save Qi. In that way everything will go well for him. He said, "Now Qi and Chu are at war. War entails defeat. Your Majesty should call up troops to help the defeated party. You will have the gain of saving Qi and avoid the evil of attacking Chu."[64] Even though Chen Zhen's purpose in telling the story of the tigers is to prevent Qin from attacking Chu, yet in fact this strategy is advantageous to Qin, and hence King Hui accepted Chen Zhen's proposed strategy.

Su Dai urged King Hui of Yan not to fight Zhao to avoid giving Qin the opportunity to "sit and watch like the fisherman." He used the story of the old fisherman getting the advantage when the snipe and the clam fight to persuade King Hui, "If now Zhao launches a war against Yan, then Zhao and Yan will be locked in battle for a long time and this will paralyze everyone . . . strong Qin will be like the fisherman."[65] This example is to prevent the other state getting the opportunity to sit on the mountain and catch both tigers.

We have already noted that the book discusses the strategy of sitting on the mountain to catch both tigers. The condition for the success of this strategy is that the two parties engaged in conflict are of roughly equal strength. The purpose of the strategy is to let other contenders for hegemony expend their strength. If the result of the strategy is that the victor ends up being much stronger, then it will be a case of rearing a tiger to court calamity (appeasement) and the sitting on the mountain to catch both tigers strategy will have failed. For instance, when Wei encircled the Zhao capital of Handan, Zhao Xixu suggested to King Xuan of Chu that he should not rescue Zhao but rather wait and watch Zhao and Wei destroy each other. Jing She proposed helping Zhao, however. He thought that if Chu did not help Zhao, then Zhao might be annihilated and this would amount to Chu helping Wei to destroy Zhao. This possibility could result in forcing Zhao to reconcile with Wei so as to avoid disaster and both would then attack Chu. Jing She suggested that King Xuan should send a small number of troops to assist Zhao and hope that both Zhao and Wei would be defeated in the battle and this would be advantageous to Chu in enlarging its sphere of influence. He said to King Xuan,

> If Wei attacks Zhao, then I fear that later it will attack Chu. If now you do not save Zhao, then Zhao will court defeat and Wei will not

fear Chu. Thus this amounts to Chu and Wei attacking Zhao together. The danger will be great indeed! How can this be a case of
"both defeated"? Wei's whole army will cut deeply into Zhao. Zhao
will see that it courts disaster and that Chu is not helping it and so
will make up with Wei and both together will attack Chu. Thus, the
king has no better course than to send a few troops to give assistance to Zhao. Zhao will rely on Chu's strength and hence carry on
the fight against Wei. Wei will be furious at Zhao's strength and will
see that Chu's assistance is not worth fearing and therefore will not
let go of Zhao. Zhao and Wei will defeat each other and Qi and Qin
will, in turn, work with Chu; then Wei can be destroyed.[66]

According to *The Stratagems of the Warring States*, "Since Chu mobilized
troops to help Zhao as Jing She advised, Handan fell; Chu took the area
between the rivers Sui and Cen [in Henan]."[67]

CONCLUSION AND MESSAGE FOR TODAY

The philosophy of contending for hegemony in *The Stratagems of the Warring States* was subject to criticism from Confucian scholars for a long
time, yet in fact the history of states' contention for hegemony has gone
on for thousands of years. Right up to the present globalized information
era, struggle for hegemony is still the core of international politics. Understanding what *The Stratagems of the Warring States* says on this issue not
only aids a deeper understanding of the real state of international politics
today but it also can bring together and enlighten studies of comprehensive national power, international systems, international strategy, and
China's rise.

A Message for Research into National Power

Political power is the basis for drawing together comprehensive national
power. In the discussions about hegemonic power in *The Stratagems of the
Warring States*, political power is the foundation, but this is different from

the analysis of the foundation of hegemonic power propounded by contemporary international relations theory. The contemporary theories see material power (territorial area, population, the economy, military affairs) as the foundation of hegemonic power. Even if in recent years the scholarly world has begun to pay attention to the importance of states' soft power, the mainstream point of view is still that hard power is the basis of soft power. Even scholars who do pay more attention to soft power mainly stress the power of cultural resources rather than the power of political manipulation. Furthermore, if we observe the present world of politics from the viewpoint of a philosophy that takes political power as the basis for comprehensive power, then we will find that its explanatory power is not inferior—and may even be superior—to that of the theory that the economy is decisive. The understanding of the comprehensive power of hegemony in *The Stratagems of the Warring States* is one that sees political power as the basis of comprehensive power. The theoretical question this raises is how to use scientific methods to test which of the two, economic or political power, is the foundation of comprehensive national power. Given that we have as yet no effective proof, we must ask what the difference in the degree of reliability is between the present assumption that economic power is the foundation of comprehensive national power and the historical assumption that military power was the foundation of national power.

Leadership is the core of a national political power. This belief is the same today as it was in the past. But when the theories positing system as the decisive factor arose in the 1970s, research on leadership shifted its focus from policy makers and the policymaking body to the system of policymaking. In the early twenty-first century, research on policy makers and the policymaking body has again become a focus of attention. International political psychology represents this trend.[68] Discussions of state leadership in *The Stratagems of the Warring States* mainly focus on the morality of the leader and his employment of policy. The message for us is that, from the beliefs of the leader, the structure of the leadership, and the state bureaucracy, we should study the relationships between leadership and national political power, between leadership and foreign policymaking, and between leadership and international mobilization capability.

The employment of worthy and competent people is an indicator of the leadership's strength or weakness. What *The Stratagems of the Warring States* says about the relationship between employment of competent persons and hegemony differs from today's ideas in two respects. The first is that the standard for assessing the moral level of the leader is whether he employs competent persons; the second is that the type of person employed determines whether hegemony can be attained and the class of that hegemony. It may be that this way of assessing national leadership by the capacity of the high-ranking officials is not perfect, but it is still an advance on the current lack of any standard to assess national political power in contemporary international relations theory. If we look at the method for assessing state leadership presented in *The Stratagems of the Warring States*, we may take the movement of talented persons among nations as an indicator to assess national political power. People naturally head for the top places just as water naturally flows downhill; hence, the movement of talented people from politically weak to politically strong states is a universal phenomenon globally. To take the direction and volume of this movement as an indicator for assessing national political power, even soft power, is perhaps reasonable.

Message for International Systems Research

Shifts in the center of the world are the result of human activity and effort, not a purely natural change. The explanations of the rise and fall of hegemonies in *The Stratagems of the Warring States* may be simply ascribed to correct human strategy and effort or lack thereof. It is not a natural succession. Su Qin thought that the rise of the three kings and the succession of the five hegemons were all due to the leaders not being content with the way things stood and hence making an effort to change things. He tells King Yi of Yan, "The rise in turn of each of the three kings and the success of the five hegemons were none of them automatic events."[69] This understanding is very different from how contemporary international relations theory seeks to find the objective causes of shifts in global hegemony. By combining what *The Stratagems of the Warring States* says about shifts in hegemony being due to human strategy and effort and contemporary theory, which holds that there are objective laws governing shifts in hegemony, we can begin by looking for the objective factors that cause the strength of leadership to increase or decline and go on to study the law of shifts in hegemony.

Hierarchical norms are the basis of international order, but they differ in different eras. In *The Stratagems of the Warring States* the understanding of social norms and social order is that social order is based on hierarchical norms. This idea is similar to that in contemporary international relations theory, which ascribes international conflict to anarchy in the international system, but it is unlike the principle in contemporary international politics that demands respect for the equality of state sovereignty. What this says about theory is that the establishment of international norms must combine the principles of equality and of hierarchy and that it should not rely only on one principle. This is like upholding the equality and fairness of a boxing match. There should be norms for judging who the winner is but also norms for distinguishing between the weights of the contestants. The former is the principle of equality, whereas the latter is that of fairness. For the most part, contemporary international relations theory relies on the principle of equality to study the role of international norms. If, however, we combined the two principles of hierarchy and equality in our research, then we could deepen our understanding of the role of international norms.

Hegemony can of itself generate legitimacy for the use of military force. What *The Stratagems of the Warring States* says about the sources of the legitimacy of the use of force by a hegemon is very similar to what we have witnessed in contemporary international political reality. This fact tells us that hegemony itself may have the role of generating legitimacy for the use of force in foreign affairs. The international responsibility, ideology, and power of a hegemon are all able to create legitimacy whereby it can use force externally: (1) When a state is accepted by a good number of other states as hegemon, these states think that that state has the duty to protect its allies militarily, uphold the current international order, and maintain its own hegemonic status; (2) One reason for accepting a hegemon is that a fair number of states accept its ideology. The dominating ideology of the hegemonic state gives rise to the conceptual superiority of its civilization, such that the hegemon has the legitimacy to use military force against states of peripheral civilizations; and (3) When a hegemon is accepted by other states, it then has the status to guide the formation of international norms. The interest in upholding the international norms formed under its guidance is for the most part at one with the interests of the hegemonic state itself. This also provides grounds for the legitimacy of using military force to uphold these kinds of interests.

Message for the Study of the Theory of a Grand Strategy

The core of successful grand strategy is creativity rather than any one model of strategy. Many of the discussions concerning strategies for attaining hegemony in *The Stratagems of the Warring States* are opposed to one another. This tells us that there must be many different ways to realize the political goal of attaining hegemony. Although contemporary international relations theories have surveyed the types of strategy for attaining hegemony found in history, they have not discovered any successful strategy for attaining hegemony that can be successfully repeated. This may be because the essence of a strategy to attain hegemony is creativity, and imitation of strategies used in the past will never be successful. Contemporary international relations theories have studied the various conditions for the success of a strategy, but these studies have overlooked creativity as the essence of any strategy for attaining hegemony, namely, that a strategy for attaining hegemony is without a fixed form. It changes according to the times and is something that the strategists must invent in accord with circumstances. In other words, it may be that the strategies for attaining hegemony found in history are of no use for the later rise of a great power. Deng Xiaoping's construction of socialism with Chinese characteristics happens to be a grand strategy of this kind. From the discovery that strategies for attaining hegemony cannot be repeated, the focal point of research in contemporary international strategic theory should, it seems, shift to the two themes of how strategies for attaining hegemony were invented and what the basic principles of inventing a successful strategy are.

A successful strategy for building alliances is based on strategic credibility. There is much in *The Stratagems of the Warring States* about successful or failed vertical or horizontal alliances. These records reflect that success in alliance formation depends on the strategic credibility of the leader of the alliances, and failure comes when the partners lack fidelity in undertaking their parts of the bargain because they do not trust the leading state. Discussions in the book about the unreliability of strategies to form alliances are strikingly similar to Jean-Jacques Rousseau's game of Stag Hunt.[70] The strategists in *The Stratagems of theWarring States* ascribe the unreliability of alliances to a lack of fidelity among the allies, whereas Rousseau ascribes it to the allies not believing in the fidelity of other allies. What this tells us is that contemporary alliance-building theory is based on study of the common interest, the function of the organization, and the concept of cooperation, but there is not much study of the role of strategic credibility within the alliance. If one were to look at how the strategic credibility of the lord of the alliance is formed, at the origins of the fidelity of the allies, and at the principle of formation of mutual trust among the allies and were to deepen contemporary study of alliance building, then this would enrich not only current study of international security cooperation but also our understanding of the success and failure of states' strategies for ascent.

Message for China's Strategy for Ascent

A strategy for China's rise must adopt the principle of balanced development of the factors of comprehensive national power. The principle of economic construction as the center is of assistance in increasing a state's material power under certain conditions, but this principle cannot become the basis of comprehensive power for Chinese national resurgence. By adopting the principle of balanced development of the factors of comprehensive state power, China will maintain balanced development of both political and economic power. It is only by constraining the worship of money formed by placing the priority on economic construction that the factors of comprehensive state power can be developed evenly. The focal point in improving political power is to improve national leadership, and the key to this lies in constructing a system for promoting superior cadres and demoting inferior ones. Seen from the point of view of increasing international political power, China must stress the construction of a system that attracts talented persons. In a globalized era, it is necessary to reflect on the experience of *The Stratagems of the Warring States* and recruit talented persons according to international standards, irrespective of their nationalities.

The strategy of China's rise must tend toward strategic creativity. A successful strategy for the rise of a major power is created by adapting to constantly changing international circumstances. Ever since 1949, when the new China was founded, China has proposed many strategic foreign policy principles according to the international environment of the time. These principles are variously used to respond to the international environment; hence, contradictions are unavoidable. Since the circumstances of international competition are constantly changing, China must adapt to the times and adjust the guiding principles of its strategy of ascent. It should not be constrained by old principles. Still less should it restrain the adjustment of its strategic principles on account of any long-lasting, unchanging theory. Following the rise of China's power status, the limitations of the principle of nonalignment have already become apparent. China can reflect on the alliance-building strategies of *The Stratagems of the Warring States* and adopt a strategy beneficial to expanding its international political support. The alliance-building strategies of *The Stratagems of the Warring States* and the Communist Party's United Front principle are very similar. This kind of principle was able to bring about victory in the War against Japanese Aggression [i.e., World War II], and it may also be successful in guiding China's rise.

This essay has analyzed and summarized many of the ideas and understandings of interstate relations in *The Stratagems of the Warring States* related to hegemony. It has undertaken its analysis of *The Stratagems of the Warring States* on the basis of the idea of contemporary international relations theory. It has not considered the historical background of discourse in the book. In fact, there are at least three different backgrounds of discourse to be found in *The Stratagems of the Warring States*. The first is that of the language and concepts used by people in the Warring States

Period. The second is the language and thought of the editor of the book, toward the end of the Western Han Dynasty (i.e., before 24 CE). The third is that of the historical status of the personages in the book and their relationship to the persons they are addressing. According to these three backgrounds of discourse, it is very probable that people may draw different conclusions and find different things in what *The Stratagems of the Warring States* says about hegemony. We think that however great the differences are in the conclusions drawn on the presupposition of different backgrounds of discourse, all are positive so long as they enrich the development of current international relations theory or can help in perfecting China's strategy for ascent. We hope that this essay will inspire more colleagues in academia to study *The Stratagems of the Warring States* from the point of view of international politics.

PART II
Comments

An Examination of the Research Theory of Pre-Qin Interstate Political Philosophy

Yang Qianru

U sing the expression of Barry Buzan, we can say that there were many "statelike units" in China with complex and varied relationships. There were clans bound together in an alliance under a leader (as in the Legends of the Five Emperors), tribal states on the periphery of the land ruled by the Son of Heaven (at the time of the Three Kings), feudal states under a central royal house (the Zhou king), as well as relationships among various family clans, tribes, and princely states. This essay groups all these forms together and looks at their interstate relations, taking this as the basis for examining pre-Qin interstate political philosophy.[1]

In terms of monarchy, the common understanding of history is that from the Western Zhou until the end of the Eastern Zhou there was only one actual state, that of the Zhou king, and all the princely states were feudal dependencies of the Zhou Son of Heaven and hence belonged to the Zhou royal house and could not be considered as independent states in their own right. But the historical reality is that from the eighth to the third century BCE the hold of the Zhou king was gradually relaxed. The Zhou court's overall grasp and authority were constantly weakened so that from the Western Zhou feudal era on, it no longer had the means to carry out its role of upholding the political order and system of power. In the Spring and Autumn Period (eighth to sixth century BCE), several large princely states already had two basic features of the modern "state": sovereignty and territory. Not only did the states have independent and autonomous sovereignty, they also had very clear borders. By the time of the Warring States Period (fifth to third century BCE), states proliferated and entered into several centuries of competition to unify all under heaven under their own rule, while the Zhou royal domain sank to the level of a small, weak state. Hence, some scholars think that the way in which the various princely states gave feudal homage to the Zhou king as their common lord from the eighth to the third century BCE was rather like the relationship of the members of today's Commonwealth to Great Britain. They accept the Queen as head of the Commonwealth but enjoy equal and independent status along with Great Britain.[2] In a PhD dissertation from the War Strategies Faculty of the International University titled "The Politics of State Alliances in the Spring and Autumn and Warring States Periods," Zhou Yi describes the states of this period as "politically behaved bodies." This description is more accurate than the term *states*.

Bearing this in mind, I think that the name "pre-Qin interstate political philosophy" is acceptable on academic grounds and is appropriate because the pre-Qin states—following the decline of the Western Zhou feudal system and the destruction of the previous harmony and balanced order between the Zhou royal house and the various states, from the Five Hegemons of the Spring and Autumn era to the Seven Powers of the Warring States up until the "great unification" of the Qin-Han—on the grounds of protecting their own security, sought to develop and resolve the relationships among themselves and the central royal house and thus they accumulated a rich and prolific experience in politics and diplomacy. This complicated and complex political configuration created the space for scholarship to look at the international system, state relations, and interstate political philosophy. The pre-Qin masters wrote books and advanced theories trying to sell to the rulers their ideas on how to run the state and conduct diplomacy and military strategy while they played major roles in advocating strategies of becoming either a humane ruler or a hegemon, making either vertical (North-South) or horizontal (East-West) alliances, or either creating alliances or going to war. Scholars who have researched the history of thought have looked only at one side and emphasized the value of the pre-Qin masters' thought as *theory* (philosophical, historical, or political), whereas most of these ideas were used to serve practical political and diplomatic purposes among the states. Their effectiveness both then and now is proven. Therefore, there is no doubt about the positive and practical role of researching the foreign relations, state politics, and military strategies of the pre-Qin classics or of applying the insights gleaned from studying these masters to international political thought by gathering together, from out of several thousand years of the legacy of historical culture, a specifically Chinese wisdom of theoretical principles and ways of thinking with a view to guiding current research and combining this with China's present rise and its diplomatic strategy.

Seen in this light, the research into pre-Qin interstate political thought led by Professor Yan is of particular value. Following the perspective of international relations theory in highlighting quantitative analysis and logical deduction, it is worthwhile to comb through the classics of the pre-Qin masters to study the intersection between international political studies and historical studies, at the same times also seeking to draw comparisons with Western international relations theory. In "A Comparative Study of Pre-Qin Interstate Politics" (chapter 1 in this volume), Yan Xuetong examines seven pre-Qin thinkers and divides the levels of their thought into three—unifying all under heaven, establishing norms, and constructing concepts[3]—and contrasts these with realism, liberalism, and constructivism, leading to a plausible and reassuring conclusion: "What pre-Qin thinkers have to say about international relations is all grounded in policy; their thought is oriented toward practical political policies. Therefore, to hold up what the pre-Qin thinkers say about the role of concepts in international relations as a mirror may help constructivism and international political psychology achieve success in the field of political policy. At the same time, it may enrich the theories of realism and liberalism."[4]

MATTERS FOR DISCUSSION

Against the background of this basic confirmation of Professor Yan's work and support for his conclusion, I would nonetheless like to raise a few points for discussion, where I hold a differing opinion.

First, his essay uses the three levels of analysis of international relations—the system, the state, and the individual—to classify the theories of Mozi, Laozi, and Xunzi as at the level of system, those of Guanzi and Hanfeizi as at the level of the state, and those of Mencius and Confucius as at the individual level. He also analyzes their views on the cause of war and how to uphold peace, and draws distinctions among their ways of thinking. This analysis is debatable. In my article "The Type and Evolution of the Pre-Qin International System," I use the perspective of how the masters constructed an ideal international system, placing Confucius and Mencius on one level, Guanzi and Xunzi on another, and Laozi and Hanfeizi on a third.[5] The basis for this is their construction and description of the international system and interstate relations. Although Mozi does not present a theory for constructing an international system, he vigorously promotes the sage kings—Yao, Shun, and Yü—from the ancient times of the Five Emperors to the Three Kings as the highest leaders of the primitive joint military-political clans, holding the ideal that "political education" and "moral improvement" can realize the "harmony of the myriad clans," and proposing abdication as the means of ensuring the peaceful transition of power between the highest ruler and his successor. Hence, I list him in a special category apart and hold that although Mozi's view of the construction of an international system is largely an impractical dream, with his ideas of "mutual love" and "against aggression" as a basis, he proposes preventing large states from annexing small ones, takes a positive attitude toward the self-defense of small states against large ones, and argues for a security outlook in which each state should assist small states morally, militarily, and in the arts of war in resisting annexation by large states. In this his ideas take on a much more practical significance. Regarding the causes of war and the path to implementing peace, I think that the pre-Qin masters are all in favor of uniting all under heaven. It is just that they differ on how to accomplish this goal.

Second, it would seem that Professor Yan's exegesis of the political thought of the pre-Qin masters is not sufficiently comprehensive. For instance, the pre-Qin masters do not necessarily view humane authority and hegemony as opposites; thus, Confucius reckons that Guanzi helped Duke Huan of Qi to establish his hegemony but still affirms Guanzi's contribution to history.[6] Even though Mencius says that there were no just wars in the Spring and Autumn Period, he still holds that undertaking war to preserve dying states, to ensure succession for those without an heir, to remove tyranny, and to stop slaughter is right. Xunzi thinks that the effective way to abolish war is to affirm hierarchical order and use this as the basis for assigning resources, so that in establishing norms, upholding peace, and guaranteeing security, large states should play a greater role and share a greater burden of responsibility. Guanzi's thought combines the good points of Daoism and Legalism and has much in common with that of Xunzi. Although he wants to implement the hegemonic power of "enriching the state and strengthening the army," he retains the "humane Way" as the supreme ideal. Even though Hanfei advocates realizing centralization and unification by strict laws, the purpose of his promoting the "rule of law" is to guarantee and realize lasting peace on the basis of an organized system established on the presupposition of universally respected international norms.

I particularly note that the essays gathered in this book categorize Laozi mainly as a conceptual determinist, believing that he lacks any realist views. This is a mistake. In fact, although Laozi proposes the reduction of desires and a return to "small states with small populations," and holds the view that war should be considered carefully and that weapons are instruments of great misfortune, this does not mean that he simply backs away from fighting. Rather, he thinks one should accumulate advantages on the terrain and adjust one's policy in response. In fact, Laozi proposes many ideas of great theoretical value and with a high degree of philosophical sophistication, such as the Way, acting according to circumstances, and nonaction, which were adopted by Confucianism, Legalism, Mohism, military thinkers, yin-yang thinkers, and the eclectics represented by the *Guanzi*, who all inherited and developed these ideas to differing degrees.[7] Furthermore, some historical personages, such as Shang Yang and the first emperor of Qin, who would later be described as using all their energy to promote hegemony and hegemonic government, when seen against the true backdrop of history may appear in a different light. According to the biography of Shang Yang in the *Records of the Historian*, when Shang Yang went to see Duke Xiao of Qin, he first proposed to him the way of the emperors and then the way of kings, but since the duke was not interested, he moved on to talk about the way of hegemons. Hence, the policy that Shang Yang advocated in Qin was a result of a realistic option, given his failure to interest the duke in the way of kings.[8] Liu Xiang in the (Western) Han Dynasty records in section 14 of the *Shuo Yuan* that after the first emperor of Qin had united all under heaven, he called together his ministers to discuss which was better: abdication in favor of worthy successors, as practiced by the Five Emperors in ancient times, or the hereditary succession of the Xia, Shang, and Zhou dynasties. He felt that his own running of the state was based on the collective wisdom of Confucians, Mohists, Legalists, Daoists, and Nominalists, who all extolled the Five Emperors and held that all under heaven belonged to all the people, and hence he felt that he should imitate the rite of abdication of the Five Emperors, but, persuaded by the academician Baobai Lingzhi, he renounced this plan.[9] Leaving aside the question of the authenticity of these two stories and looking only at their messages, we find that whether Shang Yang (who was later reputed to have been a harsh Legalist intent on going the way of enriching the state, strengthening the army, and using strict punishments and severe laws) or the first emperor of Qin (who is always referred to as a bellicose tyrant without mercy) are seen as implementing the way of kings or that of hegemons is always dependent on the value judgments of later generations and does not necessarily reflect the actual historical circumstances of the time.

In his conclusion, Professor Yan writes, "If China's foreign policy cannot improve the nation's standing as a great and responsible state, China may follow in the dust of 1980s Japan, unable to replace the United States as the leading state in the world." This implies that the goal of China's current development is to replace the United States as the world's leading state. I think that it is worth pondering whether this goal can be realized and whether it should be the goal of China's development. At an academic conference, Professor Yan mentioned that as China gradually becomes stronger it has two options: either to become part of the Western "regime" (which implies that it must change its political system and become a democracy) or to establish its own system. My problem is that, since the breakup of the Soviet Union, China is the only large country left in the socialist camp, and therefore, even if we insist that we do not want to see the Western world as our enemy or compete for hegemony with the United States, and even if we seek to establish harmonious relations with our neighboring states, we cannot prevent the United States, Japan, India, and some European countries from viewing us as their greatest threat. Against the backdrop of struggles for security of the state and core benefits, even if we accept Western values and ideology and become what they see as a "democratic state," will we then be accepted as part of the Western regime? If not, then how should "China's own system" be understood?

Furthermore, China's "rise" is a topic hotly debated by academics and the general public today. In fact, I am rather hesitant to use the word *rise* to describe China's current foreign policy strategy and the trend of its future development. *Rise* implies "suddenly shooting up" and is said of something weak that suddenly emerges. The term is generally applied to the development of economic or military power. Moreover, *rise* is a comparative term, used of the rise of the state of Qin compared to the pre-Qin times or of the rise of late nineteenth- to early twentieth-century Japan. Referring to the economic takeoff in the latter part of the twentieth century, there was the rise of the "Asian Tigers." As the core state of the ancient East Asian international system, China was in a leading position throughout the course of several thousand years of history. It is only in the last hundred years or so that China became weak, following powerful foreign invasions. At no time in the past or in the present has China made hegemony over the world the goal of its development. Rather, as a geographically large and historically ancient country with many different nationalities and the world's largest population, China must have a place within the international system that reflects its status and it must take part in international affairs on the supposition that there is no infringement of its ability to protect its core national interests. Hence, China's development must always have as its goal to uphold China's national sovereignty and independence and the integrity of its territory as well as to benefit its people. We must see that, given the great gap between the soft power and hard power of China and the United States and other developed nations, our problem—both now and far into the future—is to guarantee our own survival, development, and security, not to lead the world.

As to whether we can become the leading world state, I think that Laozi has the right and apposite answer: "I have seen that it is not possible to acquire all under heaven by striving. All under heaven is a spiritual vessel and cannot be run or grasped. To try and run it ends in failure; to try and grasp it leads to losing it."[10] This is proved by history: when, before World War II, the fascist states of Germany and Japan wanted to gain world hegemony, they precipitated a world war, with the result that they were ultimately defeated. In other words, when we study the structure and evolution of the pre-Qin international system and the thought of the pre-Qin masters regarding the international system and interstate politics, our purpose is certainly not to return to a past of flourishing heroism in a great state equal to heaven. The Western Zhou system collapsed in pre-Qin times because the ritual legal order, well-field agriculture, and five classes of mourning, which together constituted this feudal system, ceased to exist.[11] The recent idea of an "ancient East Asian international organization" with a "Confucian China" core is very similar. The experience and lessons of history tell us that we should reject a view of Han Chinese cultural values or some special view of civilization as the core to construct an "international organization." Borrowing Laozi's broad view and his systematic thought, we should seek the harmony and balance of the whole as the starting point, actively join in the existing international organization, and work to raise our international status and influence.

QUESTIONS AND PROSPECTS

I would like to make my own observations about this research and the fervor with which it is undertaken to raise some questions and to look toward future developments.

First, in the area of theory and method, historical research should be the foundation, and on this basis international political philosophy may be studied, combining methods of proof, exegesis, and quantitative and qualitative analysis. On the basis of the essays in this book, in order to differentiate itself from political history, intellectual history, and other historical methods, research in pre-Qin interstate political philosophy has, up to now, adopted a three-stage model. First, such research abstracts from concrete historical contexts (such as the historical background, the trend of the times, or concrete historical facts) and then chooses part of the works of the pre-Qin masters and expounds these texts. Second, quantitative analytical methods, such as diagrams and formulas, are used to help search for logical connections and then the findings are compared with Western international political theory. Finally, the results are brought together to see what light they shed on real politics. The researcher's goal is to use evidence-based, scientific research methods to construct an explanatory model that can adequately cover all the phenomena in the hope of making normative conclusions of universal significance. The problems I find with this approach are as follows: Is the reading of pre-Qin history and the exposition of the thought of the pre-Qin masters a matter of amassing evidence or engaging in hermeneutics? If it is a matter of evidence, then it must be grounded in accurate and strict historical testimony. At present, though, there will always be doubts about the historical authenticity of conclusions based on any exposition of the thought of the pre-Qin masters. As Professor Yan explains,

> What we are researching is contemporary international relations. We study ancient thought in order to more accurately understand the present, not the past. Since there is no way of establishing the reliability of the events recounted in the works of the pre-Qin masters, when we study them we focus on their thought rather than on the events themselves. In studying intellectual history, one often seeks to understand texts in the context of their time. This is necessary, but for international relations studies we cannot be—nor do we want to be—concerned with the real meaning of the texts because there is still no consensus regarding the real meaning of pre-Qin works and we cannot use different meanings as a basis for research and discussion. Scientific research can be undertaken only on the basis of common standards and shared ideas; hence, the evidence-based historical research method comparable to the scientific method can do nothing other than to take the literal meaning as its standard because most people do not disagree about the literal

meaning. Rather than trying to understand the words of ancient authors by relying on what someone today imagines or on historical facts the authenticity of which cannot be guaranteed, it is better to understand the thought of the ancients from the point of view of an abstract human society. If it is said that neither is able to truly reflect the real face of history of that time, then at least the latter method is more in tune with the purpose of international relations theory, because the purpose of theoretical research is to seek what is universally reasonable, not to look for particularity.[12]

I agree with this view but still think that we should promote the key points of research in this area by opening our minds and looking from another angle. In fact, no reading of history is able to free itself entirely from the subjective hermeneutical perspective of the research. Any theoretical hermeneutics based on scientific method may be able to reach conclusions that are plausible and well-founded. We can try to combine the research methods of history and international political theory. Starting from international political theory, we can use what the official historical texts of the pre-Qin period have recorded of pre-Qin history as basic textbooks—the *Spring and Autumn Annals*, *Zuo's Commentary on the Spring and Autumn Annals*, the *Records of the Historian*, the *Han History*, the *Comprehensive Mirror for Aid in Government* by Sima Guang (1019–1086)—while avoiding pedantic methods and antiquarianism, because "theory and history may sometimes make strange bedfellows," "but the fruit of their being combined together is that what they could not achieve alone may be shown to have great plausibility."[13] Otherwise this research runs the risk that, having achieved a certain amount, it then would lack the capacity to develop further.

Second, we need to correctly grasp the reality of historical texts and the thought of the pre-Qin masters, and then deepen and expand the areas and perspectives of current research. At present, study of the thought of the pre-Qin masters has focused on expounding the points of similarity and difference between them but has overlooked their common historical-cultural origin. This means that we must understand the substance of their thought in depth. For instance, in my article "The

Type and Evolution of the Pre-Qin International System," I stress that most pre-Qin thinkers take the Western Zhou system as the blueprint to construct their own ideal international system.[14] The use of legends, literary allusions, and particular cases as examples to expound their own ideas is a method that is universally adopted in the works of the masters. (In chapter 2, "Xunzi's Interstate Political Philosophy and Its Message for Today," Professor Yan calls this "simple case-selection.") Most of the theories of the masters were designed to propose plans and policies to the rulers and to serve in Realpolitik (in his essay, Professor Yan notes that the works of the masters are markedly strategic). Therefore, all find it hard to avoid utilitarianism and bias and tend to have a marked inclination to favor their own disciples. So that their own theories would be used by the rulers, the pre-Qin thinkers proposed outstanding persons who could help in the development of the country (some people even have hatred or suspicions that are biased in their emphasis and of unlimited expansion). These are all things that should be carefully distinguished in the research. Once a thinker's theory has been used by a ruler to determine the main direction of the country and the plan for its development, however, both ruler and thinker will consciously or unconsciously draw in those factors in their school of thought that can be of service so as to adapt to the actual needs. This is a manifest character of the thought of the pre-Qin masters. Just because the thought of the masters has a common historical and cultural origin, in many cases, as in the discussions of the merits of royal or hegemonic rule, the path of enriching the state and strengthening the army, and the use of benevolence, justice, and morality to establish the state, the differing opinions in fact come together into one idea and only then does it become the foundation that affirms unification in the areas of politics, the economy, and the intellectual culture of the Qin and Han times. From this it can be seen that there are no insurmountable barriers between the theories of the pre-Qin schools; rather, they draw from one another, with each stressing its own angle.

Besides the works already studied, many other pre-Qin works could be added, such as the *Book of History*, the *Sayings of the States*, the *Book of Lord Shang*, the *Spring and Autumn Annals of Yanzi*, the *Yellow Emperor's Four Classics*, and Sunzi's *Art of War*. The interstate political thought of these works is very rich. After the unification of the Qin-Han period some works and treatises on political theory, such as Lu Jia's *New Analects*, Jia Yi's *Discourse on the Passing of Qin* and *Tract on Ruling in Peace*, and Chao Cuo's *Notes on Discussions of Military Affairs* and *Tract on Eliminating the Barbarians*,[15] as well as the parts of the *Records of the Historian*, *Han History*, and *Later Han History* that deal with political thought all have great value for theory. Besides this, although the Qin-Han established a centralized unified imperial court, yet it still had long-lasting and frequent interaction with the surrounding tribes and states. Throughout its long history, China's frequent divisions have meant that the various nationalities and ruling bodies have had complicated periods of struggle and coming together, as in the times of the Three Kingdoms (222–265), the Western and Eastern Jin (265–316 and 317–420), the North and South Dynasties (420–589), the Five Dynasties and Ten Kingdoms (907–960 and 902–979 in north and south China, respectively), the entrenched opposition between the Song (960–1279) and the Liao (947–1125), Jin (1115–1234), Xi Xia (1032–1227), and Mongols (1206–1271), the wars during the Ming Dynasty (1368–1644), and both the Mongol Yuan Dynasty (1271–1367) and the Later Jin, who renamed themselves Manchu and seized power in 1644. All of these can provide ample historical material for international relations, ethnic relations, state security, military strategy, and diplomatic achievements. If more theories of value can be drawn out from all this, then it will certainly help us in understanding history in more depth and in resolving current issues. And all of this can rely on accurate historical documentation as its premise and we can ask the researcher, in addition to showing a comparatively high standard of theory, to make a practical contribution to history.

Revealing the evolution of international relations in the course of history and the similarities and differences in interstate political philosophy also implies assigning a more profound value to theory. The advantage of this is that, after going through a long period of historical verification, there is not only the hope of constructing a new and broader historical discourse but also, by using a comparative method, creating a new model of "original theory" for interdisciplinary research and opening up eye-catching new fields of discourse. I will provide one example. In the *Sayings of Zheng* section of the *Sayings of the States*, there is a discussion between the historiographer of Zhou and Duke Huan of Zheng of the rise and fall and succession in all under heaven toward the end of the Western Zhou. The historiographer understands the circumstances of all under heaven and analyzes the situation of the feudal states of the period, including the Zhou royal household. He finds a place for the weak state of Zheng to establish itself and correctly predicts the rise and fall in power of each state and the changes in their relationships. What the historiographer and Duke Huan are engaged in is an assessment of the times, a prediction of the near future, and development of a plan of strategy toward the outside world. What is worth noticing is that the author of the most important strategic plan is not a key official holding power in the state or a highly placed general, but a historian. This must be related to China's long and ancient historiographic culture and the tradition of revising and writing history books—our ancestors could value the editing and transmission of history because it clearly served practical politics. Once this point is understood, then we can understand why Laozi was formerly the historiographer of the Western Zhou and why many of Confucius's important political ideas were expounded through his editing of the historical work the *Spring and Autumn Annals*.

Third, we should avoid using a simple checklist style in comparing Chinese and Western international political thought. Western international politics and international relations theory play an important role in guiding us and are of significance as a point of reference. Currently, Chinese research in this field is mostly founded on Western theories, but it should be observed that China's and the West's historical-cultural and social backgrounds and ways of thinking are very different. In research an effort must be made to avoid a checklist style or a fixed way of thinking. The meaning of Western political theories and concepts, the theoretical system, and construction of disciplines themselves are parts of an open and constantly developing system. In many ways this system adapts to changes in actual politics and the international situation and so is constantly changing. By contrast, our study of the pre-Qin international system and interstate political philosophy has been developed on the basis of historical research. In other words, Western international relations theory is oriented toward the future, is constantly changing, and is full of uncertainties and risks, whereas pre-Qin interstate political theory must be faithfully grounded in basic historical facts and historical documents. Study of history is inevitably founded on reality, but when the fruits of its theory are used to serve actual politics it cannot respond to the needs of only one era, by taking a biased view from history books or indulging in wishful thinking to explain things. Even more to be avoided is simplistic copying and blind imitation.

Finally, on the basis of results already obtained, I think that to undertake this study the following areas remain to be explored: the evolution and laws of the international configuration in the Spring and Autumn and Warring States periods; international relations at the time of the leadership of the two great hegemons Huan of Qi and Wen of Jin during the Spring and Autumn Period; the pattern of the rise of the Five Hegemons in the Spring and Autumn era and the Seven Powers of the Warring States era and what this has to say in reality; and how the thought of the pre-Qin masters was used in the rise of the various states, and how it can be used in later history and politics.

In summary, I borrow a passage from the bibliography of the *Han History* to serve as my conclusion. While Ban Gu was verifying the origins of the thought of the pre-Qin masters and their points of similarity and difference, he recommended that "if one can learn the skills of the six arts and observe the words of the nine schools, rejecting the dross and retaining the good, then one will be able to master all possible strategies."[16] This way of putting things is very apt and sheds light on our study of the pre-Qin international system and of the interstate political thought of the pre-Qin masters and shows how it should constantly be deepened.

5

The Two Poles of Confucianism:
A Comparison of the Interstate Political
Philosophies of Mencius and Xunzi

Xu Jin

Mencius and Xunzi were two great pre-Qin Confucians, yet generations of scholars gave them radically different assessments: Mencius was raised to the status of "Second Sage" after Confucius, while Xunzi remained neglected for centuries until the late Qing Dynasty (nineteenth century). The main reason for this was that Xunzi's thought was close to that of the Legalists, and two of his disciples, Hanfeizi and Li Si, were prominent Legalist scholars and politicians. Hence, in a society dominated by Confucian orthodoxy, he was "discriminated" against.[1]

From the point of view of research in international political philosophy, however, Xunzi most certainly deserves to be highlighted. Xunzi lived at the end of the Warring States Period and died just seventeen years before the first emperor of Qin unified China in 221 BCE. Hence, he had the opportunity to personally experience, as well as understand on the basis of texts, practically the whole course of events and history of the Spring and Autumn and Warring States periods (eighth to third century BCE) and on this basis propose his own point of view and his own ideas about international politics. Therefore, he may be seen as the great synthesizer of international political philosophy of the Spring and Autumn and Warring States periods. In sorting out and studying his international political philosophy, we find that his academic importance is indisputable. If we take Xunzi as the endpoint of international political philosophy in the Spring and Autumn and Warring States periods, then Mencius is a key point in the same era but earlier than Xunzi. As a student of Mencius's international political philosophy, I have found that they have areas of agreement as well as areas where they sharply disagree. These similarities and differences show that both inherited the same academic lineage and also show how Xunzi criticized and developed the thought of his predecessor, Mencius. In this essay I make a simple synthesis and comparison of the similarities and differences in the hope that it will awaken the reader's interest.

Put simply, what Mencius and Xunzi hold in common in their international political philosophy is their methodology. What they share to some extent is their understanding of international power, and where they differ is in their understanding of state power, the origin of conflict, and the way to resolve conflict. Naturally, the contributions that their international political philosophies make to contemporary international relations theory and China's foreign policy are not identical.

AREAS OF AGREEMENT

In reflecting on the international questions they faced, Mencius and Xunzi adopted similar methods of analysis. They both set their level of analysis at that of the individual.

In Mencius's view, the type of state determines the nature of the international system and international order. In his analysis, the nature of the international system as a dependent variable has two variants, namely, the system of humane authority and that of hegemony. The dependent variable of international order also has two variants, namely, order and disorder. The independent variable of the nature of the state has two variants, namely, the sage king and the hegemon. Mencius's definition of humane authority is a state "that practices benevolence by virtue," whereas his definition of a hegemonic state is "one that pretends to benevolence but uses force."[2] In Mencius's language, the terms *sage king* and *hegemon* both refer to the nature of the state and also to the type of ruler, and can refer to the nature of the system as well. In other words, the type of ruler, the nature of the state, and the nature of the system are three ways of expressing the same thing. This is exactly the same as Xunzi's analytical frame. The specific logical relationship is that the ruler who implements humane (or hegemonic) government may make the state become humane (or hegemonic) and then go on to establish a system of humane authority (or hegemony). A system of humane authority is peaceful and hence there is order, whereas a hegemonic system is unstable and hence there is disorder.

Like Xunzi, Mencius sets his analytical level not at that of the state but rather at that of the individual. In his analysis, the nature of the state is only a mediating variable. The basic cause that determines the nature of the state is the ruler. A given type of ruler leads to a given type of state. A ruler who implements humane authority will have a humane state, whereas a ruler who implements hegemony will have a hegemonic state. In this way, the ruler himself will ultimately shape and determine the features of the entire international system. Mencius and Xunzi had good reasons for doing their analyses at the individual level. A state is a political organization formed by human beings. In the linguistic system of contemporary international relations theory, idioms such as *a state thinks* or *a state decides* use the word *state* synecdochically. In fact, a state itself cannot think or decide. It has no way of acting. What can think, decide, and act are the people in the state, especially the ruler. Therefore, Mencius thinks that the ruler and the state are of the same nature. Often in his writings he refers to the ruler in place of the state, as for instance, "O King, if you should but implement benevolent governance for the people," or "if the king goes to punish them, who will oppose the king?"[3] or "if the ruler of the state likes benevolence, he will have no enemies in all under heaven."[4] In fact, it is not the ruler himself who has no enemies in all under heaven; it is rather the state, which the ruler who likes benevolence represents.

Xunzi is a conceptual determinist whereas Mencius is a conceptual determinist with a tendency toward dialectic. They both think that the persons of the ruler and the ministers are the original motivation for all state conduct. Mencius's dialectical tendency lies in his denial that force has any importance to a state that aspires to humane authority. But he recognizes the important role of force to any state that aspires to hegemony. He says, "Using force and pretending to benevolence is the hegemon. The hegemon will certainly have a large state. Using virtue and practicing benevolence is the sage king. The sage king does not rely on having a large territory. Tang had seventy square kilometers and King Wen had a hundred square kilometers. Should you make people submit to force rather than to the heart, force will never suffice; should you make people submit to virtue, they will heartily rejoice and sincerely follow, as the seventy disciples followed Confucius."[5] This passage says that to become a hegemon a state must be large and powerful, whereas to become a humane authority a state relies not on military force but on the attractive force of morality, which causes other states readily and sincerely to submit and come to the king. Furthermore, Mencius even more than Xunzi points out clearly that it is enough to rely on the will of the ruler and the ministers. Their firm determination can effect a rapid change from hegemon to humane ruler or from humane ruler to hegemon. Mencius encourages King Xuan of Qi to implement royal government by saying, "Hence the ruler is not a humane ruler because he does not act as one, not because he cannot."[6]

Mencius and Xunzi both adopt a strict method of analysis, that is, they use a single variable to explain the changes in the logical chain of cause and effect. Both take the idea of the ruler as the first independent variable and international order as the ultimate dependent variable and construct a progressive layered logic chain of cause and effect. Therefore, figure 5.1 applies equally to Xunzi's and to Mencius's international political thought.

Finally, Mencius and Xunzi both use the method of induction on the basis of isolated cases to present their point of view. In fact, this method of research is the one commonly adopted by scholars in the pre-Qin era. In assessing this method, Yan Xuetong points out in chapter 2 of this volume, "Many of the examples he [Xunzi] chooses come from historical legends. They lack any time for the events, background, or basic account and there is no way of ascertaining their authenticity. Moreover, his examples lack the necessary variable control" and their "scientific value is poor." The veracity and plausibility of the cases are not very strong. Hence, "according to the standard of modern science his analytical method is not scientific." As a scholar educated in contemporary social sciences, I completely agree.

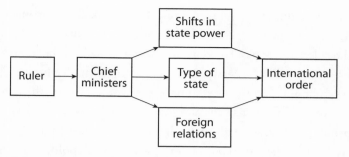

Figure 5.1 The chain of causation between the ruler and international order

If you are a scholar with a sense of history, however, then you will find Professor Yan's remarks quoted here a bit hard on the ancients. Most of the pre-Qin classics were lost in the confusion at the changeover between the Qin and Han dynasties. The works of the masters that we now see have passed through the large-scale compilation and reading of the Han Confucians. Hence, historical material that nowadays seems to be lacking in "real origins" may not necessarily have been inauthentic history at the time of the masters, or they may have generally held that these examples were real history. Their veracity is a bit like that of contemporary people who believe that the earth orbits the sun. This fact does not require us to state the time, background, process, and origins of this belief.

POINTS OF PARTIAL SIMILARITY

Mencius's and Xunzi's views of international power or world leadership have points in common and points where they differ. Neither pays attention to the structure of international power or relations between large states. Rather, they are interested in the nature of international power. The difference lies in that Mencius specifically points out the direction and policy by which a state can attain humane authority, whereas Xunzi does not specially note this. Furthermore, Mencius forcefully rejects hegemony, whereas Xunzi is not opposed to a state making efforts to attain hegemony.

Xunzi separates international power into three kinds—humane authority, hegemony, and tyranny—whereas Mencius recognizes only two kinds: humane authority and hegemony. Both think that humane authority is the highest form of power in the world. Its foundation is the morality of the ruler (the Son of Heaven). To possess humane authority is almost like possessing world leadership, or "possessing all under heaven." Mencius says, "Should you exercise humane government, then all within the four seas would lift their heads and gaze on you and seek to have you as their prince."[7] "Possessing all under heaven" refers not to using military force to conquer the world but rather to gaining such political legitimacy that the various states of the world consciously submit to one's leadership. Both scholars think that one does not acquire world leadership by seizing it, but rather it spontaneously belongs to one.[8] The conversation between Mencius and his pupil Wan Zhang over the abdication of Yao in favor of Shun illustrates this point:

> Wan Zhang said, "Yao gave all under heaven to Shun. Is that not so?"
> Mencius replied, "No. The Son of Heaven cannot give all under heaven to anyone."
> "So who gave all under heaven to Shun?"
> He replied, "Heaven gave it to him."[9]

The problem is that heaven cannot speak, so how do we know that a particular person or state has received the mandate of heaven? Mencius points out one can observe the direction of a person's mind. If the mind is directed positively, this is a sign that one has obtained the mandate of heaven, and from this one can possess world leadership. If a person's mind is directed negatively, then this means that one has lost the mandate of heaven, and from this one will lose world leadership. He says, "He appointed him to preside at the sacrifice, the hundred spirits enjoyed his offerings. This showed that heaven accepted him. He appointed him to be in charge of affairs and the affairs were well managed, so that the common people were at peace with them. This showed the people accepted him."[10] He again uses the example of Yao abdicating in favor of Shun to prove his point: "Of old, Yao presented Shun to heaven and heaven accepted him. He revealed him to the people and the people accepted him. Therefore I say, 'Heaven does not speak, it simply shows itself by deeds and actions.'"[11]

Although Xunzi argues that a state should make an effort to attain humane authority, he does not say what policies the enlightened ruler or state should adopt to this end, whereas Mencius does give a more detailed prescription. Mencius's basic suggestion is that the ruler should first raise his moral standing to become a benevolent prince and then both at home and abroad he should "implement benevolence." Mencius begins from the premise that human nature is good, holding that "all people can become a Yao or a Shun," the ruler naturally being no exception. Yao, Shun, Yü, Tang, and Wu were all ancient sage kings and the models for later rulers. From their way of behaving to their actions, they embodied the Confucian political philosophy of being "sages within and humane rulers on the outside." Hence rulers should study and imitate their every word and action. Mencius says, "If you dress in the dress of Yao, recite the words of Yao, and do the deeds of Yao, then you are quite simply Yao."[12] That is, by studying and imitating the sage kings the ruler becomes a sage king himself.

If the ruler has an idea of benevolence and justice, the next step is to implement benevolent government.[13] "Benevolent government" is a policy for both domestic and foreign affairs. In domestic matters, Mencius asks the state to restrict its excessive absorption of social resources, adopt a policy of light taxation, and ensure that the basic requirements of life are guaranteed for the common people. Once the ordinary people's basic livelihood is guaranteed, then you must promote education, lest "well-fed, adequately clad, and peacefully housed, but without education, they are close to the birds and beasts."[14] Regarding the state, education of the people serves to establish a harmonious society. Mencius thinks that teaching the people is geared toward making the ordinary people "understand human relationships," such that "there is affection between parents and children, justice between rulers and ministers, distinct roles for husband and wife, sequential order between older and younger siblings, and trustworthiness among friends."[15] Once these five areas are performed well, society will naturally be harmonious and ordered.

In his foreign policy, Mencius also stresses benevolence and justice as the main principle. He opposes the then-common practice of states employing hegemonic strategies to go to war, annexing land and increasing their populations. He especially emphasizes that the government should stop using war to annex land and people. He says, "Enacting one unjust deed, killing one innocent person, and obtaining all under heaven: they [sage kings] all would not have done such things."[16] Again, "To take from one state to give to another is something a benevolent person would not do. How much less can one do so by killing people?"[17]

On hegemony Xunzi and Mencius part company. Xunzi thinks that humane authority is the ideal form of power and hence deserves being promoted, whereas tyranny is the worst form of power and hence should be opposed. He has no moral reaction to hegemony nor is he opposed to its existence. On the contrary, he implicitly supposes that a hegemonic state must have a considerable degree of morality even if its morality falls far short of that of a humane authority. He says,

> Although virtue may not be up to the mark or norms fully realized, yet when the principle of all under heaven is somewhat gathered together, punishments and rewards are already trusted by all under heaven, all below the ministers know what they can expect. Once administrative commands are made plain, even if one sees one's chance for gain defeated, yet there is no cheating the people; contracts are already sealed, even if one sees one's chance for gain defeated, yet there is no cheating one's partners. If it is so, then the troops will be strong and the town will be firm and enemy states will tremble in fear. Once it is clear the state stands united, your allies will trust you. Even if you have a remote border state, your reputation will cause all under heaven to quiver. Such were the Five Lords. Hence Huan of Qi, Wen of Jin, Zhuang of Chu, Helü of Wu, and Goujian of Yue all had states that were on the margins, yet they overawed all under heaven and their strength overpowered the central states. There was no other reason for this but that they had strategic reliability. This is to attain hegemony by establishing strategic reliability.[18]

This passage means that even if the morality of a hegemonic state is not perfect, it understands the basic moral norms of this world. The domestic and international policy of a hegemonic state must take as its principle reliability in its strategies. Domestically it should not cheat the people and externally it should not cheat its allies.

Mencius also thinks that humane authority is the ideal form of international power and most worth aspiring to, but he is vehemently opposed to hegemony. He thinks that even if a hegemonic state succeeds in dominating the whole world, its span will be brief and illegitimate and it will not win the support of many countries because a hegemonic state "uses force to subdue people." The biggest problem with using force to subdue people is that the states that follow one "will not follow from their hearts, but because their strength is insufficient," and therefore they will look for an opportunity to rebel.[19] Moreover, although hegemons' false benevolence, fake justice, and paucity of goodness may allow them to cheat people for a while, it cannot be forever. The result of their lack of benevolence will become apparent and as a consequence they will lose the minds of the people and end up losing hegemony. Mencius goes on to say that a state that seeks hegemony for itself risks its own security, because that type of state must practice hegemonic government and this requires seeking profit in everything, and seeking profit in everything will upset the orthodox order of society. He says, "If ministers serve their prince with an eye to profit and sons serve their fathers with an eye to profit and younger brothers serve their older brothers with an eye to profit, so you end up expelling benevolence and justice between rulers and ministers, fathers and sons, and older and younger brothers and all draw close to one another with an eye to profit, such a society has never avoided collapse."[20] Furthermore, promoting hegemonic government will make all large states your enemies and they will fight with your allies. This requires an expenditure of state force and is a threat to the life and property of the people. Mencius uses the example of King Hui of Liang pursuing profit alone with the result that the power of his state went into decline to explain that profit is a danger to the state and the ordinary people. He says, "For the sake of territory, King Hui of Liang trampled his people to pulp and took them to war. He suffered a great defeat but returned again only fearful that he would not win so he urged on the son whom he loved and buried him along with the dead. This is what is called 'starting with what one does not love and going on to what one does love.'"[21] Thus, he concludes, "The three dynasties acquired all under heaven by benevolence and they lost it through lack of benevolence. This is the reason why states decline or flourish, rise or fall. If the Son of Heaven is not benevolent, he cannot retain what is within the four seas. If the feudal lords are not benevolent they cannot retain the altars of soil and grain."[22]

From Xunzi's and Mencius's analyses of hegemony set out earlier, we can see that the origin of the difference between their views on this question lies in a difference in their definitions of hegemony. Xunzi thinks that the basis of hegemony is hard power and reliability in strategy,[23] whereas Mencius thinks that the only basis for hegemony is hard power. Therefore, Xunzi accepts that the existence of hegemony has certain positive features, whereas Mencius thoroughly rejects it. What is interesting is that Xunzi's analysis of hegemony is much closer to the United States' advocacy of hegemony, namely, that a superpower must not only exercise hegemony but also be faithful in its alliances. When its allies are threatened it should not spare itself in protecting them, as in the 1960s and 1970s the United States protected South Vietnam and took part in the Vietnam War. Thus, we also find that the domino theory and Xunzi's theory of reliability in strategy have points in common. Mencius's attitude to hegemony, by contrast, is very much like that of the Chinese government. Since 1949, the various Chinese governments have firmly opposed hegemony and hegemonism.[24]

POINTS OF DIFFERENCE

Understanding of State Power

Although Mencius and Xunzi both emphasize the importance of political power and acknowledge it as the primary factor in state power, they have different opinions about the degree of importance of political power.[25] Mencius greatly respects political power and depreciates the importance of economic and military power, whereas Xunzi thinks that all three are necessary, but political power is the foundation for the exercise of economic and military power.[26]

Professor Yan says, however, that "Xunzi overlooks the importance of hard power for humane authority." I beg to disagree. Professor Yan says,

> Even if the territories of Bo and Hao ruled by the kings Tang and Wu, respectively, were small, the states of the feudal lords of that time may have been even smaller and weaker. By the Spring and Autumn Period, the scale of states had generally increased in size. Both Qi and Qin were once larger than Chu, and so Chu was not the strongest state at the time. Therefore, when Xunzi uses the example of Chu's being larger than the lands of the kings Tang and Wu and yet not being able to attain all under heaven to prove that power is not important for humane authority, his argument is less persuasive.

I think that here Professor Yan has misread Xunzi and misread history. Although it is certain that the territories of Kings Tang and Wu were larger than those of some of the feudal lords, their territories were far smaller than those ruled by King Jie of the Xia and King Zhòu of the Shang; hence, in terms of hard power they were definitely on the weaker side. For example, when King Wu led a punitive expedition against King Zhòu, he certainly had fewer troops than King Zhòu did.[27] So when Xunzi says that the kings Tang and Wu were able to attain humane authority even with territories of only one hundred square kilometers, he is speaking of their hard power in relation to that of King Jie of the Xia and King Zhòu of the Shang. Furthermore, in land area, for most of the Spring and Autumn and Warring States periods the state of Chu was the first or second largest state. It was only toward the end of the Warring States Period that it was overtaken in size by Qin. Moreover, in the Spring and Autumn Period, Chu was certainly what could be called a superpower. It contended for hegemony first with Qi and then with Jin and was very rarely eclipsed. Hence, I think that there is a certain plausibility in Xunzi's using the failure of a state as large as Chu to attain all under heaven and comparing this with the territories of Kings Tang and Wu as proof that hard power is not important to humane authority.

The difference in view of Mencius and Xunzi on the issue of state power may be owing to a difference in political philosophy. Mencius is a pure ethical idealist who believes that for the state to simply seek material goods, especially to raise its military power, is harmful. He uses the example of King Hui of Liang, who set his sights purely on profit, as quoted earlier. In contrast, a state that seeks benevolence and justice can attain humane authority over all under heaven and will have no enemies at all.

Mencius argues,

> With a territory of a hundred square kilometers, it is possible to be king. O King, if you should implement benevolent governance for the people, reduce punishments, lighten taxes and duties, allowing for deeper plowing and ensuring that weeding is well done, then the fit will spend their holidays practicing filial piety, brotherly affection, loyalty, and constancy. At home they will serve their parents and elders; outside they will serve their masters; then they can but take wooden staves in hand and attack the armored troops of Qin [in the northwest] and Chu [in the south], whose rulers steal their people's time so that they are not able to plow or hoe to support their parents. Their parents freeze and starve; their brothers, wives, and children are dispersed. They set pitfalls for their people or drown them. If the king goes to punish them, who will oppose the king? Thus it is said, "The benevolent has no enemies."[28]

This is to say that a state that speaks of benevolence and justice and implements benevolent government will be united internally. Political motivation will be strong. In contrast, a state that speaks of gain and implements hegemonic government will be rent apart internally and its political motivation will be weak. In a conflict between a king and a hegemon, the king can win without a fight.

For Mencius the pursuit of political morality is called "justice" and the pursuit of military and economic power is called "profit." The relationship between Xunzi's three factors of state power—political power, economic power, and military power—thus becomes in Mencius's thought one between justice and profit. Hence, the debate about justice and profit becomes a debate between the king and the hegemon. In other words, if the ruler speaks of justice, proposes the kingly way, and implements benevo-

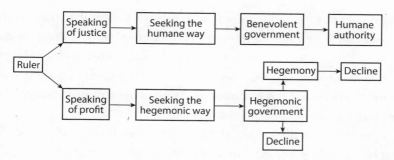

Figure 5.2 Logical relationships: justice vs. profit and humane authority vs. hegemony

lent government, then the result will be that political power will rise and ultimately one will become king of all under heaven. If the ruler speaks of profit, proposes the hegemonic way, and implements hegemonic government, although some countries may be called hegemonic, most will descend into political chaos and a diminution of state power. Moreover, even the successful hegemonies will be unable to hold on to their status for long. Their state power will rapidly decrease and they will lose their hegemonic status. The deductive relationships in Mencius's debate between justice and profit can be set out as in figure 5.2

The Origin of Conflict

Xunzi believes that human nature is evil and Mencius believes that it is good. Their viewpoints are diametrically opposed, and this leads them to equally opposed views about the origin of conflict. Xunzi thinks that there is no end to desires and that material goods cannot satisfy them. Since desires cannot be satisfied, people will go on seeking more. This quest will never end and hence it will give rise to competition, which will continue and break out in violent conflict. He says, "When man is born he has desires. Though desires are unfulfilled, yet he cannot but seek. If he seeks, and has no limits set, then he cannot but conflict with others. If he conflicts with others there will be disorder, and if there is disorder there will be poverty."[29]

It is relatively easy for an exponent of the evil of human nature to start from human desires and postulate the origin of violent conflict, but how an exponent of the goodness of human nature can postulate the origin of violent conflict requires a lot more effort to explain. The question confronting an exponent of the goodness of human nature such as Mencius is: if human nature is good, where does the evil present in real life come from? If a person could but maintain the goodness of their nature, then international conflict would not take place.

First, Mencius thinks, not that human nature is originally good, but that human beings have a natural inclination toward the good, that is, that they have an a priori basis for being good. These naturally good tendencies need to be directed, educated, and fostered before they can be fully expressed—that is, nature may move toward goodness and hence the goodness of human nature is a process. Mencius says, "It is no surprise the king is not wise. Although there are plants in the world that grow easily, yet with one day of sunshine and ten days of frost, they will not be able to grow. I see you very rarely, and the moment I leave the Jack Frosts come. I may bring out some buds, but to what good?"[30] That is, even though the king has the seeds of goodness in his heart, yet they cannot grow properly with one day of violence or ten of cold. This is especially so when Mencius leaves, since the people who lead the king to fall into injustice (the frost) will gather around him and egg him on to do wrong. Therefore, Mencius's theory of the goodness of human nature says, not that human nature is originally good, but that the heart has seeds of goodness, which may be developed to do good.[31]

Second, the fact that Mencius thinks the king can be led astray by small-minded persons shows that he acknowledges that people may be led astray by profit and desire. Mencius distinguishes two kinds of organ in the human body. The first is the "small" organs, such as the mouth, the ears, the eyes, and the nose. These organs are designed to satisfy natural desires: "The mouth is oriented to taste, the eye to colors, the ear to sounds, the nose to smells, the four limbs to ease and rest. This is nature. There is also about them what is of Heaven's decree, so the gentleman does not ascribe everything to nature."[32] The second kind is the "great" organ, the good mind, the mind of benevolence, justice, rites, and wisdom. There is a contradiction between the great and small organs: namely, the tension between benevolence and profit or between good and evil. A person becomes the sort of person he is by following the effects of the organs; that is, "those who follow the great organ are great people; those who follow the small organs are petty people."[33]

Now, why is it that some people follow the great organ (become exemplary persons) and some the small organs (become petty people)? Mencius says, "The organs of ears and eyes do not think but are veiled by things. When one thing encounters another thing, then it leads it astray. The organ of the mind does, however, think. By thinking it obtains; by failing to think it fails to obtain. These are what Heaven has given to us. Establish yourself in that which is great and then what is small cannot steal from you. This alone is what makes a great person."[34] In other words, if a person does not restrain the organs of desire, such as ears and eyes, then he will be led astray by profit. If he can use his mind to think, then he can maintain his good nature. Hence, whether one becomes an exemplary or a petty person depends on one's own choice.

Ways to Resolve International Conflict

Xunzi thinks that increasing the material goods and wealth of a society will not resolve the conflict that may arise between people, because human desires will increase along with the increases in wealth and will continue to rise. He advocates using the rationality of the mind to control desires, and he believes that the way to strengthen the rationality of the human mind is to establish social norms (rites).[35] Norms can make human desires reasonable and can also increase the capacity for satisfaction. When desires decrease and the capacity for satisfaction increases, then the two will easily come into balance. Moreover, norms can also distinguish social classes, so people will act according to the norms proper to their class and thus avoid conflict arising. Xunzi's reliance on external forces to suppress conflict is at one with his philosophical theory of the evil of human nature.[36]

I am in full agreement with what Yan Xuetong says about the role hierarchical norms can play in suppressing domestic and international conflict, but it would seem that he has overlooked one issue: given that norms are implemented and maintained by people (or by states), then how can they be implemented or maintained when there are evil persons (or evil states) that seek their own ends by flouting norms, especially when these people (or states) have considerable force?[37] Although it may be possible to wait in expectation of a true kingly state, such states occur only rarely in history, and when there are none how is one to cope? I fear that one must place one's hope in the collective response of persons or states with a sense of justice. Then force is simply the support for implementing and maintaining norms.

Mencius's resolution of international conflict is quite different from Xunzi's. Since he advocates the goodness of human nature, Mencius believes that the idea of goodness in the human mind will ultimately overcome evil desires. Of course, Mencius believes in the effectiveness of "rites" in suppressing conflict between people, but he is faced with a world in which "rites are dethroned and music is bad." Therefore, the first thing to be done is to restore the ritual order. Hence he proposes a two-step strategy. The first step is to use persuasion and education to influence the rulers so that the goodness in their minds will suppress the evil. As for who can carry out this task, Mencius believes that it is worthy people like himself. Therefore, Mencius spent his life going from state to state (he visited Zou, Lu, Qi, Wei, and Teng). On his arrival he would first preach to the rulers the way of benevolence and justice with the aim of transforming them from their tendency to "talk of profit rather than talk of justice." Through education, he would form and enlighten the goodness of their minds so that the inherent nature of benevolence, justice, rites, and wisdom would shine out and so that benevolent government would lay a foundation for thought.[38]

Once the ruler's way of thinking has been rectified, the second step is to correct distorted human relationships, that is, to restore the ritual order.[39] Mencius thinks that when the good in human nature is obscured by desire, human nature itself is distorted. When human nature is distorted, the relationships among people are also distorted. When human relationships are distorted, conflict will invariably arise. Therefore, to prevent violent conflict it is necessary to respect human relationships. The distortion of human relationships is shown in the demise of rituals among people. In human relationships there are hierarchical relationships (ruler and minister, father and son) and relationships of equality (between brothers, spouses, and friends). They can all be unified through the principle of benevolence and justice. He says, "Ministers will serve their lords with benevolence and justice; sons will serve their fathers with benevolence and justice; younger brothers will serve their elder brothers with benevolence and justice; so that ruler and minister, father and son, elder and younger brother will expel thoughts of profit and harbor benevolence and justice and draw close together."[40] With human relationships in order and the ritual order restored, and once the ruler has adopted the way of benevolence and justice, then a state will no longer harbor thoughts of gain against another. The more there are of this kind of kingdom then naturally the less there will be of international conflict.

Mencius's plan for regulating international relations is for "internal inspection" or "internal reflection." That is, he asks the individual to look into the goodness in his own mind and, by developing this goodness, to ease conflict, including international conflict. Now, Mencius is a Confucian like Xunzi but whereas Xunzi advocates a restoration of the Western Zhou system of Five Services, Mencius does not stress this. The reasons for this are twofold: first, the previously mentioned difference in their views regarding the goodness or evil of human nature, and second, a change in the times.

Xunzi lived at the end of the Warring States Period. By that time, Qin had already become the undisputed hegemon and had the power to unify China. Hence, the key political question then was in what way Qin would unify all under heaven. The previous unified world (all under heaven) had been the feudal system of the Western Zhou. Since this system had been idealized by Confucius and other Confucians as the system of Five Services, and its creation ascribed to King Wu of the Zhou and the duke of Zhou, Xunzi was bound to uphold this form of unified world.

Mencius lived in the mid–Warring States era. This was a time when the various states were in chaos and no one state could come to the fore and emerge as a hegemon, as Qin would later do. Mencius also hoped for unity in all under heaven and for a return to the feudal system of the Western Zhou, but given the conditions of international politics in his time it was very difficult to realize this hope. Hence although Mencius himself was confident about this goal, he had to realize that his duty at the time was to make people wake up and stop chaotic war. This can be seen in his dialogue with King Hui of Liang:

> Suddenly he asked me, "How can all under heaven be calmed?"
> I replied, "It can be calmed by being united."
> "Who can unite it?"
> I replied, "One who does not like killing others can unite it."
> "Who can give it to him?"
> I replied, "There is nobody in all under heaven who will not give it to him."[41]

This exchange shows that Mencius was very busy trying to put the idea of benevolence and justice into the ruler's mind and trying hard to form one ruler or several who could stop international wars. It was not yet the time for establishing international norms, since if peoples' minds were not first correct, then even if there were norms in place no one would want to implement them with any sincerity.

THE MESSAGE OF MENCIUS'S INTERNATIONAL POLITICAL PHILOSOPHY FOR TODAY

Mencius was a scholar of an idealistic moral bent and was used to converting political issues into moral ones. This meant that his political opinions could not become the first political strategic option of any state during his lifetime, when the strong devoured the weak. Xunzi was more realistic than Mencius. In his international political philosophy there is much that can be put into practice. Over time, however, the world of today has come to be unlike the jungle of the Warring States Period. The influence of morality and values cannot be discounted in international relations or in a state's foreign policy. Hence, Mencius's international political philosophy with its moral idealism still has something to contribute to the realization of China's foreign policy and to international relations theory.

Mencius praises humane authority and denigrates hegemony. He thinks that the way to unite all under heaven is by conversion of hearts rather than by force. Even if historically no humane authority has been established that has been able to leave violence behind, Mencius's viewpoint, which does not accord with history, gives us room for reflecting on what sort of great state China will develop into. If in the future China develops into a hegemonic state, then it will be a case of the rise and fall of yet another hegemon. If in the course of its rise, China can develop into a humane authority, then this will be a unique case in history of the rise of a great state. Although in recent years the Chinese government has proposed the political guidelines of "scientific development" and "taking the human being as the basis" (so its policy does have something in common with Mencius's benevolent government), in its foreign policy China lacks a universal moral ideal or high point. The lack of this moral ideal means that many countries view China's rise as that of a state thirsty for power and thus misread it as a serious threat to the stability of the international system. That is to say, China still lacks what can attract the countries of the world to naturally follow it.

Mencius stresses that a humane authority should first be a model political state in the international system. Hence, if China wants become a humane authority, it should establish itself as a model polity for the world. Only in this way will it be possible to attract other states to imitate it. Mencius thinks that the attractive power of a humane authority lies not in riches but in political ideals and in the model of social development founded on these ideals. Even though Mencius's own view of benevolence and justice may not be adopted by the Chinese government in all its details, Mencius's thought can still tell us that today, when China's GDP has already attained a considerably high standard, the Chinese government should be all the more concerned about what kind of political ideal and model of social development should be created. This is not only to build a firm foundation for China's own rapid progress but, even more, to exert sufficient international attraction to transcend the political ideals and social system of the West.

Mencius's opposition to hegemony can still serve as a reference point for the Chinese government today. In fact, the hegemony that Mencius talks about is much more about the policy of strong states and not really a reference to the status of a state in the structure of international power. Hence, while China is rising daily, the Chinese government must, on the one hand, continue to affirm its principle of opposition to hegemony while, on the other hand, being very prudent and careful and doing everything to avoid other states' thinking that we are pursuing hegemony. This requires China to stress area cooperation and multilateralism, and to uphold the authority of the United Nations and international legal norms.

Mencius's international political philosophy may be summed up in one word as "the benevolent has no enemies."[42] *Enemies* here refers not only to military enemies but also to political enemies. The greatest lesson China can draw from this is that its development should be a process not only of increasing its power but also of expanding its political ideas and model. If power alone is exalted, this will lead people to be afraid and it will not win their admiration. On the contrary, if, when power is elevated, there is creativity in the area of ideas and models, then once China has risen it will become a humane state and that kind of state will win people's admiration and respect.

Political Hegemony in Ancient China: A Review of "Hegemony in *The Stratagems of the Warring States*"

Wang Rihua

The history of ancient China's interstate politics and foreign affairs has much to say about hegemony. *The Stratagems of the Warring States* much discussion of how to contend for hegemony as well as historical instances of such contention. In chapter 3, "Hegemony in *The Stratagems of the Warring States*," Yan Xuetong and Huang Yuxing provide a detailed picture of the hegemonic philosophy of *The Stratagems of the Warring States*. Through their study the authors have summarized the foundations of hegemonic power, the role of norms in hegemony, and the basic strategy for attaining hegemony. They have also compared their findings with contemporary Western hegemonic theory and proposed that ancient China saw political power as the core of hegemony, with government by worthy and competent persons as its guarantee. They also emphasized the influence of norms on hegemony and the corresponding philosophy of contending for hegemony and hence sketched a picture of a political hegemonic theory. The present essay takes theirs as its foundation and seeks to go further in propounding the political hegemonic theory of ancient China, especially of the pre-Qin era.

ONE HEGEMONY, DIFFERENT PATHS: CONCEPTUAL LIMITS

Contemporary Western international relations theory generally defines a hegemonic state in terms of material strengths such as its capacity to make war, its military power, or its economic power. A hegemonic state may be called the dominant power, the predominant or preeminent power, or the leading power or be said to have leadership or world leadership. John Mearsheimer writes, "A hegemon is a state that is so powerful that it dominates all the other states in the system. No other state has the military wherewithal to put up a serious fight against it."[1] Robert Pahre sees the basic indicator of a hegemony in the state's share of world resources and its GNP relative to the rest of the world.[2] Joshua S. Goldstein thinks that a hegemonic state is one that has the greatest military, economic, and political strength.[3] Robert T. Gilpin believes that a hegemonic state is a state that controls or dominates the lesser states in the international system.[4] Robert O. Keohane and Joseph S. Nye think that a hegemonic state refers to "one state [that] is powerful enough to maintain the essential rules governing interstate relations, and [is] willing to do so. In addition to its role in maintaining a regime, such a state can abrogate existing rules, prevent the adoption of rules that it opposes, or play the dominant role in constructing new rules."[5] They point out that in a time of globalization and interdependence, military power plays a minor role.[6] The importance of the economy far exceeds that of the military. Immanuel Wallerstein argues that hegemony in the interstate system refers to "that situation in which the ongoing rivalry between the so-called great powers is so unbalanced that one power is truly *primus inter pares*; that is, one power can largely impose its rules and its wishes (at the very least by effective veto power) in the economic, political, military, diplomatic and even cultural arenas."[7]

The conceptions of the hegemonic state in ancient Chinese thought and in Western international relations theory are very similar. In ancient Chinese, "hegemon" (*ba*) and "lord" (*bo, father's elder brother, a senior peerage*) both refer to "the head of the feudal lords in ancient times."[8] In other words, a hegemonic state holds the highest status among the feudal states and is ranked the first state. In this sense, ancient China's hegemony and Wallerstein's "primus inter pares" are the same. In the pre-Qin classics, a hegemonic state is generally referred to directly as "hegemon," but often this term is interchangeable with "great state." This is the same as in Western international relations theory. Both hold that a hegemonic state is first a great state or a kind of great state. Ancient China customarily calls a hegemonic state a "lord of the hegemony," as "in the Spring and Autumn Period, the greatest power attained the leading role among the feudal lords."[9] This way of thinking is very similar to that of Mearsheimer.

Since ancient times, however, the Chinese word for hegemonic power and its related concepts have undergone a major shift in meaning. In the Western Zhou, "five states formed a community and the community had a leader. Ten states formed a union and the union had a general. Thirty states formed an army and the army had a ruler. 210 states formed a continent and a continent had a lord."[10] As the "head of the feudal states," being a hegemonic state was a symbol of status and honor. The status of hegemon came from a feudal gift of the kingdom. After the Spring and Autumn Period, "the Son of Heaven declined while the feudal lords emerged, and thus they are called 'hegemons.' A 'hegemon' (ba) 'grasps hold of' (ba), which refers to his grasping hold of the political education of the sage king."[11] This means that a state that relied on powerful force and managed to win hegemony was called a hegemon. Although the substance was the same as in the past, the origin was different, and thus the word hegemon replaced that of lord. Mencius was the first to understand the way of the hegemon and the way of the sage king as two different political routes, thus giving rise to "the conflict between sage kings and hegemons."[12] In contemporary Chinese, the term lord of the hegemony refers to "the person or group with the most prestige and power in a given field or geographical area," while hegemon, hegemonism, and a hegemonic state begin to be associated with words with negative connotations, such as arbitrary, control, oppress, and invade.[13] The notions of "hegemony" and "hegemonic state" used in chapter 3 and here follow the meaning of the terms in ancient Chinese, which reads them as neutral terms. It is only here that the hegemonic philosophy of ancient China can be compared to that of contemporary Western hegemonic theory.

THE BASIC STRUCTURE OF POLITICAL HEGEMONY

Hegemony is the result of competition for comprehensive state power, but the place of different factors of power in a hegemony may differ.

Western hegemonic theory in general distinguishes four theories of core factors of power. (1) Geopolitical theory: Alfred T. Mahan thinks that sea power is the core factor in world hegemony.[14] Halford J. Mackinder thinks that land power is the core factor. He constructed a famous syllogism of world hegemony: "whoever controls eastern Europe controls the heartland; whoever controls the heartland controls the world-island; whoever controls the world-island controls the world."[15] Giulio Douhet developed a theory of airpower and stressed that command of the air plays a core role in establishing world hegemony.[16] (2) Military hegemonic theory: Mearsheimer thinks that military power—especially that of the army and the capacity for war that it embodies—is the core factor of hegemony.[17] (3) Economic hegemonic theory: Wallerstein, and Keohane and Joseph Nye maintain that economic power and status in the international economy are the core factors in hegemony.[18] (4) Military-economic hegemonic theory: Paul Kennedy says that the interaction of wealth and power or of economic and military strength is the core factor in world hegemony.[19]

The Stratagems of the Warring States describes discussions among various schools of thought in interstate politics and foreign affairs during the Warring States Period. In this way it has preserved what the different schools thought about hegemony in pre-Qin times. Like Western hegemonic theorists, "the strategists of *The Stratagems of the Warring States* analyze the components of comprehensive national power. Moreover, the factors of national power they analyze are of different kinds. Unlike some scholars today, they do not see comprehensive national power as composed only of economic aspects. Among the factors of national power, they frequently mention four: political, military, economic, and geographic." Unlike Western hegemonic theory, in ancient Chinese hegemonic philosophy there is a school that puts political power as the core factor of hegemony and from this constructs the foundation for a theory of political hegemony.

The theory of political hegemony holds that the core factor of hegemony is political power, and the heart of political power is the ability of the government to govern the state and its influence. According to the summary in chapter 3, the hegemonic theory in *The Stratagems of the Warring*

States holds that "political power is the core of hegemonic power." Moreover, in the discussion of military power and geographical factors as against political power, it stresses the importance of political power: "Rely on politics; do not rely on courage."[20] Yan and Huang go on to point out that "the merits and leadership of the ruler and the chief ministers are frequently seen as the core factors in hegemonic political power." Political power is expressed mainly in two aspects: the first is the leadership, or, better, the ability to govern, of the government; the second is the virtue and self-cultivation of the important officials in the government and the political influence that flows from this.

The theory of political hegemony holds that the government's ability to govern, especially that of the ruler and important ministers, determines the fate of the hegemony. Mozi points out, "Huan of Qi was influenced by Guan Zhong and Bao Shu; Wen of Jin was influenced by Jiu Fan and Gao Yan; Zhuang of Chu was influenced by Sun Shu and Shen Yi; Helü of Wu was influenced by Wu Yuan and Wen Yi; Goujian of Yue was influenced by Fan Li and Minister Zhong. What these five princes were influenced by was correct, and so they held hegemony over the feudal lords. Their deeds and fame was passed down to later generations."[21] When Bao Shuya recommends Guan Zhong as prime minister, he says, "You, O Prince, wish to be a hegemonic king; without Guan Yiwu, it is not possible."[22] After Guan Zhong had become the prime minister of Qi, he did indeed help Qi to establish hegemony. Confucius also acknowledged that "Guan Zhong served Duke Huan, who was hegemon over the feudal lords."[23] And, "Duke Huan gathered the feudal lords from the nine directions not by troops and chariots but by the strength of Guan Zhong."[24] On the contrary, the economic and military power of Qin were both the best, yet the reason Qin was unable to be hegemon was in part because of "the clumsiness of its ministers in charge of planning."[25] Therefore, the theory of political hegemony proposes "worthy princes and enlightened prime ministers," and firmly believes that "when the worthy person is present, then all under heaven submits; and in the use of one person, all under heaven will obey."[26]

Political hegemony stresses that moral influence is of capital importance. Moral influence comes from the merit and self-cultivation of the ruler and his important chief ministers and the policies that derive from this. Virtuous conduct is the basic requirement of the lord of the covenants, or rather of the hegemonic lord: "A great state determines by justice and thereby becomes the lord of the covenants."[27] And, "Without virtue how can one be lord of the covenants?"[28] Duke Huan of Qi "relieved poverty, and paid the worthy and capable"[29] and undertook to "examine our borders, return seized territory; correct the border marks" and to "not accept their money or wealth."[30] In this way he secured the hegemony for Qi. Duke Wen of Jin "revised his administration and spread grace on the ordinary people"[31] and in this way realized the hegemony for Jin. Qin had a wealthy state and a strong army but, because the virtue of Duke Mu of Qin was inferior, in Qin "laws and commands were constantly issued." "Laws were severe and lacking in mercy, only relying on coercion to keep people submissive."[32] Therefore, "it is fitting that Mu of Qin did not become lord of the covenants."[33] Political hegemony holds that fidelity is the most important constituent component of moral influence: "fidelity so as to implement justice; justice so as to implement decrees."[34] Xunzi notes, "Huan of Qi, Wen of Jin, Zhuang of Chu, Helü of Wu, and Goujian of Yue all had states that were on the margins, yet they overawed all under heaven and their strength overpowered the central states. There was no other reason for this but that they had strategic reliability. This is to attain hegemony by establishing strategic reliability."[35]

The theory of political hegemony does not exclude the necessity of material power. The international political philosophy of ancient China held that power that was material in nature and influence that was moral in nature were two basic aspects that constituted power: "The means by which Jin became a hegemon was the military tactics of its generals and the strength of its ministers."[36] Also Mencius says, "Using force and pretending to benevolence is the hegemon. The hegemon will certainly have a large state."[37] Hence, "for a state to maintain its hegemonic status, equal emphasis must be given to virtue, awe, and fidelity."[38]

The formation of political influence is a hierarchical process. Ancient China's international political philosophy and contemporary Western international relations theory both stress the use of hierarchical analysis to observe and analyze the world, and construct a theory of world politics.

The difference between them is that in ancient China's international political philosophy there were four levels of analysis: the individual, the household, the state and the world. Among these four levels there exists a hierarchy and a relationship of cause and effect; thus

> Cultivate yourself, manage your family, administer the state, and bring peace to all under heaven.
> Of old those who wished to make their bright virtue shine in all under heaven first administered their state. Those who wished to administer their state first managed their family. Those who wished to manage their family first cultivated their person.

Or again, "When you have cultivated yourself, then manage your family; when your family is managed, then administer the state; when the state is administered, then all under heaven is at peace."[39] Different levels of material power and their corresponding levels of morality determine the levels of power in the international political system. In the Spring and Autumn Period, after Qi had attained hegemony, Duke Huan of Qi hoped to go one step further and develop to the level of humane authority. Hence he says to Guan Zhong, "I wanted to be a hegemon and, thanks to the efforts of you and your companions, I have become a hegemon. Now I want to be sage king. It is possible." Guan Zhong and his fellow ministers tactfully tell the duke that since his virtue has not yet reached the level of a sage king, Qi could not realize humane authority. Duke Huan therefore renounces pursuit of humane authority and remains content with hegemony.[40]

From this it can be seen that in the sequence of factors leading to hegemony, the greatest difference between China and the West lies in the degree of emphasis given to moral influence and its role. Western geopolitical theory, while emphasizing the geographical environment as the core factor in world hegemony, also holds that even though political power is a constituent part of comprehensive state power or geopolitical power, yet the importance of political power falls far short of that of the geographical environment. Military hegemonic theory, economic hegemonic theory, and military-economic hegemonic theory all follow the same line. Ancient China's hegemonic thought believes, however, that political power, with moral influence as its core, is an indispensable constituent of power. At the same time, it is present at each level of power, always as the pre-eminent element. But, generally speaking, hegemony tends toward a greater demand for material power, whereas humane authority sets a relatively higher standard for moral influence. Furthermore, the difference between hegemonic theory in China and in the West lies in a different understanding of the relationship of cause and effect among the different levels. Whereas both China and the West use hierarchical analysis, Western hegemonic theory tends to emphasize the influential role of the priority and structure of the international system of comparative power on hegemony: it is a case of a relationship of cause and effect that moves from the outside to the inside. Ancient China's hegemonic thought puts more emphasis on the deciding role hegemony plays in the international system: it is a case of a relationship of cause and effect that moves from the inside to the outside.

POLITICAL HEGEMONY IN THE INTERNATIONAL SYSTEM

In Western hegemonic theory, hegemony is situated at the pinnacle of the structure of internal political power. It is the highest possible form of international power. In the structure of international political power, according to the size of their power, states form a pyramidal hierarchy (see figure 6.1). Depending on the number of hegemonies involved, Western international relations theory defines the international system as one of unipolarity, bipolarity, or multipolarity.

In ancient China's hegemonic philosophy, hegemony is not the highest form of power in the system. The *Guanzi* distinguishes four levels of state power from top to bottom: sovereignty, empire, humane authority, and hegemony.[41] The main distinction that the *Xunzi* makes is between humane authority and hegemony.[42] Sovereignty and empire are both forms of state power that belong to the times of ancient Chinese myths and legends, or rather, they belong to an ideal level of power that cannot be realized in the real world. (The united kingdoms founded from the Qin onward all believed that the world they knew was the entire world and thought that the empires they founded did realize the goal of sovereignty

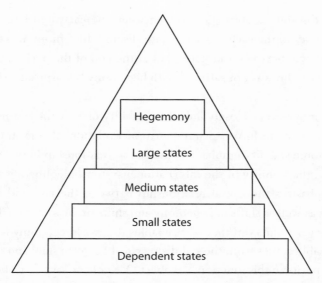

Figure 6.1 The pyramid of power envisioned in Western international relations theory

or empire.) Hence, the ancient Chinese classics, including *The Stratagems of the Warring States*, all acknowledge that the main distinction in power is between humane authority and hegemony. *Humane authority* refers to the unity of all under heaven or, rather, to the formation of a united state ruling over all the then-known world. It is the first level of power in the real world of politics. *Hegemony* refers to a power that can influence or even control other states within a fragmented world, and it is the second level of power, below that of humane authority. In other words, there is a "distinction of top and bottom" between humane authority and hegemony.[43]

Hence, in contemporary Western international relations theory, hegemony has become the main strategic goal for a state even its ultimate goal: "The overriding goal of each state is to maximize its share of world power, which means gaining power at the expense of other states. But great powers do not merely strive to be the strongest of all the great powers. . . . Their ultimate aim is to be the hegemon—that is, the only great power in the system."[44] But in ancient China's international political philosophy, hegemony is not the ultimate goal for a state. In chapter 3, Yan and Huang fail to distinguish between hegemony and humane authority in *The Stratagems of the Warring States* and also fail to distinguish between the shift in strategic goals between the early and late Warring States Period. In the early Warring States Period, hegemony was the core of the struggle between the states, but at the end of the period, the strategic goal of Qin was not satisfied with hegemony but aspired to humane authority.

Hegemony is very closely linked to stability or lack thereof in the international system. In Western international relations theory, the theory of hegemonic stability emphasizes the causal relationship between hegemony and the stability of the international system. Neoliberalism, however, emphasizes the causal relationship between the rise and fall of a hegemon as well as shifts in hegemony and shifts in the system. Charles P. Kindleberger points out that what enables the world economy to be stable invariably comes from the stabilizing role of a given state and only one state can perform this function.[45] Robert O. Keohane says that a hegemon determines norms and then encourages other members to follow them and in this way promotes international cooperation.[46] The theory of long cycles of hegemony thinks that the rise and fall of hegemonies brings about shifts in hegemony. Shifts in hegemony both give rise to wars in the system and, as a result of these wars, bring about the exchange of hegemonic power and thus lead to changes in the system.[47]

Ancient Chinese hegemonic philosophy also concentrates on the relationship between hegemony and international norms as well as the international system. Yan and Huang summarize *The Stratagems of the Warring States* on this point: "the relationship of norms to the legitimacy of hegemony, the relationship between respecting norms and using military force, and the relationship between the establishment of new norms and the preservation of old norms." According to this summary, the hegemonic philosophy of *The Stratagems of the Warring States* holds that norms provide the basis for the legitimacy of a hegemon and are a support for a hegemon's use of military force. The establishment of norms is necessary for a hegemon but it also carries a grave risk. Whether the new norms win international approval directly determines the hegemon's legitimacy. All states may aspire to be called hegemonies: "Duke Wen for this reason made his officials of different ranks and formed the laws of Beilu and so became the lord of the covenants."[48]

Hegemony is founded through a series of international norms and brings it about that the international organizations that take these norms as their center embody the hegemon's power. Likewise, international norms and international institutions will also be internalized as a constituent part of hegemony, giving rise to institutionalized hegemony. Therefore, Robert W. Cox indicates that there are three factors in hegemony: "a configuration of material power, the prevalent collective image of world order (including certain norms), and a set of institutions which administer the world order with a certain semblance of universality."[49] Ancient China's hegemonic philosophy concentrates on respecting the past, even the international norms and mechanisms left by the ancient kingdoms, and is wary of determining new norms. Political hegemonic theory holds that respect for, and even restoration of, the old international norms and mechanisms of the kingdoms is an important part of moral influence. Furthermore, if one wants to respect and uphold or restore old norms and mechanisms, then it is necessary to create new norms and mechanisms directed by a hegemony. But the establishment of new norms and mechanisms so as to restore and uphold or respect old existing norms and mechanisms at the same time whittles away at the old existing norms. Hence, political hegemonic theory falls into a dilemma.

POLITICAL HEGEMONY AND ITS FOREIGN STRATEGY

Political hegemonic theory results in a strategy of working with allies. Xunzi says, "one who befriends the feudal lords becomes a hegemon."[50] Political hegemonic theory holds that the basic indication of the firmness of hegemony is whether political influence can ultimately gain international recognition, and international recognition of a hegemony is decided by three factors: first, the establishment of alliances of friendship with most of the states within the system; second, becoming allies with the main large states in the system; and third, being able to preside at the meeting of the allies, that is, to become the lord of the covenants. "In the Spring and Autumn Period, great states used their allies to contend for hegemony and took ascendancy to the position of lord of the covenants as the standard for calling themselves a hegemon."[51] Yan and Huang go further in pointing out: "If this bloc is the strongest bloc within the world system, then the head of the bloc is the biggest hegemonic power. If that state heads the only bloc, then it is the only hegemonic power within the system." Hence, political hegemonic theory holds that to become a hegemon one must first become the lord of the covenants. "A covenant meeting can determine the public recognition of the status of a hegemon."[52] "Speaking from the history of the Spring and Autumn Period, there was no feudal lord who attained to hegemony without successfully realizing the strategy of managing a covenant meeting."[53] In the *Spring and Autumn Annals* and *Zuo's Commentary* alone there are 246 instances of covenant meetings.[54] After Duke Huan of Qi presided at a covenant meeting in Juan, "Qi began to be a hegemon."[55] At the peak of Qi's hegemony, during the forty-three years of Duke Huan's rule in Qi there were thirty-nine covenant meetings, of which the duke personally took part in twenty-one.[56] Duke Wen of Jin presided in succession at the meetings at Jiantu and Zhequan and "began to be hegemon over all the feudal lords."[57] Wu called a meeting for a covenant at the Yellow Pool and "was hegemon over the central states."[58] Thanks to the covenant meeting at Xuzhou, Yue "was termed hegemonic lord."[59] Meanwhile, though Qin had a rich state and a strong army and cleared a thousand square *li* of land, because it was not able to call together the states and preside over a covenant meeting it could only "be a hegemon over the Western nomadic tribes."[60] In the early Spring and Autumn Period, "when there was no hegemonic lord,"[61] Zheng was the most powerful and the strongest state but it could be called only a "little hegemon." "The main reason for this was because it had not yet been able to establish itself as such during the covenant meetings of the feudal lords."[62]

Political hegemonic theory holds that besides affirming hegemony, covenant meetings have two additional important political functions: the first is to control the allies and prevent them from falling away from the alliance, and the second is to determine international norms such that the will of the hegemonic state becomes the international consensus and thus institutionalizes the hegemony. The covenant meetings of the Spring and Autumn Period naturally put more emphasis on multilateral foreign relations, whereas those of the Warring States Period tended to stress bilateral foreign relations. Hence, "toward the end of the Spring and Autumn and in the early Warring States Period, the custom of covenant meetings went into decline. In the mid to late Warring States Period, the meetings evolved into vertical or horizontal alliances."[63] During the Spring and Autumn and Warring States periods, the strategy of holding covenant meetings was not only to establish bonds with allies and uphold the alliances but also to undermine opposing alliances. The frequency with which alliances were concluded between states during the Warring States Period was very great. They were also ideas on how to undermine the alliances of one's opponents. Therefore, in general during the pre-Qin period the strategy of winning allies was a matter of expediency and there was no strategic value accorded to maintaining an alliance.

Political hegemonic theory is not opposed to sending punitive expeditions abroad but it prefers the military strategy of acting in response to aggression. In contrast to humane authority, which looks more to the attractive force of moral influence to gain the willing submission of other states, political hegemonic theory tends to look to military action to gain submission from other states. Political hegemonic theory is also different from the expansionism of great power politics, however, since it prefers to use the military in response to aggression. Responding to aggression comprises two aspects. On the one hand, it indicates that when foreign relations strategies fail there is no option but to use military means. On the other hand, it means that only after one's opponent has resorted to force will one adopt military action in response. At its greatest extent, the strategy of responding to aggression is a necessary means by which hegemony can gain moral influence: "If you can stop troops and only later respond, give a hand to others to punish what is not correct, conceal your desire to use troops and rely on justice, then it is to be expected that you can reign over all under heaven by standing on only one foot." Hence, "If they truly want to make their will that of becoming lord and sage king, then they must not first engage in war or aggression."[64] In the process of winning submission from abroad, political hegemonic theory holds that it is more important to win over people than territory. Control over territory is just a part of gaining submission and it may lead to one's opponent developing nationalism and hopes for national restoration such that they become your most dangerous enemy. It is only by means of moral influence that one can win over the people's minds and thus accomplish a through submission. Therefore, political hegemonic theory is opposed to making profit one's motive or to the selfish and self-serving extension of power and bloody seizing of territory and invasion.

Political hegemonic theory stresses international duties and responsibilities. Political hegemonic theory holds that international norms must win the respect of the whole body of the nation, especially requiring that the hegemonic state itself should be the first to respect the rules and in that way it can lead other states to respect them as well. As for states that turn their backs on the norms recognized by the international community, a hegemonic state has the power and duty to punish them: "being the lord of the covenants, one may punish those who reject the decrees."[65] In the Spring and Autumn Period, international norms were expressed largely by upholding the ritual order of the Zhou court; hence the hegemon led the way in respecting the Zhou rites and had the duty to uphold the same rites: "Without ritual, how can we preside over covenants?"[66] A hegemonic state has the duty of providing security guarantees to small and medium states and in times of danger, such as famine, of providing economic assistance: "to be compassionate in great matters and overlook the small makes one fit to become lord of the covenants."[67] In the Spring and Autumn Period, the duties of the lord of the covenants included "loving your friends, being friendly with the great, rewarding your allies, and punishing those who oppose you."[68] Political hegemony holds that a hegemonic state enforces its international duty by strengthening its moral influence, and only a ruler and chief ministers of a certain merit can undertake this. Thus it is said, "The lord of the covenants has a definite duty and should have the standing that matches up to this."[69]

CONCLUSION

Ancient China's theory of political hegemony is different from the Western theories of military hegemony, economic hegemony, and military-economic hegemony. The factor of political power replaces the military, economic, and military-economic power found in the Western theories and becomes the core element of hegemony. Political hegemonic theory holds that while a rich state and a strong army are important elements in the constitution of hegemonic power, their importance is not as great as that of political power. The heart of political power is the ability of the government to govern and its moral influence. The way in which the government's ability to govern is displayed lies in the administrative ability and moral cultivation of the head of the government and his main officials, whereas moral influence is shown in the capacity of the success of the state's political and economic model to attract other states. Political hegemonic theory holds that hegemony is not the highest level of power in interstate politics.

Political hegemonic theory holds that there is a close connection between the domestic and international levels. The domestic determines the role of the international. Hence, political hegemonic theory advocates using a new model of political system to develop the economy by establishing a highly effective governing team to promote the development of the state's economic and military power. Political hegemonic theory gives priority to domestic government and advocates first managing one's own affairs well rather than directly challenging the status of the current hegemonic state. Political hegemonic theory holds that moral principles are an indispensable part of hegemony. In domestic politics, the quality and merit of the highest government leaders should be raised, whereas in the international sphere one has the duty to promote the maintenance of international norms and accept the responsibility of providing security guarantees to small and medium states and giving them economic assistance. Political hegemonic theory is a new, nonconfrontational model for the rise of a state.

PART III
Response to the Commentators

Pre-Qin Philosophy and China's Rise Today

Yan Xuetong

Since 1978, when China implemented its policy of reform and open-ing, the field of international relations studies in China has made great progress in introducing international relations theory as developed by Western scholars. There has been no systematic international relations theory created by Chinese scholars, however. For this reason, in 2005 I began to read what the pre-Qin masters had to say about interstate rela-tions and use this material to look for a way to develop a new theory. Although no systematic theory has yet been created, the few articles I have written about Chinese interstate political thought of the pre-Qin era have caught the attention of my colleagues. In this essay I wish to address five issues: (1) why I have studied this field, (2) how I summarize it, (3) how to understand it, (4) what lessons can be drawn from it, and (5) how these can be related to China's rise. I submit my views to the critique of my colleagues.

THE PURPOSE OF STUDYING PRE-QIN POLITICAL PHILOSOPHY

Some international colleagues think that my purpose in reviving pre-Qin interstate philosophy is to create a Chinese theory of international rela-tions. This is to misunderstand the reasons why I am involved in this field. Basic characteristics of science are objectivity, verifiability, and openness.

These features determine that a scientific theory must be universal. Because I believe that scientific international relations theory is also universal, ever since my first foray into the thought of the pre-Qin philosophers I have had no intention of creating a "Chinese school" of international relations theory. Rather I have three aims: to enrich current international relations theory, to deepen understanding of international political realities, and to draw lessons for policy today.

To Enrich Current International Relations Theory

Over the past quarter century, both the government and academia in China have been inspired by a strong desire to establish a Chinese international relations theory. In 1987, Chinese scholars meeting in Shanghai held the first international relations theory conference at which the goal of creating a Chinese international relations theory was mooted.[1] Given the lack of any important new theory from abroad, in 2004 at the third international relations theory conference, also in Shanghai, it was suggested that there was a duty to create a Chinese international relations theory. It was even said that "the creation of a Chinese school has already become our historic mission."[2] After this, the number of articles dealing with the need to establish a "Chinese school" of international relations theory grew and the government's attitude toward this goal became increasingly supportive. The vice-director of the Foreign Office of the Chinese Communist Party Central Committee, Qiu Yuanping, wrote an article about the necessity of constructing a Chinese international relations theory, in which she said, "As a rapidly rising major power, it is unacceptable that China does not have its own theory."[3]

Faced with the mounting calls to establish a "Chinese school," I had no choice but to ask a few questions myself: Why is it that in the twenty-five years or so since 1987, while the call for creating a Chinese international relations theory has been at a peak, there have been no Chinese scholars who have created any systematic theory? Even if now or in the future it were possible to create such a theory, would it be called the "Chinese school"? Why is it that the various schools of thought of the pre-Qin times, such as Confucianism, Daoism, Mohism, and Legalism, have not been grouped under the name "Chinese school"? I wrote a number of articles discussing why it is not possible to produce a Chinese school of international relations theory.[4] After several years spent in the study of pre-Qin interstate political philosophy, I am even more convinced that looking to pre-Qin thought to develop and enrich international relations theory is possible, but it is not possible to create a Chinese school of international relations theory. It is also possible to draw modern international relations theory and pre-Qin thought together to develop a new theory. But to view current international relations theory as Western and to keep a distance from it and set one's sights on establishing a different "Chinese school" of theory would be a waste of effort and a fruitless task.

The understandings of interstate politics of the pre-Qin philosophers and of people today are different, but this distinction is a reflection not of a difference of thought between East and West but rather a difference of understanding of international affairs. In other words, the interstate political philosophy of the pre-Qin era and contemporary international relations theory are both universal. The pre-Qin era is more than two thousand years in the past and some of the views of that time may still be used to explain today's realities, which goes to show that the views of that time were indeed strongly universal and very close to objective laws. Hence it is possible, by understanding pre-Qin thought from a universal angle, to fortify the explanatory force of current theory. Ever since I started to study pre-Qin interstate political philosophy I have sought to develop a new theory based on combining pre-Qin thought and contemporary international relations theory rather than to use pre-Qin thought as a basis for creating a new theory to replace contemporary international relations theory.

To Deepen Understanding of International Political Realities

Among the criticisms of the study of pre-Qin thought, two stand out: first, that the authenticity of the authors, text, and date of the pre-Qin works are disputed and, given these doubts about authenticity, any results based on them are unreliable; and second, that relations among the feudal lords of the Spring and Autumn and Warring States periods and relations among nation-states are different, and hence the experience drawn from the former cannot be used in the world today. Neither of these criticisms, however, can deny, from a logical point of view, that research into pre-Qin thought may deepen our understanding of today's international politics.

First, the authenticity of these works has no bearing on our ability to draw lessons from them. Even if we grant that the works of the pre-Qin masters were rewritten in the early Han Dynasty, they would still have been written more than two thousand years ago and the ideas in them reflect what people thought about interstate politics at that time or what they thought of politics in the pre-Qin era. What in all this can serve to explain today's international political reality can be accepted wholly and seen as axioms or principles of international politics. This kind of understanding can help to deepen modern international relations theory. As Hans J. Morgenthau observed, "Human nature, in which the laws of politics have their roots, has not changed since the classical philosophies of China, India, and Greece endeavored to discover these laws."[5] In other words, what is both ancient and suited to the present is the only sure foundation for creating a new theory. As for what in pre-Qin thought cannot be applied to explain today's international politics, we may see this as a particular understanding applicable to a particular international system. This kind of information can assist us in identifying the specific principles applicable to different international systems.

Second, the history of the Spring and Autumn and Warring States periods can provide us with many instructive examples. In fact, it is not just the relations among Chinese states in that period that were different from international relations today, but also relations among ancient European states. Yet no one raises any doubts about taking examples from the historical experience set out in Thucydides' *History of the Peloponnesian War* to interpret events in contemporary international relations. That book records the wars between the ancient Greek city-states, yet contemporary realist theoreticians do indeed draw much of their thinking from it and they have created a theoretical system of thought. Thucydides' maxim "the strong do what they can and the weak suffer what they must" has become the most frequently quoted saying in contemporary international relations theory.[6] In fact, there are many similarities between Chinese interstate politics of the Spring and Autumn and Warring States periods and contemporary international politics, such as: both are anarchical systems, each state has an independent military force, and at the level of the system no power has a monopoly on military force. By the Spring and Autumn and Warring States periods, the binding force of the norms of interstate conduct determined by the Zhou court was weaker than that of United Nations norms in the twenty-first century. Hence, whether considered from the viewpoint of the thoughts expressed in Chinese historical documents or of the similarities between the interstate system of the Spring and Autumn and Warring States periods and the contemporary international system, rediscovery of pre-Qin interstate thought can assist us in developing and enriching current international relations theory.

Furthermore, the differences among the interstate system of the Spring and Autumn and Warring States periods, that of ancient Europe, and that of today's world provide us with new conditions for developing new theories. Contemporary international relations theory has developed from a basis in European history and European political philosophy. Comparisons of the differences among the three systems and the differences between pre-Qin thought and contemporary international relations theory can assist us in correcting the errors and filling in the lacunae of contemporary international relations theory. For instance, Barry Buzan and Richard Little created their theory of international systems by comparing international relations in different regions of the world.[7]

To Draw Lessons for Policy Today

As a political scientist, my purpose in studying pre-Qin interstate political thought is not to understand the past so much as to draw lessons for the present, especially for the great task of China's rise. Discussion of the authenticity of the pre-Qin works and the authenticity of the historical events they refer to is a task for historians, not the reason why political scientists study ancient documents. In the twenty-first century, China faces the historic test of success or failure in its rise to becoming a superpower, while the world is faced with the uncertainty that this might bring. A study of pre-Qin interstate political philosophy may provide guidance for Chinese foreign policy as well as for the world. From China's point of view, we can draw on the experience of success or failure of rising powers from pre-Qin thought. From the point of view of the world as a whole, we can reflect on how China's rise can be of benefit to the stability of the international order and the progress of international norms.

According to pre-Qin thought, China's rise may have two different strategic goals, namely, to establish either a humane authority or hegemony. The former is a comparatively harmonious international system; the latter is the more commonly seen international system. Similarly, the world is faced with two options during China's rise: either to establish a new type of international order or to repeat an American-style hegemonic order. The establishment of a new international order requires changing not only the international power structure but also international norms.

Drawing on the lessons of pre-Qin interstate political philosophy does not necessarily lead us to exalt or restore the tribute system that was once in place in East Asia. First, scientific progress has already meant that the tribute system has lost its material base. Contemporary international communications do not need to draw support from the tribute system. Air transportation enables the leaders of major powers to meet several times a year and modern transportation has led to international commerce becoming a daily business. Hence, the tribute system is obsolete. Second, the idea of sovereign equality among nations has become a universal norm of the contemporary world and it cannot be replaced with the hierarchical degrees of the tribute system. Third, each of the pre-Qin schools of thought had its own idea of the tribute system. There was no one common view. Hence, drawing lessons from pre-Qin thought does not necessarily mean moving in the direction of a tribute system.

A WAY OF UNDERSTANDING THE PRE-QIN PHILOSOPHERS

The classification of the levels of analysis to be applied to the pre-Qin masters is a powerful academic exercise, but one that has difficulty in reaching consensus. First, the pre-Qin masters all analyze a given problem at each of the three levels of the system, the organization, and the individual. Second, their analyses of the cause of war and of how to make peace may be at two different levels. From a methodological angle this is a perfectly normal phenomenon because it is universally accepted that many causes may produce the same effect. Many different causes can lead to the same sickness and many kinds of therapeutic technique can heal the same illness. If in studying the analytical levels of the pre-Qin masters we use different kinds of standards, then our understandings may diverge. For example, analyzing the causes of war may lead to different results than analyzing the causes of peace.

Lack of uniformity in classification of levels of analysis can easily create different classifications. Yang Qianru and I differ in the analytical levels we apply to the masters. She classifies them into four categories, namely, the humane way (which is the starting point for Confucius and Mencius), the hegemonic way (which is the starting point for Guanzi and Xunzi), Laozi's and Hanfeizi's idea of the union of opposites, and Mozi's idea of transformation by virtue.[8] The basic difference between Dr. Yang's classification and mine is that we use different standards. I rely on the three levels of analysis set forth by Kenneth J. Waltz. Currently, this standard of analysis is widely used by scholars of international studies. Dr. Yang creates her own new system of classification, which differs from Waltz's; hence, our classifications of the pre-Qin masters are different. Moreover, the principles of Dr. Yang's four levels of analysis are inconsistent. She differentiates Confucius, Mencius, Guanzi, Xunzi, and Mozi on the basis of their political stance, but classifies Laozi and Hanfeizi according to their way of thinking. Inconsistency in the principles of classification means that the classifications themselves are unclear.

Xu Jin thinks that the analytical method of Xunzi should be grouped with Mencius at the level of the individual. His argument is correct. Xunzi is not as consistent in his view as Mencius is, however. Xunzi sometimes also looks at the cause of conflict from the level of the social system. In an important passage he argues, "The life of human beings cannot be without communities. If there are communities without distinctions, then there will be conflict, and if conflict then disorder, and if disorder then poverty. Hence, the failure to make distinctions is the bane of human life, whereas having distinctions is the basic good of all under heaven."[9] In line with the phrase "the ruler is the key to the management of distinctions,"[10] Dr. Xu classifies Xunzi's analysis as on the level of the individual. I think that Xunzi is a dualist who combines internal and external factors. He thinks that the internal cause of war is that human nature is evil and the external cause is the lack of distinctions in society, and it is only when the two come together that war erupts. In his criticism of Mencius's theory of the goodness of human nature, Xunzi makes human nature a constant.[11] Therefore, he takes the norms for making distinctions as a variable. If we separate the analytical levels of Xunzi by taking a variable as the standard, it is much more meaningful than if we make our classification from the angle of a constant, because a constant does not change and hence it is not adapted to the methodological role of an independent variable. For instance, neorealism also acknowledges that a cause of war is the pursuit of profit by individuals and states, but this school thinks that both are constant. Neorealists understand the cause of war from the angle of the variable of the international configuration. Therefore, this school belongs to the analytical level of the system rather than that of the individual or of the organization.[12]

I classified the philosophical viewpoints of the pre-Qin masters into the three categories of conceptual determinism, material determinism, and the dualist combination of both. Some scholars have other views of the actual categories to be used. For instance, Yang Qianru disagrees with my classification of Laozi's philosophy as conceptual determinism because to a certain extent other schools of thought—Confucian, Legalist, Mohist, Militarist, Yin-Yang, and Guanzi—inherited some of Laozi's ideas. The fact that Laozi's views were used by other schools, however, does not prove that Laozi's philosophy does not belong to conceptual determinism. Confucianism and Mohism are conceptual determinist theories, and that they inherited some ideas from Laozi simply proves that they are all conceptual determinists. Guanzi, Xunzi, and the Yin-Yang school are dualists who combine concepts and matter. That they accepted some ideas from Laozi simply proves that dualists do not reject the role of concepts, but this does not prove that Laozi is not a conceptual determinist. As for the Militarist school and Legalist personages such as Shang Yang and the first emperor of Qin who stress the role of matter, there are also records of them discussing the way of humane authority, which simply shows that they have their own view of the way of humane authority; it does not prove that they accept Laozi's ideas. Still less does it prove that Laozi is not a conceptual determinist. This is like saying that advocates of celibacy may discuss marriage, but this does not prove that they accept the idea of marriage and the family.

Dr. Xu quite reasonably thinks that Xunzi is a conceptual determinist because he regards the idea of the ruler as the determining factor in the future of a state. Nevertheless, Xunzi's analysis of social conflict is a combination of concept, matter and system. For instance, Xunzi says, "When the power exercised by two people is equal and they want the same thing and goods cannot satisfy them, then there will be conflict. Conflict will lead to disorder and disorder to poverty."[13] This passage sees the cause of conflict as lying in the three variables of social status, evil desires, and lack of material goods. Evil desires may be explained as a conceptual factor, social status as a systemic factor, and the lack of material goods as a material factor. Many historians of philosophy think that Xunzi combines Confucianism and Legalism, which from one point of view shows that Xunzi is a moderate conceptual determinist. At least he places less emphasis than Mencius does on the role of concepts.

Dr. Xu agrees with the explanation of Mencius's idea of the goodness of human nature, according to which Mencius did not argue that human nature was originally good but rather that the mind has good tendencies, which can result in good actions. In fact this explanation cannot paper over the deficiencies in Mencius's theory of human nature. First, the theory that the mind has good tendencies that can result in good actions does not exclude the twin possibilities that the mind lacks good tendencies but a person can still do good, or that a person whose mind has good tendencies may perform bad actions. In other words, whether the mind has good tendencies has no relationship to whether good is done. Second, one tendency of the mind may be to good and another to evil and hence which plays the role of motivation is wholly dependent on external circumstances. From the point of view of methodology, the nature of the mind has become a constant and is no longer a variable. Xunzi thinks that the greatest deficiency of Mencius's theory of the goodness of human nature is that it does not differentiate between nature and custom. He thinks that nature is a priori, whereas custom is a posteriori; the former is bad, whereas the latter is good.[14] Xunzi's idea that nature is evil and custom is good is also very deficient because there is a difference in the quality of a person's a posteriori merit. His idea that human nature is a priori and custom is a posteriori is worth learning from, however. From a methodological point of view, if we but acknowledge that the natural factors in society that bring about violent conflict are the same, then we can analyze what kind of social factors are beneficial to suppressing violence and what factors bring about violence. Policy makers' understanding of international relations is not a priori but a posteriori. The differences in their views are largely determined by the differences in the circumstances of their a posteriori life rather than by differences generated from a priori nature. Seen in this way, Mencius's theory of the goodness of human nature is unscientific and therefore cannot serve as the premise for creating a scientific theory of international relations.

A WAY OF DISTINGUISHING BETWEEN HUMANE AUTHORITY AND HEGEMONY

In the discussions of interstate relations by the pre-Qin masters the central theme is humane authority or hegemony. Ever since Mencius distinguished the two in terms of their basic nature, people have made even more qualifications to this distinction. Yang Qianru thinks that, according to the way of thinking of pre-Qin people, humane authority and hegemony were mutually linked and were not opposed to each other. The pre-Qin masters do not disagree that there is a mutual relationship between humane authority and hegemony, but on whether the two are opposed, different schools have different opinions. In chapter 1, I introduced the views of seven pre-Qin thinkers regarding humane authority and hegemony. Of these, Laozi, Confucius, Mozi, and Hanfeizi do not distinguish the two as having different features, but Guanzi, Mencius, and Xunzi do, especially Mencius, who stresses that the two differ in essence.

Mencius says, "Using force and pretending to benevolence is the hegemon. The hegemon will certainly have a large state. Using virtue and practicing benevolence is the sage king. The sage king does not rely on having a large territory."[15] Apart from this, pre-Qin thinkers do not differ on the features shared by humane authority and hegemony; rather, the key to the differences among these thinkers lies in the features humane authority and hegemony do not share. This point warns us that when today we study humane authority and hegemony in the pre-Qin period, the stress should be placed on the differences between the two rather than on what they share.

Is the difference between humane authority and hegemony one of nature or of degree? This is a topic worthy of study. Wang Rihua thinks that among the concepts of the pre-Qin philosophers, humane authority and hegemony differ in grade. His judgment is in accord with the truth, but it remains to be seen if the difference in grade is one of degree or of nature. Xu Jin realizes that the key difference in Mencius's and Xunzi's understandings of hegemony lies in their points of view. Mencius thinks that the two differ in nature: humane authority aims at benevolence and justice, whereas hegemony seeks power though claiming to practice benevolence and justice. Xunzi thinks that the difference between the two is one of degree. Hegemony also has benevolence and justice, but the level of these virtues is lower than in humane authority. I think that an understanding of the difference in the views of hegemony of the pre-Qin philosophers can help us to clarify the distinction between humane authority and hegemony and their differing influences on the international system.

Wang Rihua holds that the political hegemonic theory of ancient China maintains that factors at the domestic level have a determinative impact on factors at the international level. His judgment is correct, but it may mislead the reader into thinking that political hegemonic theory is a form of internal-factor determinism. When pre-Qin philosophers see political power as the core factor in hegemonic power, they mean that the fundamental cause of the uneven development of power lies in changes in the strength of leadership of governments. As a factor, however, political power, when seen from one's own state's point of view, is at the domestic level, though if it is viewed from the point of view of other states it becomes a factor at the international level. In other words, Barack Obama's inauguration, which led to a foreign policy different from that of George W. Bush and increased American political power, is a domestic factor. But for China, an increase in the international political mobilization of the United States is an international factor, because an increase in the United States' political power means a relative reduction in China's political power. Among the pre-Qin philosophers, Guanzi's view of this issue is very typical. He says, "The ruler has the Way; hegemons and sage kings have their opportunities. When one's own state is reformed and neighboring states lack the Way, this is capital for hegemons and sage kings." And again, "That by which the former sage kings ruled was that what the neighboring states did was not correct." In other words, China's pre-Qin thinkers' view of hegemony had already developed the concept of relative power in terms of international politics. When Zhu Zhiwu says, "The advantages of your neighbors are your disadvantages, O Prince," he is expressing a typical understanding of power in international politics.[16]

People later viewed Mencius and Xunzi as important Confucian thinkers, but Xunzi was very critical of Mencius and hence the differences between the two have become an important area of scholarly research. Xu Jin notes that in actual international politics, China, like Mencius, is opposed to hegemony, whereas the United States, like Xunzi, concentrates on the strategic credibility required for hegemony. Xu holds that the origin of the different attitudes toward hegemony of China and the United States, as of Mencius and Xunzi, lies in different definitions of hegemony. Seen from the specialized field of international studies, the term *hegemony* in English has no negative connotations. It means that the influence or power of a given state is much greater than that of other states.[17] It is obvious that the different political standpoints with regard to hegemony of China and the United States are influenced by the different meanings of the word *hegemony* in the two languages, but I think it is not simply a semantic issue. It is much more influenced by their different international statuses. Since the end of World War II in 1945, the United States has always enjoyed hegemony, whereas since 1840, China has repeatedly suffered from invasions by Western powers. China looks at hegemony from the point of view of the political justness of the international order, whereas the United States looks at hegemony from the point of view of the stability of the international order. In reading *Mencius* and *Xunzi* we realize that Mencius evaluates hegemony according to whether its political goals are right or not,[18] whereas Xunzi assesses hegemony in terms of the stability of the international order.

Dr. Xu holds that "there is a certain plausibility in Xunzi's using the failure of a state as large as Chu to attain all under heaven and comparing this with the territories of the kings Tang and Wu as proof that hard power is not important to humane authority." I think that if Xunzi is arguing that a state's power being greater than that of others does not necessarily mean that it can attain humane authority, then this logic is sound. But when he argues that the scale of a state's power is unrelated to its attaining humane authority, his logic is unsound. The weak occasionally defeat the strong and there are shifts in the center of international politics. Both these phenomena are often seen in international politics, but they do not prove that the scale of power has no bearing on attaining world leadership. The uneven development of power is a process and attaining humane authority or hegemony is just a process in which the contrast of power undergoes a shift. When the kings Tang and Wu were initially opposed to Jie of the Xia and Zhòu of the Shang, respectively, their hard power was indeed inferior to that of Jie and Zhòu, but when they ultimately won this battle, their hard power exceeded that of the defeated Xia and Shang dynasties. In other words, if we assess their power at the moment when King Tang of the Shang and King Wu of the Zhou ultimately attained humane authority, their hard power was the strongest within the system at that time. Similarly, when China's civil war began in 1946, the hard power of the Nationalist Party (KMT) was greater than that of the Communist Party (CCP). But in 1949, when the Communist Party acceded to the government of the state, its hard power surpassed that of the Nationalists.

A humane authority under heaven relies on its ultrapowerful moral force to maintain its comprehensive national power in first place in the system. Its hard power may not be the strongest at the time, but the level of its hard power cannot be too low. From a historical point of view, a state that is able to attain leadership of the system, whatsoever its nature, must have hard power that can be ranked among the top class. It is unthinkable that a state could attain humane authority under heaven relying purely on morality and hard power of the lowest class. In the international politics of the twenty-first century, the importance of the area of territory ruled has declined as a factor in gaining world leadership, but a population of more than two hundred million does play an important role. In other words, there is no way that a state with a population of less than two hundred million can become the leading state of the contemporary international system. Even if after the Cold War there was the idea of one super-power with several powerful satellites, including states such as the United Kingdom, France, Germany, Japan, and Russia with populations of less than two hundred million, in the twenty-first century these states have no possibility of becoming the leading states of the system. France and Germany understand that any opportunity of providing the key to a future international configuration lies not with them individually but rather with the European Union.

FACTORS ENRICHING MODERN THEORY

There are many insights in the works of the pre-Qin thinkers but they fail to constitute a complete system of interstate thought. Therefore, we principally can draw lessons from their thought to develop contemporary theory in two areas. First, we can learn from their understanding of the nature of interstate relations. Since the basis for interstate relations is human nature and human nature never changes, their understanding of the nature of interstate relations may always be valid. Second, we can learn from the concepts they use to understand interstate relations. These concepts are ancient tools of thought. Simply because they are ancient, however, they may be applicable to a broader period of history. Their suitability to this wider range of time may enlarge the scope of the effectiveness of international relations theory.

Pre-Qin thinkers generally thought that power in both international and domestic society had a hierarchical structure. This is manifestly different from the assumptions of contemporary international relations theory. Contemporary international relations theory generally holds that international society is an anarchic system—that is, international actors play similar roles and their power relationships are equal—whereas domestic society has a hierarchical structure in which actors have different roles and power is expressed in terms of relations from top to bottom.[19] If we look carefully at today's international system, however, we discover that the power relationships among members of the United Nations, the World Bank, and the International Monetary Fund are all structured hierarchically and are not equal. The United Nations distinguishes among permanent members of the Security Council, nonpermanent members of the Security Council, and ordinary member states. The World Bank and the International Monetary Fund have voting structures dependent on the contributions of the members. If we combine what contemporary international relations theory has to say about equality of power with the hierarchical idea of the pre-Qin thinkers we will arrive at a new way of thinking. For instance, in international society, relations between states are neither equal nor ranked from top to bottom. Rather they form a loose hierarchy. Domestic power relationships are determined by social norms, whereas international power relationships are determined by the capability of states. In the domestic system, hierarchical norms guide conduct in society, whereas in the international system norms of both hierarchy and equality direct state behavior.

Pre-Qin thinkers generally believe that hierarchical norms can restrain state behavior and thus maintain order among states, whereas contemporary international relations theorists think that, to restrain states' behavior, norms of equality alone can uphold the order of the international system. If we look at history, we find that relations of absolute equality between states lead to violent conflict, and relations of absolute hierarchy lead to tyranny in which the strong oppress the weak. If we unite the views of both ways of thinking, we may suppose that a combination of norms of equality and norms of hierarchy is best for upholding international order. Hierarchical norms carry with them the demand that the strong should undertake greater international responsibilities while the weak respect the implementation of discriminatory international rules. For instance, developed countries should each provide 0.7 percent of their GDP to assist developing countries, and nonnuclear states must not seek to possess nuclear weapons. Norms of equality, by contrast, guarantee that states with the same power enjoy the same international rights, while states of different grades respect the implementation of common regulations. For instance, the permanent members of the United Nations Security Council all have veto power, while all member states must refrain from using military force to annex other members. The recently developed principle of common but different responsibilities in reducing emissions of carbon dioxide (CO_2) is a typical example of the combination of equal and hierarchical norms.

The pre-Qin thinkers emphasize the influence of the leading state on the effectiveness of interstate norms, whereas contemporary theory stresses the influence of the system on the effectiveness of international norms. The former stresses that respect for norms is determined by the way in which the leading state acts according to those norms, whereas the latter concentrates on how the system itself restrains the conduct of states. If we combine the two, we can work from the nature of the leading state to understand the process of socialization, institutionalization, and internalization of international norms. According to contemporary theory, we already know that there are three steps in the formation of international norms. The first step is that new norms are put forward by major powers, the second step is that they win support from most states, and the third is that after being implemented over a long period of time they are internalized by most states. Contemporary theory still does not understand the process by which international norms are internalized, however. According to the views of the nature of humane authority and hegemony expressed by pre-Qin philosophers, we know that humane authority has the role of taking the lead in implementing and upholding international norms, whereas hegemony lacks this. Based on this realization, we can study the path by which the nature of the leading state affects the internalization of international norms after they have been established. Based on the positive influence of the multilateralist policy of Bill Clinton and the negative influence of the unilateralist policy of George W. Bush regarding the norms for preventing nuclear proliferation, we can suppose that the different leadership provided by leading states plays a role in the direction and speed of the internalization of international norms.

Hegemony is an ancient idea, and what the foundations of hegemony are is a topic that has long been debated. Wang Rihua notes that the pre-Qin thinkers saw political power as the core factor in hegemony. In this they differed from contemporary international relations theory, which sees material power as the core element in hegemony. Based on this difference, we may compare these two factors of power to see which plays the determinative role in the rise of the new China over the past sixty years. The transformation of the political system in China in 1949 and the change of China's political line in 1979 are both important turning points in the course of China's rise. At these two moments, China's international power status did not change, but both brought about long-term increases in China's military and economic strength, respectively. At the same time, annual increases in the actual strength of China's armed forces and of its economy did not bring about immediate changes in its international status, but over a long period of time there was a change in its status. A strengthening of political power can bring about an increase of material power, but an increase of material power does not necessarily mean an increase of political power. For instance, the Soviet Union had the world's second largest army in 1991 but lacked the political will to prevent the breakup of the country. Based on this comparison, we can suppose that the conversion of political power into military and economic power is the basis for a state to attain international leadership. From this we can establish a pyramidal framework for hegemonic theory in which hegemony is based on hard power, and hard power on political power. The wider and more solid the foundations of political power are, the stronger and greater the economic and military power it can generate.

Pre-Qin thought can be used not just to analyze actual international politics but also to predict trends in international politics. Yang Qianru thinks that study of the thought of the pre-Qin masters is a study of the past, whereas research in contemporary international relations theory is geared toward the future. In fact, this is not the case. Both the study of pre-Qin interstate political philosophy and contemporary international relations theory can be aimed at forecasting the future. My purpose in rereading the pre-Qin works is to find in them an analytical framework and ideas that can help us to deepen our understanding of the trends in contemporary world politics. For example, by learning from the distinction between humane authority and hegemony in the pre-Qin philosophers we were able to predict that after the election of Barack Obama as president of the United States the international political influence of the United States would increase. After Obama took office in 2009, his adoption of policies to reduce climate change won favor with traditional allies in Europe. This fact serves as preliminary support for the earlier prediction, and Obama's leadership over the next few years will show whether it holds.

APPLICATIONS TO THE RISE OF CHINA

The core issue with which pre-Qin interstate political philosophy is concerned is governing. Humane authority and hegemony are two types of governance. The current rise of China is also an issue of governance, both internally and externally. Internally it is a question of how to construct a civilized and prosperous society; externally it is how to establish a new international order. Hence, study of pre-Qin interstate political philosophy is an aid to reflecting on how to implement China's rise and to ask what kind of rising state it is to be. At the eleventh meeting of heads of the diplomatic corps, Hu Jintao proposed as the goals of foreign policy "that China should have greater political influence, greater economic competitiveness, greater cultural affinity, and greater moral impact."[20] These goals show not only that China no longer uses the policy formulated by Deng Xiaoping in 1990 of keeping a low profile as the guiding principle of its foreign policy, but also that it no longer sees increasing economic profit as the top priority in its foreign policy, and that Chinese leaders have begun to think about foreign policy in terms of how China can become the leading power in the world and what kind of world leadership it can provide. These goals also show that Chinese leaders are beginning to realize that political influence and moral impact are of great significance in attaining world leadership. When academia studies pre-Qin interstate political philosophy, it does so precisely to learn how pre-Qin thought can enrich our understanding of the foundations, strategies, and influence of China's rise.

There are opposing voices in the pre-Qin masters' view of interstate politics; hence, a big question faced by scholars today is exactly what philosophy can we learn from to guide China's rise. Ever since the publication of my book *Zhongguo Jueqi Guoji Huanjing Pinggu* (An assessment of the international environment for China's rise) in 1998, scholars in China have been discussing whether China should rise and how. In 2004, even the Chinese government joined the debate.[21] Yang Qianru thinks that the Chinese government should learn from Laozi: "All under heaven is a spiritual vessel and cannot be run or grasped. To try to run it ends in failure; to try to grasp it leads to losing it" (*Laozi* 29), and that a rise to greatness should not be a national goal. In the course of rediscovering China's ancient political philosophy, the school of conspiracy and plotting has become a strong strand in political thought. Books advocating conspiracy and plotting have become the staple studies of ancient thought in airport bookshops in China. This school proposes using the strategies of the ancients to further one's own ends. I believe that if we make national restoration or ascent our goal, we do not need the stratagems of the ancients but rather their understanding of the laws of international politics.

A national grand strategy should be formed against the background of today's realities and changes. This means that any historically successful grand strategy will become out of date because times change. The goal of national resurgence lies in ensuring that China is more advanced, more civilized, stronger, and richer, but not more crafty, devious, or smug. The goal of national resurgence requires that Chinese people do their utmost and struggle to make it happen. But if we take Laozi's nonaction as our guideline, there is no way in which China can realize its national resurgence. China must learn from thought of positive significance such as the idea of "strategic reliability being established, one can attain hegemony."[22] If this is done, then China's foreign policy will take as its goal the maintenance of strategic reliability. Maxims such as "the sage kings of old had righteous troops and did not disband their armies"[23] allow China to affirm that its use of defensive military strength is in accord with the correct interpretation of international norms.

Study of pre-Qin thought is of assistance to us in understanding history correctly. A nation that cannot face historical events correctly is one that cannot win over the hearts of other states. Yang Qianru thinks that "at no time in the past or in the present has China made hegemony over the world the goal of its development." If we believe that the Chinese people gained a modern scientific understanding of geography only in the final years of the Qing empire, then we can say that, since that time, China has not made hegemony over the world its goal. This fact does not, however, prove that before this time China did not make world hegemony its goal. The debate about humane authority among the pre-Qin masters is precisely a discussion of the issue of whether to wield humane authority or hegemony over all under heaven. Given the then lack of a modern scientific understanding of geography, the Chinese notion of all under heaven meant all the land, sea, and people under heaven. The term *all under heaven* was virtually synonymous with *the world*. The title *Son of Heaven* referred to the person who ruled over all people on the earth as the representative of Heaven. The emperors of China's feudal times called themselves Son of Heaven, which shows that they thought of themselves as rulers of the world. The idea that "under heaven's canopy there is nowhere that is not the king's land; up to the sea's shores there are none who are not the king's servants"[24] illustrates that the contention for the power of Son of Heaven was, from another point of view, a contention for world leadership. Study of pre-Qin interstate political philosophy also has the role of taking the past as a mirror so as to learn about the rise and fall of great powers, and hence to predict what kind of results different strategies of ascent may bring about. In practice, it is to learn from pre-Qin thought so as to rethink the strategy of China's rise and avoid a Soviet-style halfway collapse or a Japanese-style stagnation.

To learn from pre-Qin thought certainly does not imply rejecting Western notions of democracy. To contrast China's traditional thought with Western political thought is to overlook what they share. Yang Qianru thinks that if China were to accept the modern idea of democracy, it could not establish an international order based on humane authority of its own style. I think that in their respect for norms, the modern concept of democracy and the ancient Chinese concept of humane authority are alike. For instance, in the pre-Qin era the practical realities of humane authority were the rites and norms of the Western Zhou period, but the inner core was the universal morality required for political legitimacy. As history constantly changes, the universal moral standard also changes. For instance, inheritance by the eldest son was once the universal norm of political legitimacy, but in modern society it is no longer considered moral and it has been replaced by the norm of elections. The electoral system has become the universal political norm today. Even states that support one-party rule must have an electoral process for choosing the leader of the state. Although China supports the one-party leadership of the Communist Party, it still retains the consultative system of having eight democratic parties, so the Chinese government proclaims that China is a multiparty state. Given that democracy is the universal standard of political morality, in learning from the pre-Qin maxim "when norms are established, one can attain humane authority,"[25] China must make the moral principle of democracy one of those it promotes. In fact, in its foreign policy, China has already used the expression "jointly promoting democratization of international relations."[26] Even more important, the moral principles China emphasizes in its foreign strategy should be different from those the United States stresses in its hegemonic system.

Learning from the distinction between humane authority and hegemony in pre-Qin times, the strategy for China's rise in its foreign policy should be distinct from that of the United States in three areas. First, China should promote an international order that takes as its principle a balance between responsibilities and rights. At any given time, there are differences in power among states; hence, according to their power, states enjoy different rights and undertake different responsibilities. This is beneficial to the stability of the international order. China should not adopt the United States' current way of acting, saying that all states are equal while in practice always seeking to have a dominant international status. The United States' policy of saying one thing and doing another is, in fact, seen by international society as hypocritical hegemony.

Second, China should reflect on the principle of reversed double standards, namely, that more developed countries should observe international norms more strictly than less developed ones. For instance, the Kyoto Protocol sets different standards for the reduction of carbon dioxide emissions for developed and developing countries. China should not follow the United States in imposing a single standard on international society. This is especially so in politics, where the principle of having dual standards is more beneficial in upholding the stability of the international order than that of having one standard. There are more than two hundred political entities in the world. The differences between them are too great. Having a single standard can only lead to conflict and is not helpful in reducing friction among states.

Third, China should promote the open principle of the traditional idea of all under heaven as one, that is, China should be open to the whole world and all the countries in the world should be open to China. Ever since Europe invented the modern nation-state, nations have continually increased control of their borders. Even through some regional organizations have reduced border control among their members, the larger trend has led to the world's becoming more fragmented rather than more integrated. Border controls have become increasingly comprehensive in terms of employment, suffrage, social welfare, travel, investment, and so on. Thus, the national treatment of peoples becomes an important international political issue. After the end of the Cold War, the United States attained the position of being the only superpower, and it has constantly made its border controls stricter. After September 11, 2001, it enacted a policy of taking the fingerprints of foreigners coming into the country. Stricter border controls lead to greater suspicion between nations and more pronounced confrontation. China should promote the principle of freedom to travel, to live, and to work anywhere in the world. People tend to move to the better place, and thus nations with better conditions will be attractive to talented people. Hence, China should expand its policy of opening to international society.

Even though research into pre-Qin interstate political philosophy has attracted attention among scholars within China, it has not yet attracted the notice of international colleagues. In order to make a more rapid breakthrough, three tasks remain. The first is to translate the recent fruits of Chinese scholars into English and other languages so as to introduce what we are doing to our international colleagues. The second is to expand comparative study of China's pre-Qin interstate thought, Europe's ancient interstate thought, and contemporary international relations theory. The third is to create a new international relations theory on the basis of both pre-Qin thought and contemporary international relations theory. It may be that the third task is the most important. It is only by creating a new theory that we can fully prove the value of studying pre-Qin thought. For this reason, I hope that more Chinese and foreign scholars will take part in the field of the study of China's pre-Qin interstate political philosophy.

Appendix 1

The Spring and Autumn and Warring States Periods and the Pre-Qin Masters

Xu Jin

The last ruler of the Western Zhou kingdom, King You, was good-for-nothing and the feudal princes all rebelled against him. When he deposed the queen and heir apparent, the queen's father, Prince Shen, brought together the Rong outlying tribes, which undertook a military expedition and overthrew the government, killing King You at Mount Li (now Lintong in Shaanxi) and setting up his son, Yijiu, as king with the title King Ping. Since the capital city, Gao, had been destroyed in the fighting and the area around it occupied by the nomadic tribes, King Ping had no option but to move and settle further east at Luo Yi (now Luoyang in Henan) under the tutelage of the powerful feudal lords Duke Xiang of Qin, Prince Wen of Jin, Duke Wu of Zheng, and Duke Wu of Wei. That was in 770 BCE. History dates this as the end of the Western Zhou and the beginning of the Eastern Zhou. In 221 BCE the first emperor of Qin crushed all the feudal states in war and unified China, establishing the Qin empire. Historians commonly term the time between 770 and 221 BCE as the Spring and Autumn and Warring States periods.

THE SPRING AND AUTUMN PERIOD

The *Spring and Autumn Annals* is a historical book that records the events of the state of Lu from the first year of Duke Yin's reign (722 BCE) to the fourteenth year of Duke Ai's (481 BCE). The term *Spring and Autumn* was commonly used by historians in the Zhou era to refer to the state histories, but by the Han Dynasty only the history of Lu, edited by Confucius, survived; all others were destroyed during the Qin Dynasty. Precisely because of the historical importance of the *Spring and Autumn Annals* and because it was the earliest work recording any period of history, people later termed this era the Spring and Autumn Period. There is no disagreement among historians as to whether the Spring and Autumn Period began in 770 BCE, but there is no consensus regarding which year the period ends. The famous historian Qian Mu thought that according to the *Spring and Autumn Annals*, the Spring and Autumn Period should end with the fourteenth year of the reign of Duke Ai (481 BCE). Another historian, Guo Moruo, took the first year of the reign of King Yuan of Zhou (475 BCE) as the turning point between the Spring and Autumn and Warring States periods, as set out in the "Chronology of the Six States" in *The Records of the Historian*. Hence he thought that the Spring and Autumn Period should end in 476 BCE. The historian Jin Jingfang proposed 453 BCE as the turning point between the Spring and Autumn and Warring States periods because that was the year in which the state of Jin split into three—Zhao, Wei, and Han—which marks the formation of the Seven Powers of the Warring States Period.

Although historians are not agreed on the last year of the Spring and Autumn Period, they all think that it was a turning point for China's ancient history. In technology, China evolved at this time from the bronze to the iron age. The widespread use of iron led to progress in the development of agriculture, handcrafts, and commerce. In internal politics, the Spring and Autumn Period saw the breakup of the clan communities. The use of iron had a great impact on productivity, which brought about the breakup of the clan communities based on the well-field system. The breakup of the clan communities led to the dismantling of a bureaucracy based on blood lineages. Each state moved toward a centralized bureaucracy. Centrally coordinated administrative districts replaced feudalism. In international politics, the eastern displacement of the Zhou Son of Heaven led to a decline in the power of his successors, and so in the Spring and Autumn Period China went from unity to division and the various states emerged in constant chaos as they contended for hegemony. In culture and scholarship, the later Spring and Autumn Period saw the appearance of two great thinkers—Laozi and Confucius. Their thought opened up the discussions of the hundred schools of the Warring States Period.

THE WARRING STATES PERIOD

The name "Warring States" comes from *The Stratagems of the Warring States*, a historical work edited by Liu Xiang. Historians generally call the period from 475 BCE (according to the "Chronology of the Six States" in *The Records of the Historian*) or 453 BCE (with the division of Jin into three parts) to 221 BCE, when the first emperor of Qin unified the other six states, the Warring States Period. During the Warring States Period, the seven states of Wei, Zhao, Han, Qi, Chu, Qin, and Yan, known as the Seven Powers, were constantly at war with one another. The conflict was fierce militarily, politically, and in the area of foreign relations. Shang Yang, who transformed the legal system of Qin and developed the state into a rich and powerful one, ensured that ultimately Qin became dominant as it gradually annihilated the other six states and realized the goal of unity, by which "the king of Qin swept up the six into one" and formed a united empire where "within the seas administrative districts were created and laws were unified." Each of the seven states had sought to enrich itself and strengthen its army, and therefore some had undertaken legal reforms, including those of Li Li in Wei, Wu Qi in Chu, and Shang Yang in Qin, which all, to some extent, brought about social progress. The foreign policy of the verticalists and horizontalists represented by Su Qin and Zhang Yi was very active. During the Warring States Period, commerce and transportation reinforced each other's progress, creating several famous cities. Outstanding water conservation measures—such as Dujiangyan near Chengdu, the irrigation system of the state of Zheng, and the canal of Hong Gou—brought constant progress to agriculture and blessings to later generations. In the development of culture and thought, the hundred schools of the Warring States Period clamored for attention, creating the glorious pre-Qin civilization that has had such a great influence on later generations.

THE PRE-QIN MASTERS

During the Spring and Autumn and Warring States periods a new intelligentsia emerged, the scholar-officials. Most of them were born among the lower classes, but they were learned and talented. Some were great philosophers and thinkers. Others understood history, astronomy, the calendar, mathematics, and geography. Some were outstanding in politics and military affairs. Representatives of this group include Laozi, Confucius, Mencius, Mozi, Zhuangzi, Xunzi, Hanfeizi, the Legalists Shang Yang and Shen Buhai, the primitive agriculturalist Xu Xing (ca. 390–315 BCE) and his disciple Chen Xiang, and the military strategists Su Qin and Zhang Yi. All of these were famous thinkers, politicians, military experts, or scientists.

Because they came from different backgrounds, their views also differed, and hence, in resolving or responding to real questions, they proposed different political ideas. They wrote books to establish their ideas and were constantly debating among themselves such that the hundred schools contended for attention, giving rise to the schools of Confucianism, Daoism, Mohism, Legalism, yin-yang, Nominalism, verticalism and horizontalism, Eclecticism, Agriculturalism, and the novelists. Of these, four are important—Confucianism, Daoism, Mohism, and Legalism— and the *Analects*, *Mencius*, *Mozi*, *Laozi*, *Xunzi*, and *Hanfeizi* are the representative works of these four schools. What follows is a brief introduction to some of the most important pre-Qin masters.

Guan Zhong (719–645 BCE), personal name: Yiwu, appellation: Zhong. In the early Spring and Autumn Period, Guan Zhong was the prime minister of Qi and a famous politician, strategist, and thinker. The *Guanzi* originally had 389 sections but most of it was lost when the first emperor of Qin burned the books and buried the Confucian scholars alive. What survived was edited by Liu Xiang during the Western Han. Eliminating repetitions, the whole surviving work came to eighty-six sections, of which ten went missing before the Tang Dynasty, leaving only seventy-six today.

Laozi (600–? BCE), surname: Li, personal name: Er, appellation: Boyang. Laozi was a famous thinker of the Spring and Autumn Period. He wrote the *Daodejing* (also called the *Laozi*) and is the father of the Daoist school. It is said that Confucius studied under Laozi. The *Laozi* has throughout history been considered a classic of China's political thought, leading in the Han Dynasty to the aphorism "using the Confucian arts outside, and inside using the Yellow Emperor and Laozi," and in the Tang and Song dynasties to the exalting of Daoism to the status of state religion.

Confucius (551–479 BCE), personal name: Qiu, appellation: Zhongni. Confucius was a great thinker and educator in China. Confucian thought as represented by Confucius has had a profound and long-lasting influence on Chinese history. He was later honored as the "Most Sagely" (a sage among the sages) and "the teacher of ten thousand generations." Confucius corrected the *Odes* and the *Book of History*, edited the *Rites* and *Music*, wrote a preface for the *Book of Changes* and compiled the *Spring and Autumn Annals*. The *Analects* is the most important Confucian book. It was compiled by his disciples and their successors. It records the words and deeds of Confucius and his disciples.

Mozi (personal name: Di) was the founder of the Mohist school. Mozi lived sometime between Confucius and Mencius, but there is no agreement on the dates of his birth or death; for instance, the following have all been suggested as his dates: 490–403 BCE, 468–376 BCE, and 480–390 BCE. At first Mozi studied Confucianism, but he was not happy with the complications and expense of the rites and therefore began to form his own ideas. The *Mozi* is a book that records Mohist thought; most of it may be lecture notes written by Mozi's students, but a small part may be the work of later Mohists.

Mencius (372–289 BCE), personal name: Ke. Mencius was a great teacher and thinker in the Confucian school after Confucius. His fame increased from the Song Dynasty onward and by the time of the Yuan Dynasty he was called the "Revered Second Sage," and later people called him "Second Sage," meaning that his status was only slightly less than that of Confucius, and hence he is sometimes named alongside Confucius in the expression "Confucius and Mencius." The *Mencius*, one of the Confucian classics, is a compilation, by Mencius and his disciples, of Mencius's sayings, political ideas, and political activity.

Xunzi (312–238 BCE), personal name: Kuang. Xunzi was a famous Confucian scholar and thinker of the Warring States Period. Because two of his pupils, Hanfeizi and Li Si, both became famous Legalists, throughout history some historians have strongly doubted that Xunzi belongs among the Confucian scholars. Most chapters of the *Xunzi* summarize the scholarly world of the contentions of the hundred schools and Xunzi's own scholarly thought. A few chapters are the work of his disciples.

Hanfeizi (280–232 BCE), surname: Han, personal name: Fei. He was a famous philosopher and thinker of the Warring States Period and a representative of the Legalists. Though his teacher was Xunzi, he did not follow the Confucian school of thought. Instead he developed Legalist thought and became a successful Legalist of the late Warring States Period. The *Hanfeizi* is basically Hanfeizi's work, though a few chapters of other people's writings may have been inserted, as often happened in the transmission of ancient books.

Appendix 2

Yan Xuetong: A Realist Scholar Clinging to Scientific Prediction

Lu Xin

GROWING UP

Lu XIN: Your parents were both intellectuals. What kind of environment did you grow up in?

YAN XUETONG: I am marked by growing up in an intellectual household. My mother lectured at Hebei University and so I grew up in the university dormitory. In that environment, what people valued was not what social class you were in but your scholarship. This had a great influence on me. What I saw and heard around me made me from early on think that scholarship was the only thing worth doing.

Lu XIN: Were your parents particularly concerned about your studies?

YAN XUETONG: No. In fact, they left me to my own devices. In the environment I grew up in there was a lot of competition among children. Those who did well kept their noses to the grindstone with stubborn intensity. I was of average ability and my grades were middling. From primary school until I earned my doctorate, I think, I never won a prize or came in first in class. I never even thought of being first.

Lu XIN: What were your expectations for the future?

YAN XUETONG: I had no idea. Ever since I was young I just assumed that one studied at school and after graduation became a teacher and there was really nothing else.

Lu XIN: You would never have thought that at the age of sixteen you would be sent to a construction corps in Heilongjiang and remain there for nine years.

YAN XUETONG: Correct. Although I was surrounded by other secondary
school pupils, my whole way of life changed. I built houses and worked
on the farm. The hardships we had to put up with then are more than
you could imagine today. A lot of pupils were sent into the construction
corps and descended on the villages, which were quite unprepared for
them. For one village to house more than 150 people was beyond its
capacity. There was nowhere to live. The local people turned the cattle
out of their stalls, swept away the dung, and put mats on the floor. We
slept in the cattle shed. One winter heavy snow cut off the roads and
we were without salt or vegetables for three months. We had only
boiled beans and steamed corn cakes. Since there was no firewood, we
dismantled some of the houses and in the end we even dismantled our
own shed, leaving only one tiny stall, and that had a hole in the roof.

At that time, the Leftist ideology was in full swing. In May, water in
Heilongjiang still turns to ice. When we pulled the sowing machine,
we were not allowed to wear boots. We walked barefoot over the ice.
Our legs were covered in cuts. We carried sacks of seed that could
weigh up to eighty kilograms [about 176 pounds]. We carried them
along the raised pathways around the paddy fields. These were not
level; make a slight misstep and you fell into the water. You just thought
of climbing out and going on. When you at last struggled to the end
and lay down, your eyes could only see black and you just could not get
up. The construction corps changed me so that I can put up with any
form of hardship. Previously I could not stand even the least suffering.

LU XIN: At sixteen young men are full of life and usually curse and
swear.

YAN XUETONG: Of course. In the construction corps, if you did not curse
or swear you would soon stand out as odd and you could hardly live in
such a group. Someone who cursed other people and did so in the vil-
est possible way and used dirty words would easily be accepted by the
group. Naturally, compared with the others, I used less dirty language
and did fewer bad things than the others because, having grown up in
an intellectual household, I knew those things were not so good. For
instance, in quarrels I was generally only among the supporters and
rarely took the lead myself.

Lu Xin: I expect you found it hard to live in such a terrible environment.

Yan Xuetong: People are very adaptable. Most people survived in that environment. During the Cultural Revolution we saw people being beaten to death, so you became somewhat immune to it. My father was sent to do manual work by those opposed to academic authority. At that time many people experienced this hardship. Moreover, they showed that in the midst of hardship they were courageous. At that time we engaged in fistfights, put out fires, worked to prevent floods, sowed seed, repaired roads. You never knew what you would have to do each day. Still less did you know why you had to do it. At the time, my main feeling was that life was hopeless. I could see no future for the world. I could not even hope that tomorrow would be better than today.

The government of the time wanted us to put down roots in the border regions. At the time I was one of the few so-called cadres who resisted saying that I wanted to stay in the countryside forever. I am a person who likes to keep my promises and so I kept quiet. This may be one feature of an intellectual. I could avoid telling the truth but I could not tell lies. This maybe reflected the influence of my intellectual home, a kind of arrogant superiority.

In 1969, Lin Biao died in a plane crash trying to fly to the Soviet Union. The Voice of America predicted that war would break out on the Sino-Soviet border. When we young people learned this, we were particularly happy. We hoped that a massive war would improve the country, or at least change our own lives. Today people fear war, but at the time we hoped for immediate action, even to wage a world war. That way we could have hope. In that frame of mind, there was no difference between life and death. There was no point in living.

Lu Xin: What was the greatest influence of the construction corps on your life?

Yan Xuetong: It changed my character. When I was a child, my main characteristic was that I was very fearful and did not dare to quarrel with others. I would always retreat into my own shell. In the construction corps I changed because you had to survive in the midst of hardship. The construction corps meant hardship first and then anarchy.

Disputes broke out all the time. The youth of the construction corps formed a group that feared nothing. In that environment people became bold and dared to do anything. They held that there was nothing in the world that they could not overcome. So sometimes we did what was very daring, such as getting on a train without a ticket. When the conductor came we ran away. When we had no money to stay in a hotel, we went into the hospital and slept in a bed. When the nurse came along we slipped into another room. Just to survive we did this kind of thing. This way of life completely changed my previous character. Now I have two sides to my character. Sometimes I am afraid of nothing; at other times I am very timid. If I had not gone down to the countryside I would be a very timid person. I think that the sense of superiority I received as an intellectual is in my bones and cannot be removed. The personality changes wrought by my experience in the construction corps mean that I cannot allow that sense of superiority not to influence my whole life. For instance, my father is a real gentleman. Even if there is no one around, he will not cross the street against a red light. He insists on keeping to the principles of a gentleman. In no circumstance whatsoever would he infringe the norms of society, but I am less sensitive in this regard.

LU XIN: How long did you go on living like that before anything changed?

YAN XUETONG: In 1973 young people were permitted to join the army or go to university and so by then we began to have some hope in life. I used to study in secret. I would hide in a haystack and study English, in a place where no one could see me. This was also due to the influence of my intellectual background. I thought I should go to school and study. I never thought about what I would do after university, however. At the time we thought that policies came and went and so after graduation we might well be sent back to the countryside to teach. At the time I had not seen the great shift in the state of the nation. The government adopted the policy of reform and opening in 1978, but I did not realize that, given the educational reforms, the state was undergoing a radical transformation. I did not expect that the basic nature of China could change.

Lu Xin: Was your mind already somewhat numb?

Yan Xuetong: Not numb, just afraid. That kind of fear was with me right up until 1988, one year after I went to the United States to study for my PhD. For more than ten years I had the same nightmare: that I was in a village and applying to return to the city, and for various reasons the work unit would not let me go. From 1973, when we young people had the hope of returning to the city, this nightmare was always with me until 1988, fifteen years later. I would often wake in the middle of the night just because of this nightmare.

WORK AND STUDY

Lu Xin: In 1978, you fulfilled your dream and went to study at the Department of English in Heilongjiang University.

Yan Xuetong: At the time we tried to study twenty-four hours a day, resenting the time taken for sleep, but at last I had reached the required age. I was already twenty-five but not in a position to do what I wanted to do. At university I studied at least a little English. I just thought of studying and was not particularly interested in what went on around me. It was the time of the Democracy Wall and scar literature, which had a great influence on society, but I was not the least bit interested. I thought that study was all that mattered. Besides study I thought that nothing mattered or was of any significance.

Lu Xin: Were you able to read many books in the original English as well as in translation?

Yan Xuetong: No. To be honest, I liked science and was not particularly interested in literature. I was not interested in literature, history, or art. I read only textbooks and learned English. The only outside subject that interested me was linguistics. I felt that linguistics was scientific and logical. My graduation thesis was on linguistics. It was about how sounds through the hearing mechanism formed a system of meaningful symbols. On graduation I took an exam for an MA program in linguistics directed by Lü Shuxiang, but was unsuccessful. I liked doing things related to science. This is in line with what I was interested in later.

LU XIN: After graduation you were assigned to the Institute of Contemporary International Relations to study Africa.

YAN XUETONG: Yes. People ask me why I got into the field of international relations. In fact, it was not that I chose the subject. Rather it was the government that assigned me to that work. At the time all graduates were assigned where they went, like tools sent to different work sites. At the time in my class many people opted for practical jobs. Nobody wanted to go into research. Before it was always politically unreliable people, like Rightists, who went into research. But I asked to be sent into research. Those who assigned posts asked me what I wanted to study: America, the Soviet Union, or Japan. At the time I knew nothing about international relations. My sole interest was to be able to do some kind of study and I did not mind in what field. At the time I saw other people publishing articles, on any topic whatsoever, and felt admiration for them. I really wanted to study and publish an article and earn that sense of satisfaction.

LU XIN: In 1984 you began an MA at the Institute of International Relations. Did this period of study have a great influence on your later work?

YAN XUETONG: At the time the school did not have good classes, so basically it was a matter of self-study. I made no progress whatsoever in the field. To tell the truth, once I had completed the MA I still did not understand anything about the nature of international relations.

STUDY ABROAD

LU XIN: In 1987 you won a scholarship from the Sino-American African Association to begin work on a PhD at Berkeley. This must have been an important turning point in your academic career.

YAN XUETONG: Yes. I had a half scholarship, so my financial situation was very tight. In the summer I had to work, and without a job I could not have lived. But compared with my time in the construction corps, the hardships of life then were nothing. The real hardship was that I understood nothing in class. After class I kept on listening to the recording and still could not get what the lecturers were talking about. For instance, if the lecturer referred to "realism," I had no idea what school of thought that was. If he said "Keohane," I had no idea who that person was or what he did. Still less did I know what school of international relations theory he represented. My education in China simply did not match what I was being taught at Berkeley. There was too great a gap in the knowledge taught in the two educational systems, and I had to make up for that by teaching myself.

The requirements of a PhD program at Berkeley were very rigorous. After the first year there was an evaluation and only after passing that was one allowed to continue on to complete forty credits. After completing the forty credits there were three qualifying exams before one was permitted to take an oral exam, the equivalent of submission of a dissertation proposal. Only after this were you accepted as a prospective PhD candidate and could begin your dissertation. At each hurdle students risked being eliminated. On average, a third of the students would not get a doctorate. My wife was quite prepared for my failing to qualify and having to go back to China. But I felt that if I failed to get a degree I would lose face going home. As we say, "Once you ride a tiger, it is hard to get off!" Having been through the trial of the construction corps, I thought I was very strong, but in the first semester I did cry once at Berkeley. I really regretted coming to America to study because I did not know where it was all going. But overall this time at Berkeley was to have the greatest influence on my life. Each semester I had to read dozens of books, so many I hardly had time to sleep.

Lu Xin: After such a rigorous process, did you finally understand what international relations studies is about?

Yan Xuetong: At first I was all in a muddle. In the first semester I understood nothing. In the second, I understood but could not take notes. Only by the fourth semester did I really catch on. It was just as I felt I finally understood that the classes came to an end. The qualifying exam was a real help to me in understanding international relations studies. To prepare for the exam, I organized the knowledge I had gained in the previous two years and in that way began to understand and appreciate what international relations studies and political science are about. Strictly speaking, it was only after passing the qualifying exam that I began to enter into the field of international relations.

Lu XIN: How did the immense difficulties you faced in studying for a PhD influence you?

YAN XUETONG: The main influence of this process was that I entered into the scientific method. This is what was later to earn me some academic success. Scientific method helped me to know how to do research. This is crucial to scholarship.

I think that doctoral studies is a process of alienation. It is the same in China. People who have really studied for a doctorate will find that their academic interests change their way of looking at life. Just as work in the countryside changed me before, so the five years studying for the PhD in America also changed me. First, it reinforced my previous formation as an intellectual. Second, there was a change in what in life I was interested in. I not only admired study, I made study my hobby. If I discover something through study, then this will give me a special joy. Doctoral studies are a formation as a specialist whereas previous studies are simply the basics. Doctoral studies give one a distinct professional bent. This period of doctoral studies clarified my academic interests. Previously, I just thought of studying but did not know why. After my PhD, the purpose of my reading became clear, namely, I read only books related to international relations. Moreover, my range of interests became increasingly narrower. I studied only questions dealing with China's security and nothing else. Before, I thought that any kind of research was fine and I had no specialized focus. That was because I did not know what international studies were.

Lu XIN: From your own experience, how do you rate the influence of the different educational systems on scholars in China and America?

YAN XUETONG: I think that social science education in Chinese universities still lacks a true scientific bent. Scientific education stresses methodology. China is rather weak in research methods. We need to put more effort into learning methodology and then combine this with our excellent scholarship. Only then will we be better than America. In the field of international relations, those who return to China after earning academic degrees in the States put more stress on scientific methods. It is because we have learned them that we realize that these methods are useful. Some people who have not studied methodology are opposed to giving science any role in method. I think their ideas cannot be followed.

If PhD programs in China and America are compared, from a purely educational point of view, in twenty years Chinese institutions cannot hope to match the famous American schools. If it may be said that modernization requires two generations to be effected, then top university education will be reached in the third or fourth generation. The biggest weakness of our university education is not a lack of buildings or money but that we lack first-rate professors.

Lu Xin: At the time did you have any ideas about your own future? Many people chose to stay in the States, and at the time your whole family was there.

Yan Xuetong: I also thought of staying. But it is very difficult for Chinese scholars to earn any status in the social sciences. Political studies cannot wholly be separated from one's own political stance. That is a special feature of this field. Back in China I could work in a government research institution. At the time I thought this was well worth doing. Moreover, it may be that my sense of nationalism was stronger. This was not something I developed only in America. All people will naturally have some sense of nationalism. It is a sense of collective identity. I chose to come back not because of nationalism but because my desire for material possessions was not so great. At the time, in the United States you could earn three thousand to four thousand dollars per month. But in China you could earn only three hundred to four hundred Chinese yuan per month. Most people chose to stay in the States for economic reasons. Money also lures me, but not so much. Unlike most people, I prefer work to life. When I go abroad for meetings, I rarely go sightseeing. After the meeting, I simply go straight home. For me, the meetings are more interesting than tourism.

ACADEMIC PURSUITS

Lu Xin: How did you set yourself up academically on your return? Why did you not continue to study Africa?

YAN XUETONG: Before returning I had a talk with my PhD advisor. He was the founder of African political studies in the United States. He was very disappointed that his life's work had not had any practical effect on Africa. He said that he had originally chosen Africa because he wanted to help the continent, to help African countries modernize, but his hope was in vain. This made a great impression on me.

When I came home, the purpose of my study was to encourage study of China's foreign policy. In the States many people study China's foreign policy, but almost nobody did similar research in China itself. There was only some research done by the relevant government departments and research into the history of China's foreign affairs. Even today, Chinese scholars have written textbooks only on the history of China's foreign affairs and there is still no textbook on China's foreign policy. At the time nobody in China studied what the motives for China's determination of foreign policy were, or how China's foreign policy worked, or the reasonableness of foreign policy organizations, or what the relationship was between domestic politics and foreign policy. Even now I have not been able to do this. But I have always tried to open the door. In 1993 I wrote "Zhongguo de Anquan Huanjing" (China's security environment), and in 1995 "Zhongguo de Anquan Zhanlue" (China's security strategy). Before then there were no published articles on those topics. I have always held that Chinese scholars should assess the successes and failures of our own policy and come up with the reasons for this. Otherwise, China will never reduce the proportion of its failures.

LU XIN: During the long time you have worked at the Institute of Contemporary International Relations, what is your greatest achievement?

YAN XUETONG: The most important thing I have done is to unite academic research and foreign policy research. Without the right environment I could not have done this. Henceforth my research will tend toward scholarship and less toward policy. I am very satisfied with what I have achieved during this time in policy research. I suggested that the national interest is the starting point for foreign policy, and my book *Zhongguo Guojia Liyi Fenxi* (An analysis of China's national interest) had some influence on society. In the year I wrote that book, the term *national interest* was taboo. I took part in promoting work on multilateral security cooperation. In 1993, I criticized American security views for growing out of a "Cold War mentality." Later this idea was picked up by the media and used widely. Besides this, I spent a long time studying the Taiwan question. From 1994 on, I challenged the effectiveness of "using the economy to promote politics" and constantly maintained that it was necessary to adopt a policy of repression toward Taiwanese separatism. When on May 17, 2004, the Party Central Committee adopted a resolution declaring that the repression of Taiwan independence was the key task, the momentum of the movement for Taiwan's independence began to be curtailed.

In 1996, I argued that the post–Cold War international configuration had already been settled as one of "one superpower and many strong states." Although this view has been accepted by society, it is still debated in politics. The idea of one superpower with many strong states is clearly at variance with multipolarization. Again on the question of the structural contradiction between China and the United States, after I had proposed this idea, some people did not accept it. Later I wrote a book on the issue of the rise of China, published in 1988 as *Zhongguo Jueqi Guoji Huanjing Pinggu* (The international environment for China's rise). There were also people who did not accept the idea of China's rise. Nowadays, however, it would seem that more and more people use the idea of structural contradiction to talk about Sino-American relations and there is increasing discussion of China's rise.

LU XIN: What do you think of the many scholars who advocate founding a Chinese school of international relations theory?

YAN XUETONG: The level of China's own research in international relations studies lags far behind that of some developed countries. I think that at present the focus should be to make learning the basis for creation. International relations theory is created on a foundation of accumulated knowledge. A new theory is created by a given person, but on the basis of the accumulated learning of the whole discipline. The foundational knowledge of our international relations theory is already plentiful, but I agree that any creation in China's international relations theory must be on the basis of our ancient, traditional culture and thought. On the basis of traditional Chinese cultural thought we should mirror the experience of foreign theories and in that way we can more quickly create a worthwhile theory.

Lu XIN: How do you look on the development of China's international studies over the past few years? What do you think is lacking or what areas are there for improvement?

YAN XUETONG: If we look at the past twenty years, China has made great progress. But what is surprising is that our progress is very slow. We are basically repeating America's rate of development of fifty years ago. America took twenty years to go from a traditional to a scientific approach. We should not need twenty years to take the same step.

From an abstract point of view, our academic environment is not good. Concretely speaking, we lack really meaningful academic criticism. This is a question of the setup in China. International relations studies can hardly avoid being related to politics. When ideas do not conform to the current political view it is hard to publish them. There is also the influence of the official bureaucracy. Most people in authority are leaders of their work units, and criticism of these leaders is rather dangerous.

Meaningful academic criticism must be grounded in the critic's full understanding the other person's point of view and logical basis. The premise for critiquing other people's scholarship is that the critic knows how the point of view being critiqued has been arrived at; if not, the critique is meaningless and of no value to academic research.

ACADEMIC STANCE

Lu XIN: You have always been an out-and-out realist. What led you to this stance?

YAN XUETONG: Realist logic is clear, simple, and easy to understand. Personally, I like logic that is clear and a form of expression that is rigorous. I do not much like very complicated speech, where no one can really understand what it is all about. Dialectic method needs a premise. There is no sense in a form of dialectic by which any form of explanation is possible. Take constructivism, for instance. It stresses the mutual interaction between the environment and human behavior. That kind of explanation cannot provide us with any new knowledge because it does not tell us if human beings change the environment or if the environment changes human beings.

LU XIN: Are you not even more concerned with the usefulness of realism?

YAN XUETONG: I am more concerned with how real life and real political behavior can verify explanatory theory. I do not like what cannot be verified, because there is no way of knowing if its conclusions are valid. For instance, in making predictions I like to set a timeframe: within five years, or within three years. I do not like referring to the "long term," the "medium term," or the "short term." That way of speaking is too vague. We have no way of knowing how long the time span is: one month, a year, a decade could all be seen as the short term; ten years, a hundred years, or a thousand could all be seen as the long term. I think that kind of prediction is a form of magic. In international relations studies there is a lot of magic already. When positing an international trend, some people propose three to five possibilities. The development of anything can give rise to many possibilities, but the question is which is the most probable. To produce a lot of possibilities and to say that none of them can be ruled out amounts to saying nothing at all.

LU XIN: Many of the people who went through the Cultural Revolution are like you in being confirmed realists. Could one reason for this be that there was too much pessimism, and once pessimism goes beyond a certain point people feel that practicality is what is most reasonable? What do you think?

YAN XUETONG: The experience of the Cultural Revolution and the experience of the Movement of Going to the Countryside were not the same. People who once went to the countryside are not pessimistic. Rather, they are very sure of themselves. The latter experience gave people the confidence to overcome all obstacles. And this confidence is built precisely on the basis of an estimation of the difficulties faced, on the basis of always preparing for the worst case. Hence, many people who went down to the countryside are realists with regard to life.

People who have not experienced hardship are more liable to adopt an optimistic attitude toward international politics. I think that the experience from the gate of the university to graduate school and that of practical hard work such as in reform through labor are very different. Young people who have learned constructivism in China cannot possibly arrive at a consensus on terrorism with young Palestinians engaged in armed struggle. When I was studying for my PhD in Berkeley, we had one Palestinian auditing the course. After class I asked him privately why people should want to get involved in terrorism. He asked in reply why Chinese people engaged in guerrilla warfare during the Japanese occupation. That left a deep impression on me. This is a case of someone who lives without knowing what it feels like to have a sore back.

Because in my academic work I insist on scientific method, I think theory must be based on reality. A theory removed from reality may sound fine, but it is in fact not objective. It cannot help us to really understand the world. Indeed, it may lead us to misunderstand. If you look at the current Chinese scholars engaged in studying international trends, you may well find that a high proportion of them make their assessments based on theories. If we constantly reflected on the mistakes in our prediction of international trends, it would assist in ensuring the progress of our international relations studies. Since many people are not accountable for any mistakes in their predictions, they take an optimistic view of the international situation. It may sound great, progressive, civilized, or moral to be optimistic about the international situation, but I think that to make assessments of the international situation that do not conform to reality and then to fail to verify them is not worthy of a scholar.

Lu XIN: Some people describe you as a specialist in making predictions on international questions. Which are the occasions you are most proud of?

YAN XUETONG: I predicted that Lee Tenghui would go from covert to overt support for a policy of independence for Taiwan. I predicted that the Kuomintang would be defeated and Chen Shui-bian would be elected. I predicted he would be reelected for a second term in office. I predicted that Pakistan would certainly carry out a nuclear test in response to India's. In 1997, I predicted that the Clinton government would not agree to restoring reciprocal state visits between China and the United States. In 2005, I predicted that Sino-Japanese relations would continue to deteriorate. When I moved to Tsinghua University, I began to make quantitative predictions and the percentage of my predictions that were correct rose.

I think that predicting is especially enjoyable and very challenging. A forecaster must constantly keep an eye on shifts in circumstances, always worrying what to do if he is wrong and ready to analyze why he is wrong, so people are always kept on their toes. It is a little like playing the stock market. The difference is that there is no material benefit involved, only mental enjoyment. Using scientific, quantitative prediction methods allows us constantly to increase the accuracy of our predictions. Our current quantitative predictions have already reached world-class level, especially in our method of quantitative assessment of bilateral relationships. Our work can stand alongside that of others in the world.

Lu XIN: You seem to be particularly enthusiastic speaking about this issue. Maybe it has something to do with your personality. You like being challenged.

YAN XUETONG: This may be wherein the special feature of international relations studies lies. To study international relations means to predict the developing trends in the international situation. Everybody judges you on whether your predictions are accurate or not. The predictions are objective and are a most plausible proof. Making public predictions is a risky business. Making public predictions about the international situation is a bit like adults playing games——it is real and enjoyable. Especially so when we use scientific methods to make a prediction. According to the results we can summarize the experience of our method and improve our method of prediction. It is especially meaningful to invent a method of research, just as interesting as inventing a new weapon.

Lu XIN: But at the same time you have many critics and opponents.

YAN XUETONG: That is because our study of international relations is still at the same level as the big debate in America in the 1960s, namely, a debate between science and tradition. Currently, the traditional school is mainstream in China and the scientific school is subsidiary. There are not many people who can use quantitative methods, and those who can make quantitative predictions are even rarer. Yet I think that the development of this field in China will be like that in the States. There is no getting away from the increasingly scientific way of studying international relations. The scientific school will become mainstream. Knowledge lacking predictive power cannot become a science. Faulty predictability simply shows that the scientific nature of this science is not yet strong. Predictive power is an important criterion in judging whether a given discipline is scientific or not. Philosophy has no predictive power, so philosophy is not science.

In making predictions we do not simply rely on our minds to think. Our current quantitative predictions achieve an accuracy rate of 65 percent or more. If to this are added predictions that are not so risky, then our accuracy rate is more than 80 percent. We do hear criticism, but this criticism is meaningless because it is from laypeople. For instance, people say that even if we reached a prediction accuracy of 99 percent, we still could not rule out the 1 percent of other possibilities. It would still amount to two possible outcomes, which is not substantively different from predicting two possible outcomes. Of course, prediction accuracy can never reach 100 percent. What attains 100 percent accuracy is a law, which does not need prediction. Predictive science progresses step by step. For instance, accuracy going up from 65 percent to 75 percent is a sign of progress in knowledge for humanity and an improvement in the strength of prediction. It should not be said that an accuracy rate of 80 percent is essentially the same as a rate of 50 percent. Our predictions cannot possibly be 100 percent accurate. The accuracy of our predictions cannot reach 100 percent, but our accuracy rate is more than 70 percent, which is much higher than a rate of 50 percent.

The use of scientific method also carries an important social significance. It shows people that international studies need the scientific method. Not just anybody can do it. Before studying the method, most students imagine that anyone can do international relations studies, but after studying the method they learn that the study of international relations is a specialized science.

Lu Xin: In fact, in China more weight is given to the tradition of the arts. Have you sought to find a point of meeting between the sciences and the arts?

Yan Xuetong: Yes, but it is very hard. To combine scientific method and traditional Chinese thought requires a good foundation in classical Chinese. There are very few scholars of my age in China whose knowledge of classical Chinese is good. We have even regressed in our ability to read classical Chinese. It is very difficult for people of my age to combine ancient Chinese thought and modern social sciences research. My own knowledge does not extend that far. I once thought of combining the Eight Trigrams and scientific prediction, but after trying I realized I did not know what the principle of the Eight Trigrams was.

Lu Xin: Some people say that you are a hawk.

Yan Xuetong: This is said with regard to my views on Taiwan. I think the issue of Taiwan touches on China's very existence, so it is essential to maintain a hard line. One of my colleagues sums up my views as "Republican in foreign affairs and Democrat in domestic affairs." That is not quite accurate, but I do find that I am inconsistent in my views of foreign and domestic policy.

Lu Xin: How are you a nationalist? Some scholars avoid talking about this.

Yan Xuetong: I think I am a rather typical nationalist. Some people think that *nationalism* is a bad word. I disagree. *Nationalism* and *patriotism* are just like *surplus value* and *profit*: different names for the same thing. *Patriotism* and *nationalism* in fact refer to the same thing.

Lu Xin: What influence do you think your strong nationalism has on your scholarship?

Yan Xuetong: A great influence. For example, hegemony is a perennial issue in international studies. American scholars concentrate on studying how to maintain a durable hegemony, and many Chinese scholars also study hegemony from this angle. I advise my doctoral students in studying how to replace one hegemony with another. My nationalism affects my choice of research topic and the aspect of the topic I study. I choose topics in international relations that are strongly relevant to China. Among these relevant questions, I choose to study what is most relevant to China's core interest. I do not think that a feeling of nationalism leads me to say what is not true. As I said before, my principle is that I can keep silent rather than telling the truth, but I cannot tell lies or say something against my conscience.

LU XIN: How do you cope with the relationship between academic research and actual politics?

YAN XUETONG: Previously, Chinese international relations studies was more inclined toward policy and tended to overlook theory. Only now are there some people engaged in theoretical research. Research work should be allocated out. People engaged in theory should keep to theory without getting into policy; people engaged in policy need only to understand theory and should apply themselves wholly to policy. They do not need to bother much about creating theories. The third kind of person works on getting theory and policy to cooperate. The study of international relations is like other disciplines: it is becoming more specialized, more normalized, and more compartmentalized. I think the main problem faced by China's international relations studies is not that of combining theory and policy, but that it is not yet sufficiently specialized. Many people lack their own specialized research direction. They write articles in many fields and fail to enter into any area in depth. My suggestion is that one should concentrate on one's own specialty and say little about what lies outside one's own area. Specialization in small areas is a measure of whether our study of international relations is becoming more scientific. When we find that there are more and more small areas of special study within the discipline of international relations, when the specializations are more finely defined, that will be a sign that we have developed.

INFLUENCES ON YAN'S ACADEMIC CAREER

LU XIN: How do you see the personality of a scholar and his particular interests influencing academic research?

YAN XUETONG: People's personalities differ and what they are interested in differs, so they are inclined to study different things. This contributes to diversity in scholarship. For instance, I like hard issues such as power, war, peace, and security, but some people prefer soft issues: culture, ethics, guidelines, and international norms.

I tend to be fairly direct myself and so my articles are also quite direct. I do not like going around corners. Also, I prefer things that adhere to strict logic. Some people say I simply adhere to formal logic and do not care for dialectical logic. I do not like dialectical logic because it lacks an objective standard. Formal logic admits objective verification, whereas dialectical logic does not. Formal logic is rigorous. If there is a problem with any step in the argument, then the conclusion does not stand. But dialectical logic can make any kind of argument correct with no logical steps. Anything can make a conclusion reasonable. Using dialectical logic, all conclusions can be rendered correct or incorrect. From a scientific point of view, what is reasonable depends on there being what is not reasonable. If there is nothing that is not reasonable, then how can we know what is reasonable?

Some people think my colors are too definite. This is a personal matter. I am prepared to admit mistakes in scholarship. In *Shijie Zhishi* (World Affairs), I published an article stating where my predictions had gone wrong. I think there are two reasons why people make ambiguous predictions. The first is that they have not yet grasped their own field of knowledge. Their knowledge is inadequate to make a judgment about a particular issue. The second is that they are concerned with political gains and losses. I am not afraid of making a mistake. This is related to my scientific approach. All scientists know that research is a process of constantly making errors. Research is to find where the errors are and to analyze them. The individual stance and point of view of someone who upholds a scientific approach are definitely clear. People who think that the study of international relations is politics rather than science have difficulty adopting a clear stance. I never posit two very different possible outcomes because I reckon that amounts to saying nothing.

International relations are complicated. It is difficult to arrive at an accurate conclusion. Even using scientific method it is hard to be very accurate, but at least the use of scientific method will increase our knowledge more than not using it. For instance, we suppose that when the trade of a given state with another amounts to 10 percent to 30 percent of its total trade, it is in a situation of dependency. The range 10 percent to 30 percent is not precise, but it helps us to know the upper and lower limits of dependency, namely, that if one state's trade with another state is more than 30 percent of the first state's trade, the first state is clearly dependent on the second, whereas if it is less than 10 percent, that does not constitute dependence. This is better than a notion of dependency that does not rely on figures. Using scientific method does not necessarily mean that we can define the critical point at which things change in nature, but it can allow us to summarize the critical area. This is better than not knowing the critical area at all.

Lu Xin: How to you understand the term *scholar*? How do you define yourself?

Yan Xuetong: First, a scholar is not the same as a literatus. The difference is that a literatus writes articles to express his thought whereas a scholar uses scientific method to argue for a logical idea. A scholar may think of many things but not commit all of them to writing. A scholar does not write articles about what he has not studied. A literatus writes articles on anything he has an interest in. A literatus's writing is not constrained by his specialty. A literatus is bold enough to express his opinion on any matter beyond his specialty, whereas a scholar make remarks only on his own specialty. A scholar always restricts himself to a very narrow area of knowledge.

Furthermore, a scholar is not the same as a specialist. A specialist is someone who has very independent views in one particular field of knowledge. His level of specialization must go well beyond that of common scholars. I think that being a scholar is a mark of a person's character, including features such as being hard-working, careful, and serious and not drawing rash conclusions. A specialist has reached a high standard for a scholar in a particular specialty. There can be only a very few specialists in any given field. It cannot be that all scholars are specialists, just as not all actors are artists. I think that I am a scholar and only on a very few specific questions can I claim to be a specialist.

Lu Xin: Because of the special characteristics of international relations, many scholars in the field belong to think tanks. What do you think about this?

YAN XUETONG: A think tank serves to provide professional advice on policy. I do not think that I myself have any direct impact of China's policy makers. I just reckon that my articles have some influence on a few people who work in the relevant government departments. Maybe they have an indirect influence on policy, but I do not have a direct influence.

The influence of a scholar comes through his published articles. In the Chinese political establishment there is no system of think tanks, strictly speaking. In France, by contrast, the government provides every minister with a sum of money to hire policy advisors. This is rather like the old Chinese system of personal legal assistants. These policy advisors constitute a think tank. Since the founding of the new China in 1949, the state has not allowed high officials to have their own personal advisors or to rely on nongovernmental advisory organizations. Even their secretaries are strictly limited to the government departmental staff. Scholars may take part in conferences and air particular views, and they may influence the way other people think, but this does not mean that they play the role of a think tank. To exist, a think tank requires a clear and definite organized channel of communication. Advisors who are unpaid are not part of a think tank in the proper sense of this term.

LU XIN: Do you think a scholar could be part of a think tank or be a policy advisor?

YAN XUETONG: Not only can he, he should be. Giving advice on policy is the responsibility of the intelligentsia to society. I think that if we were to revive the personal legal assistant system and establish a system of think tanks it would enable policymaking to be more scientific.

I want to be both a scholar and a policy advisor myself. The term *intelligentsia* means someone who has received an education in the humanities, has a sense of responsibility to society, and undertakes criticism of the government. So it is said that the allotted task of the intelligentsia is to critique government policy. The intelligentsia are not those who have merely studied or are professionally engaged in study. The meaning of *intelligentsia* is primarily people with a sense of social responsibility. Nobel Prize winners do not necessarily belong to the intelligentsia. The term comes from Russia and refers to those people who met in cafés to discuss affairs of state. They constantly critique the government and take on society's burdens. They are not people who have made great scientific discoveries. The use of the term in China tends to obscure the true nature of the intelligentsia, because it refers merely to people who can read. Moreover, the genuine intelligentsia are not just critical of the government; they also tell the government what to do and how to do it. The standard of good policy advice is that it is practical, effective, and less costly.

Lu XIN: According to your definition, does China today have a system of think tanks and, if so, would you be willing to take part?

YAN XUETONG: If there were, I would take part. The research institutions attached to our government agencies are not think tanks in the strict sense. Their main task is to carry out policies, not to furnish ideas. To undertake the work of a think tank is to exercise social responsibility. This kind of work influences academic research but it has a broader social significance. Academic research alone cannot have such a direct social role.

Lu XIN: Scholars of your generation have a marked sense of social responsibility. Unconsciously you have a sense of "being concerned for all under heaven." In my view, important historical events leave an indelible mark on people of the generation that experienced them. A scholar, then, will naturally be influenced as to what he produces. How do you see the matter?

YAN XUETONG: The Cultural Revolution is without a doubt the greatest and most influential historical event people of my generation in China experienced. This is something all people of my generation experienced. The Cultural Revolution gravely damaged China's traditional culture. I think that the greatest social danger in China today is hypocrisy. The Cultural Revolution destroyed the millennial ethical tradition of China: its sincerity. People of my generation still have some degree of sincerity because before the Cultural Revolution we had lived in traditional Chinese culture, which valued sincerity in all fields. From the Cultural Revolution onward it has not been so. In politics, people were obliged to say what was false. It was clear that no one wanted to go to the countryside, but every young person was required to say that he desired to stay on the farm for his whole life. It was clear that there was a severe lack of household necessities but each work unit glossed things over and said how wonderful life was. It was clear that a professor knows more than a peasant, but professors were obliged to say that they wanted to go to the village to learn from the peasants. The government forced people to tell lies. You were punished if you did not do so. At the time, I did not say I wanted to stay in the countryside forever, so my recommendation to go to university was annulled by the political instructor of our farm.

This spirit of telling lies left by the Cultural Revolution has had a very bad influence on our study of international relations. The reason why international relations studies is viewed as a form of magic, in which the phenomenon of telling lies is particularly serious, is largely because we lack an overall environment of sincerity. To tell lies now not only does not result in punishment, it even wins society's approval. In the Song Dynasty, China already had a silver check that was like today's personal checks, but now we dare not practice the system of personal checks because of a lack of honesty in society. If China wants to resolve the problem of counterfeiting, it must start by opposing the telling of lies.

Lu XIN: How do you assess the state of your knowledge?

YAN XUETONG: I have two serious shortcomings in my knowledge. The first is that, because of the Cultural Revolution, I did not receive a proper secondary education, with the result that my knowledge of the natural sciences is very poor. I do not have the necessary knowledge of mathematics, physics, or chemistry. This severely restricts the scope and depth of my research. Second, because the May Fourth movement denied traditional culture and because in the 1950s China promoted simplified characters and educational reform, people of my generation are very poor in their knowledge of classical Chinese works. We find reading the old classics very difficult. Inadequacies in knowledge of the natural sciences and of traditional Chinese writings mean that the foundations of my scholarship are narrow; hence, I cannot hope to achieve great academic success.[1]

Appendix 3

Why Is There No Chinese School of International Relations Theory?

Yan Xuetong

In 1987, Huan Xiang, who once served as Zhou Enlai's secretary of foreign affairs, suggested building a Chinese theory of international relations (IR) during an IR theory conference in Shanghai.[1] Since then, Chinese scholars have conducted an internal debate about the necessity and possibility of creating a "Chinese school" of IR theory.[2] During the past thirty years, Chinese scholars have developed a variety of views about the establishment of a Chinese school of IR theory but have created nothing that merits such a title. This phenomenon suggests the question of why there is not a single theory or a series of theories under the rubric of "Chinese school," even though so many Chinese scholars have been advocating one for the past thirty years. This essay attempts to answer this question.

LACK OF A THEORY NAME COINED BY ITS CREATORS

Until now, all known IR theories have been labeled by people other than the creators of the theories themselves. Realism was not named by Hans J. Morgenthau, nor were neo-Marxism by Karl Marx, neorealism by Kenneth Waltz, neoliberalism by Robert Keohane and Joseph S. Nye, constructivism by Alexander Wendt, or the English school by Hedley Bull and Barry Buzan. Waltz mentioned that he hates for others to call his theory *neorealism* and has tried very hard to replace it with *structuralism*.

Unfortunately, he failed to make the name *structuralism* more popular than *neorealism*. In China, most students are often confused by the terms *structuralism* and *functionalism* because they are familiar with the term *neorealism* and hear less about the term *structuralism*. This phenomenon discourages us from expecting that Chinese IR theorists will be able to popularize theories with self-generated titles within the academic community.

This phenomenon is not limited to modern IR studies. It also is evident with ancient Chinese thinking. None of the best-known Chinese theories possess a name coined by their creators. For instance, *Confucianism* was not coined by Confucius, nor was *Taoism* by Laozi, *Legalism* by Shang Yang, or *Mohism* by Mozi. In modern Chinese history, Mao Zedong did not coin the term *Mao Zedong Thought* or *Maoism*. Instead, *Mao Zedong Thought* was coined by Liu Shaoqi and *Maoism* by foreigners.

Thus, it is highly likely that those who are trying to name their own theories under the classification of "Chinese group or school" meet with one of two outcomes: either their theories remain unknown or unrecognized in academic circles or their theories become known by a title that excludes the term *Chinese*.

COUNTRIES ARE RARELY NAMED IN THEORY TITLES

In most cases, a theory of social science is named after its core arguments, creator, or the institution of the creator. For example, neoconservatism derived its name from its stance and arguments, the Truman doctrine from the U.S. president Harry S. Truman, and the Chicago school from the University of Chicago. It is often the case that an IR theory is named after a city because that city has only one advanced university for IR theories. In many cases, advanced universities are named after the city in which they are located. Thus, it is hard to tell if a theory is named after the university or the city. For instance, the term *Florida school* refers to the early stages of constructivism developed by scholars at the University of Florida. The Copenhagen school got its name from the Copenhagen Peace Research Institute.

The case of the English school is debatable. According to Barry Buzan, the term *English school* was not coined in England. The world *English* does not mean "of the United Kingdom."[3] The term *English* has several meanings, and at least two when it refers to geographical location—that is, England and the United Kingdom. England is simply a part of the United Kingdom. When *English school* is translated into Chinese, it becomes *ying-guo xuepai* (school of the United Kingdom). The translation seems to have misled some Chinese scholars into believing that they can develop some IR theories named the "Chinese school."

It is reasonable to name a theoretical school after the name of a university or a city because there is often only one dominant school of IR thought within a city or a university. It would be difficult, however, to use a town or university to name a school of IR theory when there are two or more dominating schools in that town or university. For instance, there is no IR theory named after Berkeley because Waltz and Ernst Hass developed two influential theories—namely, neorealism and cognitive theory—at the University of California, Berkeley. These two groups possess some fundamental differences, and therefore neither has been named after Berkeley. I give this summary with no intention to imply that IR institutions within the United States are less diversified. Actually, that there are so many different theories, even within one research program, indicates the cultivating and diversifying factors of the U.S. IR academic environment.

CHINA'S DIVERSITY IS TOO GREAT FOR A SINGLE IR THEORY

Like the United States, China is rich in both population diversity and philosophical thought. Therefore, it is impossible that a single school of thought or theory can represent the entirety of Chinese thinking. In the last three thousand years, no school of thought has been more powerful than Confucianism. Even Confucianism, however, cannot represent all of Chinese thought. As a result, there is no school of thought within China that has been labeled the "Chinese school." In modern Chinese history, Mao Zedong Thought could be viewed as the most influential school of political theory. Yet, even this school did not gain the name *Chinese school*.

The term *Chinese* seems too broad to fit any theories developed by Chinese scholars. The size of the Chinese population and the length of Chinese history make it very difficult for any school of theory to represent all of this diversity. The title *Chinese* is so massive that no school of theory is able to bear its weight.

We may find some schools of thought or theories have *Chinese* at the beginning of their names, but this was always added as an adjective modifying the original name. "Chinese Socialism" or "Socialism with Chinese characteristics" remains the best-known of these schools of thought. In this case, *Chinese* is just a modification of the given school of theory rather than a reference to a particular school of thought. Some foreign scholars have named my own theories "Chinese neo-communism" or "Chinese neoconservatism."[4] (I prefer to have my theories labeled "Chinese realism," because the basic assumptions of neo-comm or neocon are fundamentally different from my basic arguments.) No matter what the label, however, *Chinese* in these terms means only a branch of that school rather than an independent school.

Currently, those ideas on IR theories developed by scholars at our institute (the Institute of International Studies, Tsinghua University) are referred to as the "Tsinghua school" among the Chinese academic community. The diversity of ideas and thought in Beijing makes it impossible for the Tsinghua school to adopt the name *Beijing school*. It is similar to the situation in Washington, DC, as the city's name is rarely used as a label for any one school of thought. The name of a capital is often used for a governmental political stance or ideology—such as the Washington Consensus and the Beijing Consensus—rather than for an academic theory.

GIVING BIRTH IS MORE IMPORTANT THAN GIVING A NAME

It is understandable that Chinese scholars are uneasy that no influential IR theories have been developed by Chinese scholars. The positive side of this situation is that Chinese scholars have realized their weakness in theoretical studies, while the negative side is that most Chinese scholars do not understand why they have been unable to create theoretical achievements like those of their American colleagues. Every IR theory should be considered like a baby. Before we give birth, we cannot be sure of the name we should give the baby. In my opinion, what Chinese scholars should worry about most is not the name but rather giving birth to the baby.

Why have Chinese scholars not given birth to an IR theory? I suggest three possible academic reasons and one political reason. First, Chinese scholars lack basic methodological training and they have yet to develop systematic explanations for international phenomena. Second, Chinese IR scholars, at least in some cases, lack training in traditional Chinese political thought. As a result, they are unable to master Western or Chinese political theories as Western scholars do with their own traditional political thought. Third, there are too few theoretical debates among Chinese scholars; thus they cannot improve theories by learning from critiques. The political reason remains that China is not as strong as the United States. Thus, Chinese IR concepts and ideas are unable to garner the same attention from the rest of the world.

The hope of Chinese IR theoretical study lies in rediscovering traditional Chinese IR thought. Chinese scholars have an advantage in reading Chinese ancient writings and, thus, are able to have a more nuanced and perhaps better understanding than their Western colleagues. Recently, more and more Chinese scholars have developed an interest in rediscovering ancient Chinese IR concepts, with an increasing number of journals publishing articles under the title "Ancient Chinese IR Thought." It is my hope that Chinese scholars will develop strong IR theories in the next five years. This being said, however, even if Chinese scholars achieve this goal in the future, it is not to be expected that these new theories will fall under the name *Chinese school*.

REVOLUTION VERSUS MODIFICATION OF IR THEORY

In the past thirty years, we have witnessed Chinese scholars advocating a Chinese school of IR, but few of them have created any new theories. Some Chinese scholars have their own names attached to an original theoretical argument, such as Zhao Tingyang to "Tianxia" and Zheng Bijian to "Peaceful Rise," but they are not affiliated with the group advocating a "Chinese school." Building a new school of thought in IR requires hard work to deepen our understanding of international reality. Rather than pursuing a national school of thought in IR, Chinese scholars should focus on investigating theoretical and empirical puzzles in existing IR literature and, hopefully, contributing to the theory building of IR scholarship in the future.

There are three metatheoretical perspectives in appraising scientific progress. Thomas Kuhn believes that the great leaps of progress made by science are not cumulative and continuous but rather revolutionary, in that an old paradigm is overthrown by a new one.[5] Some Chinese scholars hold the Kuhnian view of science and hope that the Chinese school of IR can somehow replace Western IR theory as a new paradigm of IR. This revolutionary view of scientific progress in IR has two problems, however.

First, the prerequisite for the Kuhnian paradigm shift is that the existing dominant paradigm shows unfixable flaws. It is still too early to proclaim the death of Western IR theory, though it faces many empirical and theoretical puzzles. Second, the application of Kuhn's metatheory within IR has been criticized extensively because of Kuhn's problematic claim of "incommensurability" between paradigms.[6]

In appraising IR theory, Lakatos's methodology of scientific research programs (MSRP) and Laudan's puzzle-solving research tradition are two prevailing metatheories. Lakatos defines a series of theories as a research program, which consists of an irrefutable "hard core," negative heuristics, positive heuristics, and a protective belt of auxiliary hypotheses.[7] Instead of arguing for one dominant paradigm in the scientific community, as Kuhn does, Lakatos believes that there may be many coexisting research programs in the scientific field.

In IR, we see the coexistence of three dominant research programs: realism, liberalism, and constructivism. Lakatos argues that the difference between two research programs lies in their different irrefutable "hard cores," that is, key assumptions protected by the rules of negative heuristics. If Chinese scholars intend to develop their own research program, different from existing ones, they should first develop a different hard core for their theory. Here, traditional Chinese thought may be of assistance to Chinese scholars in developing a different research program in IR.

Some scholars criticize Lakatos's MSRP in the application of social sciences such as IR. For example, the method of defining a hard core for social science theory remains a debated question. In IR, as Elman and Elman point out, even for the most widely accepted research program, such as neorealism, scholars could not achieve consensus on what the hard core is.[8] Therefore, some scholars, such as Waltz, question the applicability of Lakatos's MSRP to IR research and advocate Laudan's metatheory of research traditions.[9]

Laudan criticizes Lakatos's MSRP as too strict and argues that theories should be loosely grouped into different research traditions, according to shared key assumptions and methods.[10] Research traditions are neither explanatory nor predictive, nor directly testable. Although not falsifiable, a research tradition can be assessed by its fruitfulness, that is, whether theories of a research tradition can solve more empirical and theoretical puzzles. The problem-solving criterion is more liberal than Lakatos's MSRP. Still, some scholars criticize Laudan's criterion as too permissive to be used in appraising and guiding the development of IR theory.

Chinese scholars, I argue, should rely on both Lakatos's MSRP and Laudan's problem-solving criterion to guide their research. The final goal of Chinese scholars is to develop a new research program, that is, a series of theories with a shared hard core, as Lakatos's MSRP suggests. The first step for Chinese scholars, however, is to follow Laudan's suggestion that they focus on solving existing theoretical and empirical puzzles by wisely using traditional Chinese thought and literature. For example, traditional Chinese thinking offers a different understanding of hegemony than mainstream IR theory does. Different typologies of hegemony within traditional Chinese thought may shed some light on our understanding of the rise and the fall of U.S. hegemony within the system. If Chinese scholars can successfully solve existing research puzzles in IR from a similar perspective, then this shared view has the potential to develop into a new hard core for a new research program.

Although I am not sure whether it will be named the "Chinese school" of IR, the contribution of traditional Chinese thought to IR should and will be recognized. The positive trend is that more and more Chinese scholars are devoting their energies to studying traditional Chinese thought on IR. They are working to enrich modern IR theories with traditional Chinese thought, using modern methodology.

In fact, the *Chinese Journal of International Politics* and *Guoji Zhengzhi Kexue* (Scientific Studies of International Politics) are two IR journals within China that consistently publish papers using this modern methodology. During 2007–2009, they published several articles on traditional Chinese IR thinking. If we envision IR as a scientific inquiry, then IR theory should be universally applied. If we do not need a Chinese school of physics or chemistry, why should we need a Chinese school of IR theory?

Notes

Introduction

1. Quoted from the interview with Yan Xuetong in appendix 2 of this book.

2. Mark Leonard, *What Does China Think?* (London: Fourth Estate, 2008), 139, 90–91.

3. Quoted from chapter 4.

4. Yan recognizes that predictions in intenational relations cannot be 100 percent accurate, but he argues that it is important to strive for as much accuracy as possible with the use of scientific methods, and he notes that most of his predictions have been correct. In 2008, however, he publicly apologized to readers for having (wrongly) predicted that military conflict between Taiwan and mainland China would break out in the 2000–2008 period. In that article he explains why the situation changed for the better, predicts peaceful relations over the following eight years (even if the United States continues to sell arms to Taiwan), and ends with the hope that he will not have to note another mistaken prediction in 2016 (www.chinaelections.org/newsinfo.asp?newsid =129345).

5. See www.fcnl.org/issues/item.php?item_id=2252&issue_id=54.

Chapter 1

1. Many scholars doubt the authenticity of the works of the pre-Qin masters. Whether the ideas in these writings are those of the masters themselves or are ones attributed to them several hundred years later does not, however, affect our being able to learn from them and use them to enrich contemporary international relations theory. The time when these ideas were formed does not affect our use of them to understand today's international politics. Hence, in this chapter I assume that the words recorded in these works are indeed those of the masters themselves.

2. Liu Zehua and Ge Quan, eds., *Zhongguo zhengzhi sixiangshi yanjiu* [Studies in the history of Chinese political thought] (Wuhan: Hubei Educational Press, 2006), 1; Liang Qichao, *Xianqin Zhengzhi Sixiangshi* [A history of pre-Qin political thought] (Beijing: Zhonghua Shuju and Shanghai Shudian, 1986) (based on the 1936 edition by Zhonghua Shuju; original version published 1922).

3. Liang, *Xianqin Zhengzhi Sixiangshi*, 155, 156. His quotations come from *Mencius* 1 *King Hui of Liang* A6 (cf. James Legge, *The Chinese Classics* [London and Oxford: Frowde and Oxford University Press, 1895], 2:136) and *Mozi* 11 *Conforming to Superiors* A.

4. Liang, *Xianqin Zhengzhi Sixiangshi*, 157–159. Quotations are from *Laozi* 31 and *Mencius* 7 *Exhausting the Mind* B2 (cf. Legge, *The Chinese Classics*, 2:478).

5. Yang Kuan, *Zhanguo Shi* [A history of the Warring States] (Shanghai: Shanghai People's Press, 2003), 473–485.

6. Ibid., 477.

7. Yang Youqiong, *Zhongguo Zhengzhi Sixiangshi* [A history of Chinese political thought] (Shanghai: Commercial Press, 1937); Sa Mengwu, *Zhongguo Zhengzhi Sixiangshi* [A history of Chinese political thought] (Beijing: Oriental Press, 2008); Cao Deben, ed., *Zhongguo Zhengzhi Sixiangshi* [A history of Chinese political thought] (Beijing: Higher Education Press, 1999); Xiao Gongquan, *Zhongguo Zhengzhi Sixiangshi* [A history of Chinese political thought] (Beijing: New Star Press, 2005).

8. Liu Zehua and Ge Quan, eds., *Zhongguo Gudai Sixiangshi* [A history of ancient Chinese thought] (Tianjin: Nankai University Press, 2001), 56.

9. Liu Zehua, *Zhongguo Zhengzhi Sixiangshiji* [An anthology of the history of Chinese political thought] (Beijing: People's Press, 2008), 176. Quotation from *Guanzi* 23 *Conversations of the Hegemon* (cf. W. A. Rickett, *Guanzi: Political, Economic, and Philosophical Essays from Early China* [Princeton, NJ: Princeton University Press, 1985], 1:357).

10. He Maochun, *Zhongguo Waijiao Tongshi* [A history of China's external relations] (Beijing: Chinese Academy of Social Sciences Press, 1996), 37–43.

11. Ibid., 41.

12. Ye Zicheng, *Chunqiu Zhangguo Shiqi de Zhongguo Waijiao Sixiang* [Chinese diplomatic thought in the Spring and Autumn and Warring States periods] (Hong Kong: Hong Kong Social Sciences Press, 2003), 10.

13. Ibid., preface.

14. Ibid., 30, 37, 54.

15. Sun Xuefeng and Yang Zixiao, "Hanfeizi de Guojiajian Zhengzhi Sixiang" [Hanfeizi's interstate political thought], *Guoji Zhengzhi Kexue* [Scientific Studies of International Politics], no. 2 (2008): 96n4.

16. Chen Qi and Huang Yuxing, "Chunqiu Shiqi de Guojiajian Ganshe" [Intervention between states in the Spring and Autumn Period], *Guoji Zhengzhi Kexue* [Scientific Studies of International Politics], no. 1 (2008): 70n167.

17. Piao Bingjiu, "*Liji* de Hexie Shijie Sixiang" [A harmonious world according to the *Record of rites*], *Guoji Zhengzhi Kexue* [Scientific Studies of International Politics], no. 3 (2008): 69–70.

18. Liu Jiangyong, "*Guanzi* Guojiajian Zhengzhi Sixiang Chutan" [A preliminary study of interstate political thought in the *Guanzi*], *Guoji Zhengzhi Kexue* [Scientific Studies of International Politics], no. 3 (2008): 55.

19. Chen Yudan, "Guoji Guanxixue Zhong de Jingdian yu Chanshi" [Classic readings in international relations, with a commentary], *Guoji Zhengzhi Kexue* [Scientific Studies of International Politics], no. 3 (2008): 111.

20. *Mozi* 19 *Against Aggression* C.

21. *Laozi* 80.

22. *Guanzi* 23 *Conversations of the Hegemon* (cf. Rickett, *Guanzi*, 1:357, 361).

23. *Hanfeizi* 6 *Having Standards*.

24. *Hanfeizi* 49 *Five Vermin*.

25. *Analects* 12 *Yan Yuan* 1.

26. *Analects* 14 *Xian Asked* 42.

27. *Mencius* 4 *Li Lou* A3 (cf. Legge, *The Chinese Classics*, 2:293–294).

28. *Xunzi* 11 *Humane Authority and Hegemony*.

29. *Xunzi* 10 *Enriching the State*. *Distinction* refers to class or grade.

30. *Hanfeizi* 49 *Five Vermin*.

31. *Guanzi* 15 *Importance of Issued Orders* (cf. Rickett, *Guanzi*, 1:245–246).

32. *Xunzi* 10 *Enriching the State*.

33. Ibid.

34. Ibid.

35. *Mozi* 14 *Impartial Love* A.

36. *Mozi* 12 *Conforming to Superiors* B.

37. *Analects* 16 *Ji Shi* 1.

38. *Mencius* 4 *Li Lou* A3 (cf. Legge, *The Chinese Classics*, 2:294).

39. *Laozi* 46.

40. *Laozi* 80.

41. *Laozi* 46.

42. *Laozi* 31.

43. *Mozi* 14 *Impartial Love* A.

44. *Hanfeizi* 49 *Five Vermin*.

45. *Hanfeizi* 46 *Six Crimes*.

46. Zhang Lu, "Zhongxi Zhengyi Zhanzheng de Sixiang Bijiao" [A comparative study of just war thought in China and the West], *Xiandai Guoji Guanxi* [Contemporary International Relations], no. 4 (2005): 17.

47. *Laozi* 31.

48. *Hanfeizi* 36 *Problems* 1.

49. Huang Shouan, Duan Fude, et al., *Zhongguo Gudai Jiu Da Sixiang Xuepai Jiyao* [A summary of the nine schools of thought in ancient China] (Beijing: People's Liberation Army Press, 2002), 31.

50. *Xunzi* 9 *Humane Governance*.

51. *Xunzi* 23 *Human Nature Is Evil*.

52. *Xunzi* 15 *Debating the Military*.

53. *Guanzi* 17 *Methods of Warfare* (cf. Rickett, *Guanzi*, 1:270).

54. *The Elder Dai's Record of Rites: Employing Troops*.

55. Huang Pumin, "Xianqin Zhuzi Junshi Sixiang Yitong Chutan" [A preliminary comparative study of the military thought of the pre-Qin masters], *Lishi Yanjiu* [Historical Research], no. 5 (1996): 76.

56. *The Elder Dai's Record of Rites: Employing Troops*.

57. *Mencius* 6 *Gaozi* B7 (cf. Legge, *The Chinese Classics*, 2:436).

58. *Mencius* 7 *Exhausting the Mind* B2 (cf. Legge, *The Chinese Classics*, 2:478).

59. Ye, *Chunqiu Zhangguo Shiqi de Zhongguo Waijiao Sixiang*, 177.

60. *Laozi* 80.

61. *Laozi* 3.

62. Francis Fukuyama, *The End of History and the Last Man* (Harmondsworth: Penguin, 1992), 336.

63. *Mozi* 15 *Impartial Love* B.

64. *Mozi* 11 *Conforming to Superiors* A.

65. Ibid.

66. *Xunzi* 10 *Enriching the State.*

67. *Xunzi* 9 *Humane Governance.*

68. *Analects* 14 *Xian Asked* 41.

69. *Analects* 12 *Yan Yuan* 1.

70. *Guanzi* 15 *Importance of Issued Orders* (cf. Rickett, *Guanzi*, 1:247).

71. *Hanfeizi* 49 *Five Vermin.*

72. *Hanfeizi* 53 *Implementing Commands.*

73. *Guanzi* 15 *Importance of Issued Orders* (cf. Rickett, *Guanzi*, 1:245).

74. *Hanfeizi* 9 *Eight Evils.*

75. *Hanfeizi* 49 *Five Vermin.*

76. *Guanzi* 23 *Conversations of the Hegemon* (cf. Rickett, *Guanzi*, 1:357).

77. *Analects* 16 *Ji Shi* 1.

78. *Xunzi* 9 *Humane Governance.*

79. *Mencius* 2 *Gongsun Chou* A3 (cf. Legge, *The Chinese Classics*, 2:196–197).

80. *Laozi* 46.

81. *Laozi* 51.

82. *Laozi* 54.

83. *Guanzi* 23 *Conversations of the Hegemon* (cf. Rickett, *Guanzi*, 1:362).

84. *Analects* 14 *Xian Asked* 22.

85. *Xunzi* 15 *Debating the Military.*

86. *Mencius* 2 *Gongsun Chou* B8 (cf. Legge, *The Chinese Classics*, 2:223).

87. *Laozi* 31.

88. *Mozi* 14 *Impartial Love* A.

89. *Hanfeizi* 1 *The First Meeting with the King of Qin.*

90. *Mozi* 13 *Conforming to Superiors* C.

91. *Mozi* 20 *Economy in Expenditure* A.

92. *Guanzi* 1 *Shepherding the People* (cf. Rickett, *Guanzi*, 1:56).

93. *Guanzi* 23 *Conversations of the Hegemon* (cf. Rickett, *Guanzi*, 1:357).

94. Ibid. (cf. Rickett, *Guanzi*, 1:358).

95. *Record of Rites*: Li Yun.

96. Ibid.

97. *Odes* II *Minor Odes* 6.1 North Mountain (cf. Legge, *The Chinese Classics*, 360).

98. *The Doctrine of the Mean and Harmony* 28 (cf. Legge, *The Chinese Classics*, 424).

99. *Analects* 16 *Ji Shi* 2.

100. *Xunzi* 18 *Correcting: A Discussion.*

101. Ibid.

102. Ibid.

103. *Mencius* 7 *Exhausting the Mind* B13 (cf. Legge, *The Chinese Classics*, 483).

104. *Laozi* 57.

105. *Laozi* 29.

106. *Hanfeizi* 49 *Five Vermin*.

107. *Hanfeizi* 1 *The First Meeting with the King of Qin*.

108. *Hanfeizi* 49 *Five Vermin*.

109. *Hanfeizi* 54 *Yardsticks for the Mind*.

110. *Mozi* 21 *Economy in Expenditure* B.

111. *Mozi* 3 *On Dyeing*.

112. *Guanzi* 23 *Conversations of the Hegemon* (cf. Rickett, *Guanzi*, 1:356).

113. *Guanzi* 17 *Methods of Warfare* (cf. Rickett, *Guanzi*, 1:270).

114. *Guanzi* 23 *Conversations of the Hegemon* (cf. Rickett, *Guanzi*, 1:357).

115. *Mencius* 2 *Gongsun Chou* A3 (cf. Legge, *The Chinese Classics*, 2:196).

116. *Xunzi* 11 *Humane Authority and Hegemony*.

117. *Xunzi* 9 *Humane Governance*.

118. *Xunzi* 11 *Humane Authority and Hegemony*.

119. *Analects* 14 *Xian Asked* 16.

120. *Analects* 14 *Xian Asked* 17.

121. *Analects* 14 *Xian Asked* 42.

122. *Analects* 15 *Duke Ling of Wei* 5.

123. *Laozi* 66.

124. *Laozi* 78.

125. *Laozi* 66.

126. *Stratagems of the Warring States* 3 (*Qin* 1) 7.

127. *Guanzi* 23 *Conversations of the Hegemon* (cf. Rickett, *Guanzi*, 1:359–360).

128. *Laozi* 59.

129. *Mencius* 1 *King Hui of Liang* A7 (cf. Legge, *The Chinese Classics*, 2:147).

130. *Xunzi* 9 *Humane Governance*.

131. *Hanfeizi* 54 *Yardsticks for the Mind*.

132. *Mozi* 8 *Appointing the Worthy* A.

133. *Analects* 12 *Yan Yuan* 7.

134. *Laozi* 59.

135. *Analects* 2 *The Practice of Governance* 1.

136. *Mencius* 1 *King Hui of Liang* A5 (cf. Legge, *The Chinese Classics*, 2:135, 136).

137. *Xunzi* 11 *Humane Authority and Hegemony*.

138. *Mozi* 8 *Appointing the Worthy* A.

139. *Hanfeizi* 6 *Having Standards*.

140. *Hanfeizi* 49 *Five Vermin*.

141. *Hanfeizi* 27 *Employing People*.

142. *Guanzi* 16 *Conforming to the Law* (cf. Rickett, *Guanzi*, 1:259).

143. *Guanzi* 64 *Comments on Attendant Circumstances*.

144. *Guanzi* 23 *Conversations of the Hegemon* (cf. Rickett, *Guanzi*, 1:360).

145. *Hanfeizi* 6 *Having Standards.*

146. *Guanzi* 23 *Conversations of the Hegemon* (cf. Rickett, *Guanzi*, 1:357).

147. *Mencius* 4 *Li Lou* A3 (cf. Legge, *The Chinese Classics*, 2:293–294).

148. *Xunzi* 11 *Humane Authority and Hegemony.*

149. *Xunzi* 11 *Humane Authority and Hegemony.*

150. *Mozi* 3 *On Dyeing.*

151. *Guanzi* 23 *Conversations of the Hegemon* (cf. Rickett, *Guanzi*, 1:360).

152. Ibid. (cf. Rickett, *Guanzi*, 1:357).

153. *Analects* 2 *The Practice of Governance* 19.

154. *Mencius* 2 *Gongsun Chou* A5 (cf. Legge, *The Chinese Classics*, 2:199, 201).

155. *Xunzi* 24 *The Prince.*

156. *Laozi* 57.

157. *Laozi* 3.

158. *Hanfeizi* 49 *Five Vermin.*

159. *Hanfeizi* 46 *Six Crimes.*

160. Robert Kagan, "The Benevolent Empire," *Foreign Policy*, no. 111 (June 1998): 26.

161. Walter Lippmann, *U.S. Foreign Policy: Shield of the Republic* (Boston: Little, Brown & Co., 1943), 10; Paul Kennedy, *The Rise and Fall of the Great Powers: Economic Change and Military Conflict from 1500 to 2000* (New York: Random House, 1987), 535.

162. Jack Snyder, *The Myths of Empire: Domestic Politics and International Ambition* (New York: Cornell University Press, 1991), 60–61.

163. *Guanzi* 23 *Conversations of the Hegemon* (cf. Rickett, *Guanzi*, 1:357).

164. Alexander Wendt, *Social Theory of International Politics* (Cambridge: Cambridge University Press, 1999), chapter 7.

CHAPTER 2

1. Ye Zicheng, *Chunqiu Zhangguo Shiqi de Zhongguo Waijiao Sixiang* [Chinese diplomatic thought in the Spring and Autumn and Warring States periods] (Hong Kong: Hong Kong Social Sciences Press, 2003), 315–330.

2. This essay concentrates on Xunzi's interstate political philosophy from the perspective of international relations theory and hence has no intention of discussing historical issues and textual criticism. Historians generally rely on Wang Xianqian's (1842–1918) *Xunzi jijie* [Collected notes on the "Xunzi"] (1891); therefore, in this essay quotations from the *Xunzi* are from Wang Xianqian's edition, as edited by Shen Xiaohuan and Wang Xingxian. The reading of the texts cited is indebted to Yang Liuqiao, *Xunzi guyi* ["Xunzi": Notes and translation] (1985); Wang Tianhai, *Xunzi xiaoshi* ["Xunzi": Edited and annotated]; Jiang Nanhua and Yang Hanqing, *Xunzi quanyi* [A complete translation of the "Xunzi"]; and Gao Changshan's translation and edition of *Xunzi*.

3. Xunzi's ideas formed in the Warring States Period. The feudal states of the time were very much like modern states in having the three factors of a people, a territory, and a government, but they lacked sovereignty. Therefore there is a slight difference

between the terms *interstate* of that time and *international* today. But now the term *international* is widely used to express the meaning of "among states," whereas the term *interstate* is seldom used in modern international relations literature. In this essay, *interstate* is used for ancient times and *international* for the present.

4. The term *ba* used by Xunzi is similar to the English word *hegemony* as it is used in contemporary international relations discourse. It has no pejorative sense. Thus in this essay the term *hegemony* has no connotation of wishing to invade or bully small states.

5. *Xunzi* 11 *Humane Authority and Hegemony.*

6. Ibid.

7. *Xunzi* 24 *The Prince.*

8. *Xunzi* 9 *Humane Governance.*

9. Alexander Wendt, *Social Theory of International Politics* (Cambridge: Cambridge University Press, 1999), 250.

10. *Xunzi* 11 *Humane Authority and Hegemony.*

11. *Xunzi* 9 *Humane Governance.*

12. *Xunzi* 18 *Correcting: A Discussion.*

13. Yan Xuetong, *Zhongguo Guojia Liyi Fenxi* [An analysis of China's national interest] (Tianjin: Tianjin People's Press, 1997), 4–6.

14. *Xunzi* 18 *Correcting: A Discussion.*

15. *Xunzi* 11 *Humane Authority and Hegemony.*

16. Pp = perceived power, C = critical mass, E = economic capability, M = military capability, S = strategic purpose, W = will to pursue national strategy. See Ray S. Cline, *World Power Assessment 1977: Calculus of Strategic Drift* (Boulder, CO: Westview, 1977).

17. *Xunzi* 7 *Confucius.*

18. *Xunzi* 10 *Enriching the State.* Xunzi came from an agricultural society in which agriculture was seen as the most important part of the state economy and artisans and merchants were seen as secondary, just as in an industrial society, industry is seen as the most important part of the national economy and the service industry is seen as secondary. Similarly, in the knowledge economy, the service industry is seen as the most important sector of the national economy and agriculture is seen as secondary.

19. *Xunzi* 9 *Humane Governance.*

20. *Xunzi* 10 *Enriching the State.*

21. Ibid.

22. Lu Yang, "Feizhou na shenme zhengjiu ziji?" [What can Africa do to save itself?], http://news.xinhuanet.com/world/2005-07/22/content_3252643.htm.

23. *Xunzi* 9 *Humane Governance.*

24. *Xunzi* 10 *Enriching the State.*

25. *Xunzi* 15 *Debating the Military.*

26. *Xunzi* 13 *The Way of the Ministers.*

27. *Xunzi* 12 *The Way of the Rulers.* Yü was the founding king of the Xia Dynasty and Jie the last king of the same dynasty.

28. Ibid.

29. *Xunzi* 11 *Humane Authority and Hegemony.*

30. Ibid. Shun was a king who reigned before the Xia Dynasty and is revered as a sage.

31. *Xunzi* 18 *Correcting: A Discussion.*

32. Ibid. Zhòu was the last king of the Shang Dynasty.

33. Ibid.

34. Ibid.

35. *Xunzi* 11 *Humane Authority and Hegemony.*

36. *Xunzi* 9 *Humane Governance.*

37. *Xunzi* 18 *Correcting: A Discussion.*

38. *Xunzi* 11 *Humane Authority and Hegemony.*

39. *Xunzi* 9 *Humane Governance.*

40. Ibid.

41. Hans J. Morgenthau and Kenneth W. Thompson, *Politics among Nations: The Struggle for Power and Peace,* 5th edition (New York: Alfred A. Knopf, 1972), 225–229.

42. *Xunzi* 23 *Human Nature Is Evil.*

43. Morgenthau and Thompson, *Politics among Nations,* 4.

44. *Xunzi* 23 *Human Nature Is Evil.*

45. *Xunzi* 19 *Rites: A Discussion.*

46. *Xunzi* 22 *Correcting Names.*

47. Ibid.

48. *Xunzi* 27 *Overall Summary.*

49. *Xunzi* 23 *Human Nature Is Evil.*

50. *Xunzi* 19 *Rites: A Discussion.*

51. Robert O. Keohane and Joseph S. Nye, *Power and Interdependence,* 3rd edition (New York: Longman, 2001), 294.

52. Ibid., 295.

53. *Xunzi* 10 *Enriching the State.*

54. *Xunzi* 9 *Humane Governance.*

55. Ibid.

56. According to Wang Xianqian's *Xunzi jijie* [Collected notes on the "Xunzi"], the system of Five Services was centered on the royal city of the Zhou Son of Heaven and extended outward to form an international system from center to periphery. The area within 250 kilometers of the royal city was the area for "domain service," where the king's fields were sown to provide food for the Son of Heaven. A further 250 kilometers out was the "feudal service," which provided labor and border guards. A further 1,250 kilometers out was the "tributary service," which belonged to the states of the central plain. Every 250 kilometers of the tributary service was one *qi,* in the order: feudal *qi,* domain *qi,* baron's *qi,* fiefdom *qi,* and border *qi,* which promoted culture and education and provided military service. Even farther out were the "formal service" and the "wasteland service," each of 500 kilometers. It is not clear if the latter two were at the same distance from the royal city or one was farther away. The "formal service" comprised the two areas of the Man and the Yi, each of 250 kilometers. The tribes had to

perform roughly the same kind of service but at reduced levels of taxation. The "wasteland service" was divided into two territories, the "settled service" and the "wild service," each of 250 kilometers. The norms for the tribes were simple and the people could move freely. Scholars differ in their opinions on the geographical areas of the Five Services. See Ye, *Chunqiu Zhangguo Shiqi de Zhongguo Waijiao Sixiang*, 28.

57. *Xunzi* 18 *Correcting: A Discussion*.

58. Ibid.

59. Hu Jintao, "Nuli Jianshe Chijiu Heping, Gongtong Fanrong de Hexie Shijie: Zai Lianheguo Chengli 60 Zhounian Shounao Huiyishang de Jianghua" [Work hard to establish a lasting, peaceful, universally prosperous, and harmonious world: A speech at the summit to commemorate the sixtieth anniversary of the founding of the United Nations], *Renmin Ribao* [People's Daily], 16 September 2009, 1.

60. "Zhongyang Waishi Gongzuo Huiyi Zai Jing Juxing" [Central foreign affairs working meeting held in Beijing], *Renmin Ribao* [People's Daily], 24 August 2006, 1.

61. "Zhonggong Zhongyang Guanyu Goujian Shehuizhuyi Hexie Shehui Ruogan Zhongda Wenti de Jueding" [The decision of the Central Committee of the Chinese Communist Party dealing with key questions in the construction of a harmonious socialist society], *Renmin Ribao* [People's Daily], 19 October 2006, 1–2.

62. Hu, "Nuli Jianshe Chijiu Heping, Gongtong Fanrong de Hexie Shijie," 1.

63. Zhu Rongji, "Zhengfu Gongzuo Baogao" [Government work report], in *16 Da Yilai Zhongyao Wenxian Xuanbian [Shang]* [A selection of important documents since the Sixteenth Party Congress, part 1] (Beijing: Zhongyang Wenxian Press, 2005), 188.

64. Mao Zedong, *Mao Zedong Xuanji* [Selected works of Mao Zedong] (Beijing: People's Press, 1991), 2:526, 535.

65. L. S. Stavrianos, *The World since 1500: A Global History* (London: Prentice-Hall International, 1966), 36–37.

66. *Xunzi* 11 *Humane Authority and Hegemony*.

CHAPTER 3

1. *The Stratagems of the Warring States* was edited by Liu Xiang (77–8 BCE) and contains historical material from historiographers and strategists of the Warring States Period. Scholars are divided on issues such as the identity of the author, the authenticity of what is recorded, and the meaning of the text. Where there are divergent opinions on the identity of the personages mentioned, the authors of this essay follow the majority opinion. Quotations are based on the 1978 edition published in Shanghai. On editorial questions, see Hu Ruhong, *"Zhanguoce" Yanjiu* [Study of "The stratagems of the Warring States"] (Changsha: Hunan People's Press, 2002), 10–12; Luo Genze, *Luo Genze Shuo Zhuzi* [Luo Genze on the masters] (Shanghai: Shanghai Guji Press, 2001), 382; and Fu Yuzhang, *Zhongguo Gudai Shixueshi* [A history of the historiography of ancient China] (Hefei: Anhui University Press, 2008), 17.

2. Bai Shouyi, *Zhongguo Shixueshi Lunji* [Collected essays on the history of Chinese historiography] (Beijing: Zhonghua Shuju, 1999), 37.

3. On these two terms, see p. 225.

4. Xiong Xianguang, trans., *"Zhanguoce" Yanjiu yu Xuanyi* ["The stratagems of the Warring States": Studies and selected texts in translation] (Chongqing: Chongqing Press, 1988); Gao Xiaoying, "*Shi Ji* yu *Zhanguoce* de Bijiao Yanjiu" [A comparative study of the *Historical records* and *The stratagems of the Warring States*] (M.A. thesis, Anhui University, 2005), 6–7, 11–12.

5. Wang Jingxiong, Shang Jinglong, and Guan Xiu, *"Zhanguoce" yu Lunbianshu* ["The stratagems of the Warring States" and the art of debate] (Shanghai: Shanghai Guji Press, 2002), 407.

6. Zhang Yanxiu, "*Zhanguoce* Zhuti Sixiang Shitan" [Topics in *The stratagems of the Warring States*], *Guanzi Xuekan* [Guanzi Journal], no. 2 (1999): 64.

7. Zhang Yanxiu, *Zonghengjia Shu: "Zhanguoce" yu Zhongguo Wenhua* [Verticalists and horizontalists: "The stratagems of the Warring States" and Chinese culture] (Kaifeng: Henan University, 1998), 25–27.

8. Jia Chuantang, "*Zhanguoce* Rencai Lun" [Talented persons in *The Stratagems of the Warring States*], *Zhengzhou Daxue Xuebao (Zhexue Shehuikexue Ban)* [Journal of Zhengzhou University: Philosophy and Social Sciences], no. 5 (1987): 49.

9. Xu Jieling, *Chunqiu Bangjiao Yanjiu* [Interstate relations in the Spring and Autumn era] (Beijing: Chinese Academy of Social Sciences Press, 2004), 129.

10. Guo Dan, "*Zuozhuan*" *Guoce Yanjiu* [State strategy in "Zuo's commentary"] (Beijing: Renmin Wenxue, 2004), 170, 173.

11. Wang Fuhan and Meng Ming, eds., *Wenbai Duizhao Quanyi "Zhanguoce"* [A translation of "The stratagems of the Warring States" into modern Chinese] (Beijing: Zhongyang Minzu Xueyuan Press, 1993), 7.

12. Hu Ruhong, *"Zhanguoce" Yanjiu*, 160–161.

13. Yu Rubo, "*Zhanguoce* Moulue Sixiang Xiyao" [Strategic planning in *The stratagems of the Warring States*], *Junshi Lishi Yanjiu* [Military History Research], no. 1 (1990): 96.

14. Wang and Meng, *Wenbai Duizhao Quanyi "Zhanguoce,"* 3.

15. *Stratagems* 14 (*Chu* 1) 17.

16. *Stratagems* 3 (*Qin* 1) 7.

17. *Stratagems* 3 (*Qin* 1) 2.

18. *Stratagems* 3 (*Qin* 1) 5.

19. *Stratagems* 19 (*Zhao* 2) 1. Although the *Records of the Historian* says that Su Qin's interlocutor was Prince Xiao of Zhao, mainstream contemporary historians think that Su Qin could not have lived before the time of King Huiwen of Zhao, and therefore the text adopted here refers to King Huiwen. See Wang Gesen and Tang Zhiqing, eds., *Qiguo Shi* [The history of the state of Qi] (Jinan: Shandong People's Press, 1992), 410; and Yang Kuan, *Zhanguo Shi* [The history of the Warring States] (Shanghai: Shanghai People's Press, 2003), 342–343. On Su Qin's activities in Zhao, see Shen Changyun et al., *Zhaoguo Shigao* [A sketch history of the state of Zhao] (Beijing: Zhonghua Shuju, 2000), 184–186.

20. *Stratagems* 17 (*Chu* 4) 9.

21. *Stratagems* 22 (*Wei* 1) 7. The Jin of this quotation is actually Wei. When Jin split into three, Wei held the old capital and therefore continued to call itself "Jin."

22. *Stratagems* 22 (*Wei* 1) 7.

23. Ibid.

24. Huang Shuofeng, *Zonghe Guoli Xinlun: Jianlun Xinzhongguo Zonghe Guoli* [A new theory of comprehensive state power: Comprehensive state power in the new China] (Beijing: Chinese Academy of Social Sciences Press, 1999), 10.

25. *Stratagems* 11 (*Qi* 4) 6.

26. *Stratagems* 13 (*Qi* 6) 3.

27. *Stratagems* 29 (*Yan* 1) 9.

28. *Guanzi* 17 *Methods of Warfare*. On the tasks of the emperor, sage king, and hegemon, see *Gudai Hanyu cidian* [A dictionary of ancient Chinese] (Beijing: Commercial Press, 2001), 310, 1603, and 105, respectively.

29. *Stratagems* 29 (*Yan* 1) 12.

30. *Stratagems* 17 (*Chu* 4) 9.

31. *Stratagems* 3 (*Qin* 1) 2.

32. *Stratagems* 3 (*Qin* 1) 5.

33. *Stratagems* 1 (*Eastern Zhou*) 15. [*Da ling zhao* is the sixteenth rank of nobles in a scheme of one to twenty (twenty being the highest) initiated by Shang Yang in Qin.]

34. *Stratagems* 3 (*Qin* 1) 2.

35. *Stratagems* 5 (*Qin* 3) 9.

36. *Stratagems* 20 (*Zhao* 3) 14.

37. *Stratagems* 22 (*Wei* 1) 11.

38. *Stratagems* 3 (*Qin* 1) 7. The nine tripods and map-cum-registry are the symbols of the kingship of the Zhou Son of Heaven. They are rather like the scepter and seal of modern politics. If you have these two things, then you have the formal legitimacy to issue commands to the feudal lords in the name of the Son of Heaven.

39. Ibid.

40. *Stratagems* 7 (*Qin* 5) 1. Editors disagree on the identity of the king of Qin referred to in this passage. Gao You (ca. 168–212) thought that it was the first emperor of Qin but later commentators think it was King Wu. I adopt the latter position. For a discussion of these problems, see Miao Wenyuan, *Zhanguoce Kaobian* [A critical edition of "The stratagems of the Warring States"] (Beijing: Zhonghua Shuju, 1984), 70.

41. *Stratagems* 25 (*Wei* 4) 18.

42. *Stratagems* 33 (*Zhongshan*) 10. The King Zhao of Qin referred to here is King Zhaoxiang of Qin. Lin Jianming, *Qinshi Gao* [A sketch history of Qin] (Shanghai: Shanghai People's Press, 1981), 266–267.

43. *Stratagems* 30 (*Yan* 2) 11.

44. *Stratagems* 3 (*Qin* 1) 5.

45. *Stratagems* 3 (*Qin* 1) 7.

46. *Stratagems* 19 (*Zhao* 2) 4.

47. *Stratagems* 11 (*Qi* 4) 10. Historians differ on the date and historical background of Su Qin's persuading Qi not to follow Qin in calling himself emperor. See Miao, *Zhanguoce Kaobian*, 120.

48. *Stratagems* 23 (*Wei* 2) 11.

49. *Stratagems* 4 (*Qin* 2) 2.

50. Li Shaojun, ed., *Guoji Zhanlue Baogao* [Report on international strategies] (Beijing: Chinese Academy of Social Sciences Press, 2005), 1.

51. *Stratagems* 7 (*Qin* 5) 1.

52. *Stratagems* 5 (*Qin* 3) 9.

53. Ibid.

54. *Stratagems* 29 (*Yan* 1) 1.

55. *Stratagems* 5 (*Qin* 3) 2.

56. *Stratagems* 12 (*Qi* 5) 1.

57. *Stratagems* 19 (*Zhao* 2) 1.

58. *Stratagems* 3 (*Qin* 1) 3.

59. *Stratagems* 28 (*Han* 3) 5. Prince Zhaoxi of Han is Prince Zhao of Han.

60. For the logic of following a strong state, see Robert Powell, *In the Shadow of Power: States and Strategies in International Politics* (Princeton, NJ: Princeton University Press, 1999), 195; and Randall L. Schweller, *Deadly Imbalances: Tripolarity and Hitler's Strategy of World Conquest* (New York: Columbia University Press, 1998), 69.

61. *Stratagems* 3 (*Qin* 1) 5.

62. *Stratagems* 12 (*Qi* 5) 1.

63. Ibid.

64. *Stratagems* 4 (*Qin* 2) 2.

65. *Stratagems* 30 (*Yan* 2) 12.

66. *Stratagems* 14 (*Chu* 1) 5.

67. Ibid.

68. Rose McDermott, *Political Psychology in International Relations* (Ann Arbor: University of Michigan Press, 2004); Jerold M. Post, *Leaders and Their Followers in Dangerous World: The Psychology of Political Behavior* (Ithaca, NY: Cornell University Press, 2004); Jerold M. Post, ed., *The Psychological Assessment of Political Leaders, with Profiles of Saddam Hussein and Bill Clinton* (Ann Arbor: University of Michigan Press, 2003).

69. *Stratagems* 29 (*Yan* 1) 5.

70. James E. Dougherty and Robert L. Pfaltzgraff Jr., *Contending Theories of International Relations: A Comprehensive Survey*, 5th edition (New York: Addison Wesley Longman, 2001), 506. In the game of Stag Hunt, a group of participants hunt a stag. If one or more of them defects to chase a rabbit instead, then the stag will escape through the gap in the line. This shows that when the participants lose faith in the fidelity of the others to keep to the cooperative task, and seek their own small gains instead of the greater gain of the whole group, then collective cooperation will fail.

CHAPTER 4

1. Engels writes that the state "is a product of society at a certain stage of development." It has two main features: "it divides its subjects according to territory," and it "is the establishment of a public power which no longer directly coincides with the

population organising itself as an armed force" (Friedrich Engels, "The Origin of the Family, Private Property, and the State," in *The Marx-Engels Reader*, ed. Robert C. Tucker [NewYork: Norton, 1978], 752).

2. Pei Monong points out that those international relations in the Spring and Autumn and Warring States periods were intertwined and complex and changeable. The diplomacy of each state was very highly advanced. The *Rites of Zhou* became like today's international law. See Pei Monong, "Introduction," in *Chunqiu Zhanguo Shidai de Waijiao Qunxing* [Diplomatic constellations in the Spring and Autumn and Warring States periods] (Chongqing: Chongqing Press Group, 1994).

3. This is how I think Professor Yan's thought should be understood: in its domestic and foreign policy and its determination and choice of developing military strategy, there are three levels to a state—first, unifying all under heaven; second, establishing norms (that is, first using material power, and second determining the order of power). The third level, constructing concepts, is of a higher order.

4. Yan Xuetong, "The Similarities and Differences of the Schools of Pre-Qin Interstate Political Thoughts," in *Thoughts of World Leadership and Implications,* ed. Yan Xuetong and Xu Jin (Beijing: World Knowledge Press, 2009), 265, 286.

5. Yang Qianru, "The Type and Evolution of the Pre-Qin International System," *International Political Science* 21, no.1 (2010): 110.

6. *Analects* 14 *Xian Asked* 17: "The master said, 'But for Guanzi, we would still be wearing our hair loose and buttoning our robes on the left.'" (*Translator's note*: wearing hair loose and buttoning clothes on the left were seen as uncivilized.)

7. Qi Haixia has dealt with Laozi's strategy for winning all under heaven in her paper "Laozi de xiaoguo guamin sixiang [Laozi's idea of small states with small populations]" and hence I do not discuss it further here.

8. "Duke Xiao met Wei Yang, who spoke eloquently for a long time. Duke Xiao gradually fell asleep and did not listen. . . . Wei Yang said, 'I spoke to the duke about the way of emperors but his mind was not open to understand.' Five days later he asked to see Yang again. Yang went to see Duke Xiao again. This time was better but he still did not hit on what was wanted. . . . Yang said, 'I spoke to the duke about the ways of kings but he did not take it in. He asked to see me again.' Yang went to see Duke Xiao again. Duke Xiao praised him but did not employ him. He left and went away. . . . Yang said, 'I spoke to the duke about the way of hegemons. He is interested in using that. He will certainly see me again, I know it.' Wei Yang went to see Duke Xiao again. The duke spoke with him and, without realizing, moved forward to sit with him. Though he spoke of many things, the duke did not tire for the whole day. . . . Yang said, 'I spoke to you, O Prince, of the way of emperors and kings like under the Three Dynasties, yet you said, "It is too far away. I cannot wait for that. Moreover worthy princes must first bring it about that their personal merit shines throughout all under heaven, how can I wait so many centuries to become an emperor or king?" So I spoke to the prince of how to strengthen the state and the prince liked that very much. Yet it is difficult for his virtue to match that of the Yin [Shang] and Zhou dynasties'" (*The Records of the Historian: Biography of Lord Shang*).

9. "The first emperor of Qin, having annexed all under heaven, called his ministers and asked them, 'The Five Emperors of old practiced abdication in favor of the worthy; the Three Kings practiced hereditary succession. Which should it be? I will do whatever is right.' The seventy scholars did not reply. Baobai Lingzhi spoke in reply, 'Offices of all under heaven should be given to the worthy; but the household of all under heaven belongs to hereditary succession. Hence the Five Emperors treated all under heaven as an office, whereas the Three Kings held it as a household.' The first emperor of Qin looked up to heaven and sighed, 'My virtue comes from the Five Emperors; I will be the official of all under heaven. Who is it who may succeed me?' Baobai Lingzhi replied, 'Your Majesty uses the way of Jie and Zhòu and yet you want to use the abdication of the Five Emperors; this is something that your majesty cannot do. . . . Your Majesty is what one may describe as a self-made king. How dare you compare your virtue to that of the Five Emperors and want to treat all under heaven as an office?' The first emperor fell silent and did not reply. He looked troubled. After a long time he said, 'What Lingzhi has said leads all of you to disrespect me.' He desisted from his plan and did not use abdication" (*Shuo Yuan* 14 *Zhigong* 5).

10. *Laozi* 29.

11. *Translator's note*: *Well-field agriculture* refers to the system whereby one central field was held in common and the surrounding eight fields portioned out. The resulting nine-square pattern resembles the Chinese character for *well*. Mourning was prescribed for three years, one year, nine months, five months, or three months, depending on one's relationship to the deceased.

12. Yan, "The Similarities and Differences of the Schools of Pre-Qin Interstate Political Thoughts," 261.

13. Barry Buzan and Richard Little, *International Systems in World History: Remaking the Study of International Relations* (Oxford: Oxford University Press, 2000), 10. Buzan notes that contemporary international relations studies use only realism, thus overlooking the faults of historicism: "The discipline of International Relations has been mainly focused on contemporary history and current policy issues. The fast-moving nature of the subject and the pressing demand for expertise on current events, encourage a forward- rather than a backward-looking perspective. Consequently . . . [it] impose[s] the present on the past. . . . Social scientists of a positivist predisposition anxious to emulate the natural sciences, also seek to identify laws that are immune to historical variation. . . . But as with historicism, this story [the history of contemporary international relations] can only be told in this way by ignoring or distorting great swaths of the past" (ibid., 18, 19, 20). I think that this point applies also to the theoretical lacunae in the current study of pre-Qin interstate political thought.

14. Yang Qianru, "The Type and Evolution of the Pre-Qin International System," *International Political Science* 21, no.1 (2010): 110.

15. *Translator's note*: The following are all Han Dynasty politicians: Lu Jia (fl. 207–180 BCE), Jia Yi (201–169 BCE), and Chao Cuo (d. 154 BCE). On Lu Jia and the *New Analects*, see *The Cambridge History of China* 1:709–710, 731–732. On Jia Yi and Chao Cuo, see ibid., 1:148–149.

16. *The History of the Former Han Dynasty* 30 *Gazette of Literature*.

CHAPTER 5

1. Liang Qichao, *Xianqin Zhengzhi Sixiangshi* [A history of pre-Qin political thought] (Tianjin: Tianjin Guji Press, 2003), 117–118; Xiao Gongquan, *Zhongguo Zhengzhi Sixiangshi* [A history of Chinese political thought] (Beijing: New Star Press, 2005), 73–78; Lü Simian, *Xianqin Xueshu Gailun* [An outline of pre-Qin scholarship] (Beijing: Dongfang Press, 1996), 84.

2. *Mencius 2 Gongsun Chou* A3 (cf. Legge, *The Chinese Classics* [London and Oxford: Frowde and Oxford University Press, 1895], 2:196).

3. *Mencius 1 King Hui of Liang* A5 (cf. Legge, *The Chinese Classics*, 2:135, 136).

4. *Mencius 4 Li Lou* A7 (cf. Legge, *The Chinese Classics*, 2:298).

5. *Mencius 2 Gongsun Chou* A3 (cf. Legge, *The Chinese Classics*, 2:196–197).

6. *Mencius 1 King Hui of Liang* A7 (cf. Legge, *The Chinese Classics*, 2:142).

7. *Mencius 3 Duke Wen of Teng* B5 (cf. Legge, *The Chinese Classics*, 2:274).

8. Both think that one can win leadership of a state by seizing it. Mencius says, "There are those lacking benevolence who have acquired states; but there has never been anyone lacking benevolence who acquired all under heaven" (*Mencius 7 Exhausting the Mind* B13 [cf. Legge, *The Chinese Classics*, 2:483]).

9. *Mencius 5 Wan Zhang* A5 (cf. Legge, *The Chinese Classics*, 2:354).

10. Ibid. (cf. Legge, *The Chinese Classics*, 2:356).

11. Ibid. (cf. Legge, *The Chinese Classics*, 2:355–356). Mencius goes on to explain in detail that Shun's taking the place of Yao was due to the mandate of heaven: "Shun served Yao for twenty-eight years. This was not something a human being could do, only heaven. Yao died and after three years' mourning, Shun left Yao's son and went to the south of the South River. The feudal lords of all under heaven came to pay court not to Yao's son but to Shun. Those who had court hearings did not go to Yao's son but to Shun. Those who sang elegies did so not for Yao's son but sang and danced for Shun. Therefore I say, 'This is of heaven.' Later, he went to the central state and took the throne of the Son of Heaven. If he had stayed in Yao's palace and dismissed Yao's son, this would be usurpation rather than a matter of heaven giving it. The *Great Oath* says, 'Heaven sees as my people see; heaven hears as my people hear'" (ibid. [cf. Legge, *The Chinese Classics*, 2:357]).

12. *Mencius 6 Gaozi* B2 (cf. Legge, *The Chinese Classics*, 2:426).

13. The ruler ought also to have a process for selecting good ministers, but Mencius thinks that the type of ruler decides what type of ministers he has; hence, a prince of benevolence and justice will certainly select ministers of benevolence and justice.

14. *Mencius 3 Duke Wen of Teng* A4 (cf. Legge, *The Chinese Classics*, 2:251).

15. Ibid. (cf. Legge, *The Chinese Classics*, 2:252).

16. *Mencius 2 Gongsun Chou* A2 (cf. Legge, *The Chinese Classics*, 2:194).

17. *Mencius 6 Gaozi* B8 (cf. Legge, *The Chinese Classics*, 2:440).

18. *Xunzi 11 Humane Authority and Hegemony*.

19. *Mencius 2 Gongsun Chou* A3 (cf. Legge, *The Chinese Classics*, 2:196).

20. *Mencius 6 Gaozi* B4 (cf. Legge, *The Chinese Classics*, 2:429–430).

21. *Mencius 7 Exhausting the Mind* A1 (cf. Legge, *The Chinese Classics*, 2:477–478).

22. *Mencius* 4 *Li Lou* A3 (cf. Legge, *The Chinese Classics*, 2:293–294).

23. This is Yan Xuetong's view; see chapter 2, p. 88–89.

24. The term *hegemonism* does not exist in English. English-speaking readers may not understand the official Chinese translation, *hegemonism*. In Chinese, *hegemonism* refers to a strong state (not necessarily a hegemonic state) seeking to humiliate weak states or to a strong state forcing a weak state to do something it does not want to do. Official Chinese texts generally use the three expressions *imperialism*, *hegemonism*, and *great power politics* together to show that they have virtually identical meanings.

25. Both coincide in using the historical case of King Wen becoming king with a territory of only one hundred square kilometers to prove the role of political power in the rise of a state to world leadership.

26. This essay does not specifically discuss the role of armed force insofar as it relates to the state's military power. Regarding the use of armed force, both Mencius and Xunzi support just war. For an analysis of the conditions under which Mencius supports a state's using armed force, see Daniel A. Bell, *Beyond Liberal Democracy: Political Thinking for an East Asian Context* (Princeton, NJ: Princeton University Press, 2006), 49–56.

27. Yang Kuan, *Xizhou Shi* [A history of the Western Zhou] (Shanghai: Shanghai People's Press, 2003), 95.

28. *Mencius* 1 *King Hui of Liang* A5 (cf. Legge, *The Chinese Classics*, 2:134–136).

29. *Xunzi* 19 *Rites: A Discussion.*

30. *Mencius* 6 *Gaozi* A9 (cf. Legge, *The Chinese Classics*, 2:409–410).

31. Yang Zebo, *Mengzi Pingzhuan* [Mencius: A biography] (Nanjing: Nanjing University Press, 1998), 327–331.

32. *Mencius* 7 *Exhausting the Mind* B24 (cf. Legge, *The Chinese Classics*, 2:489).

33. *Mencius* 6 *Gaozi* A15 (cf. Legge, *The Chinese Classics*, 2:417–418).

34. Ibid. (cf. Legge, *The Chinese Classics*, 2:418).

35. Although Xunzi does not deny the role of education and moral example, he nonetheless stresses the role of rites.

36. I say that rites are a kind of external force but do not thereby imply that rites are a purely external force imposed on one. In reference to the human person, rites are an external thing with a certain compulsory role, but rites may also be internalized (by being united with happiness), so that people live gently in a spirit of respect and obedience.

37. According to Xunzi's theory that human nature is evil, evil persons or states will very easily emerge.

38. On this point, Mencius's concept is very like the idea of a "norm entrepreneur" discussed by the constructivist Martha Finnemore. Norm entrepreneurs hope to give leaders of countries norms so that they can accept, inherit, and internalize them to form new norms. Finnemore studies only successful examples of norm entrepreneurs, whereas the *Mencius* records the failures of Mencius in trying to promote norms. Examples of failure in fact are even more deserving of our attention because they can show where the limits of the norm entrepreneur lie. Martha Finnemore and Kathryn Sikkink, "International Norms Dynamics and Political Change," *International Organization* 52, no. 4 (1998): 887–917.

39. Human relationships are the core of the rites; hence, the restoration of ritual order and respect for human relationships are two sides of the same coin.

40. *Mencius* 6 *Gaozi* B5 (cf. Legge, *The Chinese Classics*, 2:430).

41. *Mencius* 1 *King Hui of Liang* A6 (cf. Legge, *The Chinese Classics*, 2:136–137).

42. *Mencius* 1 *King Hui of Liang* A5 (cf. Legge, *The Chinese Classics*, 2:136).

CHAPTER 6

1. John J. Mearsheimer, *The Tragedy of Great Power Politics* (New York: Norton, 2001), 40.

2. Robert Pahre, *Leading Questions: How Hegemony Affects the International Political Economy* (Ann Arbor: University of Michigan Press, 1999), 4.

3. Joshua S. Goldstein, *Long Cycles: Prosperity and War in the Modern Age* (New Haven, CT: Yale University Press, 1988), 125.

4. Robert T. Gilpin, *War and Change in World Politics* (Cambridge: Cambridge University Press, 1983), 29.

5. Robert O. Keohane and Joseph S. Nye, *Power and Interdependence*, 3rd edition (New York: Longman, 2001), 38.

6. Ibid., 23.

7. Immanuel Wallerstein, *The Politics of the World Economy: The States, the Movements, and the Civilizations* (Cambridge: Cambridge University Press, 1984), 38.

8. Wang Li, ed., *Gu Hanyu Zidian* [A dictionary of ancient Chinese] (Beijing: Zhonghua Shuju, 2000), 1619.

9. Dictionary Editing Office, Institute of Language, Chinese Academy of Social Sciences, ed., *Xiandai Hanyu cidian* [A dictionary of modern Chinese] (Beijing: Commercial Press, 2005), 23.

10. *Record of Rites* 5 Humane Governance: Part 3.

11. Zheng Xuan (127–200 CE) in commentary on *Zuo's Commentary* 8 *Duke Cheng Year 2*.

12. Liu Zehua, *Zhongguo Zhengzhi Sixiangshi (xian Qin)* [An anthology of the history of Chinese political thought (pre-Qin)] (Hangzhou: Zhejiang People's Press, 1996), 198.

13. Dictionary Editing Office, *Xiandai Hanyu cidian*, 22–23.

14. A. T. Mahan, *The Influence of Sea Power upon History, 1660–1783* (Boston: Little & Brown, 1890).

15. Halford J. Mackinder, *Democratic Ideals and Reality: A Study in the Politics of Reconstruction* (Washington, DC: National Defense University Press, 1942), 106.

16. Giulio Douhet, *Diario critico di Guerra* (Torino: G. B. Paravia, 1921).

17. Mearsheimer, *The Tragedy of Great Power Politics*.

18. Keohane and Nye, *Power and Interdependence*; Robert O. Keohane, *After Hegemony: Cooperation and Discord in the World Political Economy* (Princeton, NJ: Princeton University Press, 2005); Immanuel Wallerstein, *Mercantilism and the Consolidation of the European World Economy, 1600–1750* (New York: Academic Press, 1980).

19. Paul Kennedy, *The Rise and Fall of the Great Powers: Economic Change and Military Conflict from 1500 to 2000* (New York: Random House, 1987).

20. *Stratagems* 3 (*Qin* 1) 2.

21. *Mozi* 3 *On Dyeing*.

22. *Records of the Historian* 32 *Dukes of Qi*.

23. *Analects* 14 *Xian Asked* 17.

24. *Analects* 14 *Xian Asked* 16.

25. *Stratagems* 3 (*Qin* 1) 5.

26. *Stratagems* 3 (*Qin* 1) 2.

27. *Zuo's Commentary* 8 *Duke Cheng Year 8* (cf. Legge, *The Chinese Classics* [London and Oxford: Frowde and Oxford University Press, 1872], 5:366).

28. Note in *Zuo's Commentary* 8 *Duke Cheng Year 7*.

29. *Records of the Historian* 32 *Dukes of Qi*.

30. *Guanzi* 20 *Xiao Kuang* (cf. W. A. Rickett, *Guanzi: Political, Economic, and Philosophical Essays from Early China* [Princeton, NJ: Princeton University Press, 1985], 1:336).

31. *Records of the Historian* 39 *House of Jin*.

32. *Stratagems* 3 (*Qin* 1) 1.

33. *Records of the Historian* 5 *Qin*.

34. *Zuo's Commentary* 8 *Duke Cheng Year 8* (cf. Legge, *The Chinese Classics*, 5:366).

35. *Xunzi* 11 *Humane Authority and Hegemony*.

36. *Zuo's Commentary* 7 *Duke Xuan Year 12* (cf. Legge, *The Chinese Classics*, 5:317).

37. *Mencius* 2 *Gongsun Chou* A3 (cf. Legge, *The Chinese Classics*, 5:196–197).

38. Sun Jiazhou, "Tianzi, Bazhu, Zhuhou: Chunqiu Bazheng Yanjiu" [The Son of Heaven, hegemonic lord, and the feudal princes: A study of the struggle for hegemony in the Spring and Autumn Period], *Guizhou Shehui Kexue* [Guizhou Social Sciences], no. 2 (1993): 104.

39. *The Great Learning* (cf. Legge, *The Chinese Classics*, 1:357ff.).

40. *Guanzi* 51 *Little Questions*.

41. *Guanzi* 17 *Methods of Warfare* (cf. Rickett, *Guanzi*, 1:270).

42. *Xunzi* 11 *Humane Authority and Hegemony*.

43. Ibid.; *Xunzi* 12 *The Way of the Rulers*.

44. Mearsheimer, *The Tragedy of Great Power Politics*, 2.

45. Charles P. Kindleberger, *The World in Depression, 1929–1939* (Berkeley: University of California Press, 1986), 365.

46. Keohane, *After Hegemony*, 137–138.

47. George Modelski, *Long Cycles in World Politics* (London: Macmillan, 1987); George Modelski, ed., *Exploring Long Cycles* (Boulder, CO: L. Rienner; London: Frances Pinter, 1987); Goldstein, *Long Cycles*; Immanuel Wallerstein, *The Modern World System: Capitalist Agriculture and the Origins of the European World Economy in the Sixteenth Century* (New York: Academic Press, 1974); Wallerstein, *Mercantilism and the Consolidation of the European World Economy*.

48. *Zuo's Commentary* 10 *Duke Zhao Year 29* (cf. Legge, *The Chinese Classics*, 5:732). *Beilu* is the name of a place in the state of Jin; its location is unknown.

49. Robert W. Cox, "Social Forces, States and World Orders: Beyond International Relations Theory," in *Neorealism and Its Critics*, ed. Robert O. Keohane (New York: Columbia University Press, 1986), 206.

50. *Xunzi* 9 *Humane Governance*.

51. Zhang Quanmin, "Shilun Chunqiu Huimeng de Lishi Zuoyong" [The historical role of alliance meetings in the Spring and Autumn Period], *Jilin Daxue Shehui Kexue Xuebao* [Journal of Jilin University Social Sciences], no. 6 (1994): 46.

52. Song Liheng, "Lun Huimeng Zai Chunqiu Zhengbazhong de Teshu Gongneng" [The special role of alliance meetings in the contest for hegemony in the Spring and Autumn Period], *Jilin Shifan Daxuexuebao (Renwen Shehui Kexue Ban)* [Journal of Jilin Normal University: Humanities and Social Sciences], no. 6 (2003): 91.

53. He Pingli, "Luelun Chunqiu Shiqi Huimeng, Zhengba Zhanzheng yu Zhanzhengguan" [A brief discussion of alliances, hegemonic wars, and views of war in the Spring and Autumn Period], *Junshi Lishi Yanjiu* [Research in Military History], no. 2 (2008): 109.

54. Xu Jieling, *Chunqiu Bangjiao Yanjiu* [Interstate relations in the Spring and Autumn era] (Beijing: Chinese Academy of Social Sciences Press, 2004), 85.

55. *Zuo's Commentary* 3 *Duke Zhuang Year 15* (cf. Legge, *The Chinese Classics*, 5:93).

56. He Pingli, "Luelun Chunqiu Shiqi Huimeng, Zhengba Zhanzheng yu Zhanzhengguan," 109.

57. Note on *Zuo's Commentary* 5 *Duke Xi Year 29*. [*Translator's note*: Jiantu was part of Zheng, now in Henan Province; Zhequan may be the city of Luoyang, also in Henan Province.]

58. *Records of the Historian* 31 *Lords of Wu*.

59. From the conclusion by Sima Qian in *Records of the Historian* 41 *King Goujian of Yue*.

60. *Records of the Historian* 5 *Qin*.

61. Note on *Zuo's Commentary* 7 *Duke Xuan Year 16*.

62. Li Ruilan, *Chunqiu Zhanguo Shidai de Lishi Bianqian* [Historical changes in the Spring and Autumn and Warring States periods] (Tianjin: Tianjin Guji Press, 1994), 36.

63. Zhang Erguo, "Xian Qin Shiqi de Huimeng Wenti" [The issue of alliance meetings in the pre-Qin era], *Shixue Jikan* [Journal of Historical Studies], no. 1 (1995): 18.

64. *Stratagems* 12 (*Qi* 5) 1.

65. *Zuo's Commentary* 10 *Duke Zhao Year 23* (cf. Legge, *The Chinese Classics*, 5:698).

66. *Zuo's Commentary* 9 *Duke Xiang Year 9* (cf. Legge, *The Chinese Classics*, 5:441).

67. *Zuo's Commentary* 10 *Duke Zhao Year 1* (cf. Legge, *The Chinese Classics*, 5:577).

68. *Zuo's Commentary* 10 *Duke Zhao Year 13* (cf. Legge, *The Chinese Classics*, 5:653).

69. Chen Zhiyong, "Shixi Chunqiu Mengshi Dui Chunqiu Shiren de Yingxiang Ji Shiren Dui Mengshi yu Mengzhu de Pingjia" [The influence of oaths on people in the Spring and Autumn Period and contemporary criticism of oaths and lords of alliances], *Zhongguo Lishi Bowuguan Guankan* [Journal of the Museum of Chinese History], no. 2 (2000): 23.

Chapter 7

1. Ni Shixiong et al., *Dangdai Xifang Guoji Guanxi Lilun* [Contemporary Western theories of international relations] (Shanghai: Fudan University Press, 2001), 487.

2. Guo Shuyong, ed., *Guoji Guanxi: Huhuan Zhongguo Lilun* [International relations: A call for a Chinese theory] (Tianjin: Tianjin People's Press, 2005), 1.

3. Qiu Yuanping, "Guanyu Zhongguo Guoji Zhanlue Yanjiu de Ruogan Kanfa" [A view of Chinese international strategy], in *Zhongguo Guoji Zhanlue Pinglun* [An assessment of China's international strategy] (Beijing: Shijie Zhishi Press, 2009), 5.

4. Yan Xuetong, "Guoji Guanxi Lilun Shi Pushi de" [International relations theories are universal], *Shijie Jingji yu Zhengzhi* [World Economics and Politics], no. 2 (2006): 1; Yan Xuetong, "Why Is There No Chinese School of International Relations Theory?" in *Wangba Tianxia Sixiang Ji Qidi* [Ruling over all under heaven: Theory and lessons], ed. Yan Xuetong, Xu Jin, et al. (Beijing: Shijie Zhishi Press, 2009), 294–301.

5. Hans J. Morgenthau and Kenneth W. Thompson, *Politics among Nations: The Struggle for Power and Peace,* 5th edition (New York: Alfred A. Knopf, 1972), 4.

6. Phil Williams, Donald M. Goldstein, and Jay M. Shafritz, *Classic Readings of International Relations* (Boston: Wadsworth, 1998), 225. The quotation from Thucydides comes from *The Peloponnesian War*, book 5, chapter 17 (Melian Dialogues) (New York: Modern Library, 1951), 331.

7. See Barry Buzan and Richard Little, *International Systems in World History: Remaking the Study of International Relations* (Oxford: Oxford University Press, 2000).

8. See chapter 4.

9. *Xunzi* 10 *Enriching the State.*

10. Ibid.

11. *Xunzi* 23 *Human Nature Is Evil.*

12. Kenneth N. Waltz, *Theory of International Politics* (Boston: McGraw-Hill, 1979), 60–78.

13. *Xunzi* 9 *Humane Governance.*

14. *Xunzi* 23 *Human Nature Is Evil.*

15. *Mencius* 2 *Gongsun Chou* A3 (cf. Legge, *The Chinese Classics* [London and Oxford: Frowde and Oxford University Press, 1895], 2:196–197).

16. *Zuo Zhuan* 5 *Duke Xi Year* 30 [Cf. Legge, *The Chinese Classics*, 5:217].

17. *Webster's New Collegiate Dictionary* (Springfield: G. & C. Merriam, 1977), 531; cf. Ian Clark, "Towards an English School Theory of Hegemony," *European Journal of International Relations* 15, no. 2 (June 2009).

18. See Daniel A. Bell, *Beyond Liberal Democracy: Political Thinking for an East Asian Context* (Princeton, NJ: Princeton University Press, 2006), chapter 2.

19. Waltz, *Theory of International Politics*, 81–82, 93, 97.

20. *Renmin Ribao* [People's Daily], 21 July 2009, 1.

21. "Zhongguo Heping Jueqi de Guoji Huanjing yu Guoji Zhanlue" [The international environment and international strategy for the peaceful rise of China], *Jiaoxue yu Yanjiu* [Education and Research], no. 4 (2004): 5–20.

22. *Xunzi* 11 *Humane Authority and Hegemony.*

23. *Mr. Lu's Spring and Autumn Annals* 7.2 *The Origin of Weapons.*

24. *Odes* II *Minor Odes* 6.1 *North Mountain* (cf. Legge, *The Chinese Classics*, 4:360).

25. *Xunzi* 11 *Humane Authority and Hegemony*.

26. Hu Jintao, "Gaoju Zhongguo Tese Shehuizhuyi Weida Qizhi Wei Duoqu Quanmian Jianshe Xiaokang Xin Shengli Er Fendou" [Holding the great banner of Socialism with Chinese characteristics and struggling to achieve the new victory of the construction of a prosperous society], *Renmin Ribao* [People's Daily], 25 October 2007, 4.

APPENDIX 2

1. This translation is based on the original interview, which was shortened when it was published. It was published under the title "Yan Xuetong: Zhizhuo yu Kexue Yuce de Xianshi Zhuyizhe" [Yan Xuetong: A realist scholar clinging to scientific prediction], *Shijie Jingji yu Zhenzhi* [World Economics and Politics], no. 7 (2005): 57–62.

APPENDIX 3

1. Ni Shixiong et al., *Dangdai Xifang Guoji Guanxi Lilun* [Contemporary Western theories of international relations] (Shanghai: Fudan University Press, 2001), 487.

2. Shi Bin, "Guoji Guanxi Yanjiu 'Zhongguohua' de Zhenlun" [Debate about the "localization" of international studies in China], in *Zhongguo Guoji Guanxi Yanjiu (1995–2005)* [IR studies in China (1995–2005)], ed. Wan Yizhou (Beijing: Peking University Press, 2006), 521–527.

3. Barry Buzan, "Yingguo Xuepai Jiqi Dangxia Fazhan" [The English school and its development], *Guoji Zhengzhi Yanjiu* [International Politics Quarterly] 2 (2007): 101.

4. Mark Leonard, *What Does China Think?* (London: Fourth Estate, 2008), 90.

5. Thomas Kuhn, *The Structure of Scientific Revolutions*, 2nd edition (Chicago: University of Chicago Press, 1970).

6. Terence Ball, "From Paradigms to Research Programs: Toward a Post-Kuhnian Political Science," *American Journal of Political Science* 20, no. 1 (1976): 151–177.

7. Imre Lakatos, "Falsification and the Methodology of Scientific Research Programmes," in *Criticism and the Growth of Knowledge*, ed. Imre Lakatos and Alan Musgrave (New York: Cambridge University Press, 1971), 91–196.

8. Colin Elman and Miriam Elman, *Progress in International Relations Theory* (Cambridge, MA: MIT Press, 2003).

9. Stephen Walt, "The Progressive Power of Realism," *American Political Science Review* 91, no. 4 (1997): 931–935.

10. Larry Laudan, "From Theories to Research Traditions," in *Progress and Its Problems: Towards a Theory of Scientific Growth,* ed. Larry Laudan (Berkeley: University of California Press, 1977), 70–120.

ENGLISH AND ITALIAN WORKS

Bell, Daniel A. *Beyond Liberal Democracy: Political Thinking for an East Asian Context.* Princeton, NJ: Princeton University Press, 2006.

Buzan, Barry, and Richard Little. *International Systems in World History: Remaking the Study of International Relations.* Oxford: Oxford University Press, 2000.

Clark, Ian. "Towards an English School Theory of Hegemony." *European Journal of International Relations* 15, no. 2 (June 2009).

Cline, Ray S. *World Power Assessment 1977: Calculus of Strategic Drift.* Boulder, CO: Westview, 1977.

Cox, Robert W. "Social Forces, States and World Orders: Beyond International Relations Theory." In *Neorealism and Its Critics*, ed. Robert O Keohane. New York: Columbia University Press, 1986.

Dougherty, James E., and Robert L. Pfaltzgraff Jr. *Contending Theories of International Relations: A Comprehensive Survey.* 5th edition. New York: Addison Wesley Longman, 2001.

Douhet, Giulio. *Diario critico di Guerra.* Torino: G. B. Paravia, 1921.

Engels, Friedrich. "The Origin of the Family, Private Property, and the State." In *The Marx-Engels Reader*, ed. Robert C. Tucker. New York: Norton, 1978.

Finnemore, Martha, and Kathryn Sikkink. "International Norms Dynamics and Political Change." *International Organization* 52, no. 4 (1998): 887–917.

Fukuyama, Francis. *The End of History and the Last Man.* Harmondsworth: Penguin, 1992.

Gilpin, Robert T. *War and Change in World Politics.* Cambridge: Cambridge University Press, 1983.

Goldstein, Joshua S. *Long Cycles: Prosperity and War in the Modern Age.* New Haven, CT: Yale University Press, 1988.

Kagan, Robert. "The Benevolent Empire." *Foreign Policy*, no. 111 (June 1998): 24–35.

Kennedy, Paul. *The Rise and Fall of the Great Powers: Economic Change and Military Conflict from 1500 to 2000.* New York: Random House, 1987.

Keohane, Robert O. *After Hegemony: Cooperation and Discord in the World Political Economy.* Princeton, NJ: Princeton University Press, 2005.

———, ed. *Neorealism and Its Critics.* New York: Columbia University Press, 1986.

Keohane Robert O., and Joseph S. Nye. *Power and Interdependence.* 3rd edition. New York: Longman, 2001.

Kindleberger, Charles P. *The World in Depression, 1929–1939*. Berkeley: University of California Press, 1986.

Legge, James. *The Chinese Classics*. London and Oxford: Frowde and Oxford University Press, vol. 1, *Confucian Analects, the Great Learning, the Doctrine of the Mean* (1893); vol. 2, *Mencius* (1895); vol. 4, *Odes* (1872); vol. 5, *The Chunqiu with Zuo's Commentary* (1872).

Lippmann, Walter. *U.S. Foreign Policy: Shield of the Republic*. Boston: Little, Brown & Co., 1943.

Mackinder, Halford J. *Democratic Ideals and Reality: A Study in the Politics of Reconstruction*. Washington, DC: National Defense University Press, 1942.

Mahan, A. T. *The Influence of Sea Power upon History, 1660–1783*. Boston: Little & Brown, 1890.

McDermott, Rose. *Political Psychology in International Relations*. Ann Arbor: University of Michigan Press, 2004.

Mearsheimer, John J. *The Tragedy of Great Power Politics*. New York: Norton, 2001.

Modelski, George, ed. *Exploring Long Cycles*. Boulder, CO: L. Rienner; London: Frances Pinter, 1987.

———. *Long Cycles in World Politics*. London: Macmillan, 1987.

Morgenthau, Hans J., and Kenneth W. Thompson. *Politics among Nations: The Struggle for Power and Peace*. 5th edition. New York: Alfred A. Knopf, 1972.

Pahre, Robert. *Leading Questions: How Hegemony Affects the International Political Economy*. Ann Arbor: University of Michigan Press, 1999.

Post, Jerold M. *Leaders and Their Followers in a Dangerous World: The Psychology of Political Behavior*. Ithaca, NY: Cornell University Press, 2004.

———, ed. *The Psychological Assessment of Political Leaders, with Profiles of Saddam Hussein and Bill Clinton*. Ann Arbor: University of Michigan Press, 2003.

Powell, Robert. *In the Shadow of Power: States and Strategies in International Politics*. Princeton, NJ: Princeton University Press, 1999.

Rickett, W. A. *Guanzi: Political, Economic, and Philosophical Essays from Early China*, vol. 1. Princeton, NJ: Princeton University Press, 1985.

Schweller, Randall L. *Deadly Imbalances: Tripolarity and Hitler's Strategy of World Conquest*. New York: Columbia University Press, 1998.

Snyder, Jack. *The Myths of Empire: Domestic Politics and International Ambition*. New York: Cornell University Press, 1991.

Stavrianos, L. S. *The World since 1500: A Global History*. London: Prentice-Hall International, 1966.

Wallerstein, Immanuel. *Mercantilism and the Consolidation of the European World Economy, 1600–1750*. New York: Academic Press, 1980.

———. *The Politics of the World Economy: The States, the Movements, and the Civilizations*. Cambridge: Cambridge University Press, 1984.

Waltz, Kenneth N. *Theory of International Politics*. Boston: McGraw-Hill, 1979.

Wendt, Alexander. *Social Theory of International Politics*. Cambridge: Cambridge University Press, 1999.

Williams, Phil, Donald M. Goldstein, and Jay M. Shafritz. *Classic Readings of International Relations*. Boston: Wadsworth, 1998.

CHINESE WORKS

Bai Shouyi. *Zhongguo Shixueshi Lunji* [Collected essays on the history of Chinese historiography]. Beijing: Zhonghua Shuju, 1999.

Cao Deben, ed. *Zhongguo Zhengzhi Sixiangshi* [A history of Chinese political thought]. Beijing: Higher Education Press, 1999.

Chen Qi and Huang Yuxing. "Chunqiu Shiqi de Guojiajian Ganshe" [Intervention between states in the Spring and Autumn Period]. *Guoji Zhengzhi Kexue* [Scientific Studies of International Politics], no. 1 (2008): 33–73, 167.

Chen Yudan. "Guoji Guanxixue Zhong de Jingdian yu Chanshi" [Classic readings in international relations, with a commentary]. *Guoji Zhengzhi Kexue* [Scientific Studies of International Politics], no. 3 (2008): 102–114.

Chen Zhiyong. "Shixi Chunqiu Mengshi Dui Chunqiu Shiren de Yingxiang Ji Shiren Dui Mengshi yu Mengzhu de Pingjia" [The influence of oaths on people in the Spring and Autumn Period and contemporary criticism of oaths and lords of alliances]. *Zhongguo Lishi Bowuguan Guankan* [Journal of the Museum of Chinese History], no. 2 (2000).

Fu Yuzhang. *Zhongguo Gudai Shixueshi* [A history of the historiography of ancient China]. Hefei: Anhui University Press, 2008.

Gao Xiaoying. "*Shi Ji* yu *Zhanguoce* de Bijiao Yanjiu" [A comparative study of the *Historical records* and *The stratagems of the Warring States*]. M.A. thesis, Anhui University, 2005.

Guo Dan. "*Zuozhuan*" *Guoce Yanjiu* [State strategy in "Zuo's commentary"]. Beijing: Renmin Wenxue, 2004.

Guo Shuyong, ed. *Guoji Guanxi: Huhuan Zhongguo Lilun* [International relations: A call for a Chinese theory]. Tianjin: Tianjin People's Press, 2005.

He Maochun. *Zhongguo Waijiao Tongshi* [A history of China's external relations]. Beijing: Chinese Academy of Social Sciences Press, 1996.

He Pingli. "Luelun Chunqiu Shiqi Huimeng, Zhengba Zhanzheng yu Zhanzhengguan" [A brief discussion of alliances, hegemonic wars, and views of war in the Spring and Autumn Period]. *Junshi Lishi Yanjiu* [Research in Military History], no. 2 (2008).

Hu Jintao. "Gaoju Zhongguo Tese Shehuizhuyi Weida Qizhi Wei Duoqu Quanmian Jianshe Xiaokang Xin Shengli Er Fendou" [Holding the great banner of Socialism with Chinese characteristics and struggling to achieve the new victory of the construction of a prosperous society], *Renmin Ribao* [People's Daily], 25 October 2007, 4.

———. "Nuli Jianshe Chijiu Heping, Gongtong Fanrong de Hexie Shijie: Zai Lianheguo Chengli 60 Zhounian Shounao Huiyi Shang de Jianghua" [Work hard to establish a lasting, peaceful, universally prosperous, and harmonious world: A speech at the summit to commemorate the sixtieth anniversary of the found-ing of the United Nations]. *Renmin Ribao* [People's Daily], 16 September 2009.

Hu Ruhong. *"Zhanguoce" Yanjiu* [Study of "The stratagems of the Warring States"]. Changsha: Hunan People's Press, 2002.

Huang Pumin. "Xianqin Zhuzi Junshi Sixiang Yitong Chutan" [A preliminary compara-tive study of the military thought of the pre-Qin masters]. *Lishi Yanjiu* [Histori-cal Research], no. 5 (1996): 75–90.

Huang Shouan, Duan Fude, et al. *Zhongguo Gudai Jiu Da Sixiang Xuepai Jiyao* [A summary of the nine schools of thought in ancient China]. Beijing: People's Liberation Army Press, 2002.

Huang Shuofeng. *Zonghe Guoli Xinlun: Jianlun Xinzhongguo Zonghe Guoli* [A new theory of comprehensive state power: Comprehensive state power in the new China]. Beijing: Chinese Academy of Social Sciences Press, 1999.

Jia Chuantang. *"Zhanguoce* Rencai Lun" [Talented persons in *The stratagems of the Warring States*]. *Zhengzhou Daxue Xuebao (Zhexue Shehuikexue Ban)* [Journal of Zhengzhou University: Philosophy and Social Sciences], no. 5 (1987): 45–52.

Li Ruilan. *Chunqiu Zhanguo Shidai de Lishi Bianqian* [Historical changes in the Spring and Autumn and Warring States periods]. Tianjin: Tianjin Guji Press, 1994.

Li Shaojun, ed. *Guoji Zhanlue Baogao* [Report on international strategies]. Beijing: Chi-nese Academy of Social Sciences Press, 2005.

Liang Qichao. *Xianqin Zhengzhi Sixiangshi* [A history of pre-Qin political thought]. Bei-jing: Zhonghua Shuju and Shanghai Shudian, 1986 [based on the 1936 edition by Zhonghua Shuju; original version published in 1922].

———. *Xianqin Zhengzhi Sixiangshi* [A history of pre-Qin political thought]. Tianjin: Tianjin Guji Press, 2003.

Lin Jianming. *Qinshi Gao* [A sketch history of Qin]. Shanghai: Shanghai People's Press, 1981.

Liu Jiangyong. "*Guanzi* Guojiajian Zhengzhi Sixiang Chutan" [A preliminary study of in-terstate political thought in the *Guanzi*]. *Guoji Zhengzhi Kexue* [Scientific Stud-ies of International Politics], no. 3 (2008): 36–56.

Liu Zehua. *Zhongguo Zhengzhi Sixiangshi Ji* [An anthology of the history of Chinese po-litical thought]. Beijing: People's Press, 2008.

———. *Zhongguo Zhengzhi Sixiangshi (xian Qin)* [An anthology of the history of Chinese political thought (pre-Qin)]. Hangzhou: Zhejiang People's Press, 1996.

Liu Zehua and Ge Quan, eds. *Zhongguo Gudai Sixiangshi* [A history of ancient Chinese thought]. Tianjin: Nankai University Press, 2001.

———, eds. *Zhongguo Zhengzhi Sixiangshi Yanjiu* [Studies in the history of Chinese po-litical thought]. Wuhan: Hubei Educational Press, 2006.

Lü Simian. *Xianqin Xueshu Gailun* [An outline of pre-Qin scholarship]. Beijing: Dongfang Press, 1996.

Luo Genze. *Luo Genze Shuo Zhuzi* [Luo Genze on the masters]. Shanghai: Shanghai Guji Press, 2001.

Mao Zedong. *Mao Zedong Xuanji* [Selected works of Mao Zedong], vol. 2. Beijing: People's Press, 1991.

Miao Wenyuan. *Zhanguoce Kaobian* [A critical edition of "The stratagems of the Warring States"]. Beijing: Zhonghua Shuju, 1984.

Ni Shixiong et al. *Dangdai Xifang Guoji Guanxi Lilun* [Contemporary Western theories of international relations]. Shanghai: Fudan University Press, 2001.

Pei Monong. "Introduction." In *Chunqiu Zhanguo Shidai de Waijiao Qunxing* [Diplomatic constellations in the Spring and Autumn and Warring States periods]. Chongqing: Chongqing Press Group, 1994.

Piao Bingjiu. "*Liji* de Hexie Shijie Sixiang" [A harmonious world according to the *Record of rites*]. *Guoji Zhengzhi Kexue* [Scientific Studies of International Politics], no. 3 (2008): 57–70.

Qiu Yuanping. "Guanyu Zhongguo Guoji Zhanlue Yanjiu de Ruogan Kanfa" [A view of Chinese international strategy]. In *Zhongguo Guoji Zhanlue Pinglun* [An assessment of China's international strategy]. Beijing: Shijie Zhishi Press, 2009.

Sa Mengwu. *Zhongguo Zhengzhi Sixiangshi* [A history of Chinese political thought]. Beijing: Oriental Press, 2008.

Shen Changyun et al. *Zhaoguo Shigao* [A sketch history of the state of Zhao]. Beijing: Zhonghua Shuju, 2000.

Song Liheng. "Lun Huimeng Zai Chunqiu Zhengbazhong de Teshu Gongneng" [The special role of alliance meetings in the contest for hegemony in the Spring and Autumn Period]. *Jilin Shifan Daxuexuebao (Renwen Shehui Kexue Ban)* [Journal of Jilin Normal University: Humanities and Social Sciences], no. 6 (2003).

Sun Jiazhou. "Tianzi, Bazhu, Zhuhou: Chunqiu Bazheng Yanjiu" [The Son of Heaven, hegemonic lord, and the feudal princes: A study of the struggle for hegemony in the Spring and Autumn Period]. *Guizhou Shehui Kexue* [Guizhou Social Sciences], no. 2 (1993).

Sun Xuefeng and Yang Zixiao. "Hanfeizi de Guojiajian Zhengzhi Sixiang" [Hanfeizi's interstate political thought]. *Guoji Zhengzhi Kexue* [Scientific Studies of International Politics], no. 2 (2008): 81–97.

Wang Fuhan and Meng Ming, eds. *Wenbai Duizhao Quanyi "Zhanguoce"* [A translation of "The stratagems of the Warring States" into modern Chinese]. Beijing: Zhongyang Minzu Xueyuan Press, 1993.

Wang Gesen and Tang Zhiqing, eds. *Qiguo Shi* [A history of the state of Qi]. Jinan: Shandong People's Press, 1992.

Wang Jingxiong, Shang Jinglong, and Guan Xiu. *"Zhanguoce" yu Lunbianshu* ["The stratagems of the Warring States" and the art of debate]. Shanghai: Shanghai Guji Press, 2002.

Xiao Gongquan. *Zhongguo Zhengzhi Sixiangshi* [A history of Chinese political thought]. Beijing: New Star Press, 2005.

Xiong Xianguang, trans. *"Zhanguoce" Yanjiu yu Xuanyi* ["The stratagems of the Warring States": Studies and selected texts in translation]. Chongqing: Chongqing Press, 1988.

Xu Jieling. *Chunqiu Bangjiao Yanjiu* [Interstate relations in the Spring and Autumn Period]. Beijing: Chinese Academy of Social Sciences Press, 2004.

Yan Xuetong. "Guoji Guanxi Lilun Shi Pushi de" [International relations theories are universal]. *Shijie Jingji yu Zhengzhi* [World Economics and Politics], no. 2 (2006).

———. "Why Is There No Chinese School of International Relations Theory?" In *Wangba Tianxia Sixiang Ji Qidi* [Ruling over all under heaven: Theory and lessons], ed. Yan Xuetong, Xu Jin, et al. Beijing: Shijie Zhishi Press, 2009.

———. *Zhongguo Guojia Liyi Fenxi* [An analysis of China's national interest]. Tianjin: Tianjin People's Press, 1997.

Yang Kuan. *Xizhou Shi* [A history of the Western Zhou]. Shanghai: Shanghai People's Press, 2003.

———. *Zhanguo Shi* [A history of the Warring States]. Shanghai: Shanghai People's Press, 2003.

Yang Youqiong. *Zhongguo Zhengzhi Sixiangshi* [A history of Chinese political thought]. Shanghai: Commercial Press, 1937.

Yang Zebo. *Mengzi Pingzhuan* [Mencius: A biography]. Nanjing: Nanjing University Press, 1998.

Ye Zicheng. *Chunqiu Zhangguo Shiqi de Zhongguo Waijiao Sixiang* [Chinese diplomatic thought in the Spring and Autumn and Warring States periods]. Hong Kong: Hong Kong Social Sciences Press, 2003.

Yu Rubo. "*Zhanguoce* Moulue Sixiang Xiyao" [Strategic planning in *The stratagems of the Warring States*]. *Junshi Lishi Yanjiu* [Military History Research], no. 1 (1990).

Zhang Erguo. "Xian Qin Shiqi de Huimeng Wenti" [The issue of alliance meetings in the pre-Qin era]. *Shixue Jikan* [Journal of Historical Studies], no. 1 (1995).

Zhang Lu. "Zhongxi Zhengyi Zhanzheng de Sixiang Bijiao" [A comparative study of just war thought in China and the West]. *Xiandai Guoji Guanxi* [Contemporary International Relations], no. 4 (2005): 15–20.

Zhang Quanmin. "Shilun Chunqiu Huimeng de Lishi Zuoyong" [The historical role of alliance meetings in the Spring and Autumn Period]. *Jilin Daxue Shehui Kexue Xuebao* [Journal of Jilin University Social Sciences], no. 6 (1994).

Zhang Yanxiu. "*Zhanguoce* Zhuti Sixiang Shitan" [Topics in *The stratagems of the Warring States*]. *Guanzi Xuekan* [Guanzi Journal], no. 2 (1999): 63–69.

———. *Zonghengjia Shu:"Zhanguoce" yu Zhongguo Wenhua* [Verticalists and horizontalists: "The stratagems of the Warring States" and Chinese culture]. Kaifeng: Henan University Press, 1998.

"Zhonggong Zhongyang Guanyu Goujian Shehuizhuyi Hexie Shehui Ruogan Zhongda Wenti de Jueding" [The decision of the Central Committee of the Chinese Communist Party dealing with key questions in the construction of a harmonious socialist society]. *Renmin Ribao* [People's Daily], 19 October 2006.

"Zhongguo Heping Jueqi de Guoji Huanjing yu Guoji Zhanlue" [The international environment and international strategy for the peaceful rise of China]. *Jiaoxue yu Yanjiu* [Education and Research], no. 4 (2004): 5–20.

"Zhongyang Waishi Gongzuo Huiyi Zai Jing Juxing" [Central foreign affairs working meeting held in Beijing]. *Renmin Ribao* [People's Daily], 24 August 2006.

Zhu Rongji. "Zhengfu Gongzuo Baogao" [Government work report]. In *16 Da Yilai ZhongyaoWenxian Xuanbian [Shang]* [A selection of important documents since the Sixteenth Party Congress, part 1]. Beijing: Zhongyang Wenxian Press, 2005.

Contributors

Daniel A. Bell is a professor of ethics and political philosophy at Tsinghua University (Beijing). He has published four books (including one edited volume) on East Asian politics and philosophy with Princeton University Press. E-mail: Daniel.a.bell@gmail.com.

Huang Yuxing is a graduate student in the Political Science Department at Boston College. He graduated from Tsinghua University in 2009. E-mail: hyx05tsinghua@gmail.com.

Edmund Ryden, PhD (SOAS, London University), teaches in the Law Department at Fujen University, Taiwan. He translated Zhang Dainian's *Key Concepts in Chinese Philosophy* (Yale University Press, 2002) and Chen Lai's *Tradition and Modernity* (Brill, 2009), as well as the *Laozi: Daodejing* (Oxford University Press, 2008). E-mail: 035477@mail.fju.edu.tw.

Sun Zhe is a professor in the Department of International Studies, and the director of the Center for U.S.-China Relations at Tsinghua University (Beijing). He is the author and editor of eighteen books on comparative politics and U.S.-China relations. He received his PhD in political science from Columbia University in 2000.

Wang Rihua is an associate professor of political philosophy at Guandong School of Administration (Guangzhou, China). He received his PhD from Peking University in 2008. His current research focuses on ancient Chinese international thought and foreign policy. E-mail: wangrihua@gmail.com.

Xu Jin is a research fellow at the Institute of World Economics and Politics, Chinese Academy of Social Sciences. He received his PhD from the International Relations Department at Tsinghua University in 2008. His current research focuses on traditional Chinese international political thought, Chinese foreign policy, and the law of war. E-mail: xuj@cass.org.cn.

Yan Xuetong is a professor and director of the Department of International Studies, Tsinghua University (Beijing), and the editor in chief of the *Chinese Journal of International Politics*. Before joining Tsinghua University, he was a senior fellow at the Institute of Contemporary International Relations during 1992–2000. He also serves as a vice chairman of the China Association of International Relations Studies as well as the China Association of American Studies, and as a board member of several organizations, including the China Diplomacy Association, the China Association of Peaceful Unification, the

China UN Association, the China Arms Control Association, the China-U.S. Friendship Association, and the China Association of Asia-Pacific Studies. He is the author and editor of eighteen books on international relations theory, international security, and Chinese foreign policy. Professor Yan received his PhD in political science from the University of California, Berkeley, in 1992. E-mail: yanxt@mail.tsinghua.edu.cn.

Yang Qianru is a postdoctoral researcher in the Chinese Traditional Culture School at Renmin University of China (Beijing). She received her PhD from the History Department at Beijing Normal University in 2009. Her current research focuses on Chinese history and historiography. E-mail: shirley_yqr@sohu.com.

Index